Minh Chung

KOREAN TREASURES

Rare Books, Manuscripts and Artefacts in the
Bodleian Libraries and Museums of Oxford University

VOLUME 2

Bodleian Library
UNIVERSITY OF OXFORD

For Quyen, Kien, Manh, Thuc and Banh

이 책은 2018년도 한국학중앙연구원
해외한국학 지원사업의 지원에 의하여
발행되었음 (AKS-2018-P08)

This Publication was supported by the
Academy of Korean Studies Grant (AKS-2018-P08)

First published in 2019 by the Bodleian Library
Broad Street, Oxford OX1 3BG
www.bodleianshop.co.uk

ISBN: 978 1 85124 526 0

Text © Bodleian Library, University of Oxford, 2019.
All images, unless specified, © Bodleian Library, University of Oxford, 2019.

Jacket design by Dot Little at the Bodleian Library
Designed and typeset by Ocky Murray in Minion
Printed and bound by Great Wall Printing Co. Ltd., Hong Kong on 157gsm Neo matt art paper

British Library Catalogue in Publishing Data
A CIP record of this publication is available from the British Library

CONTENTS

Preface 4

Note to the reader 5

1. Maps 8

2. Coins, amulets and chatelaines 44

3. Christianity in Korea 74

4. Clothes and accessories 102

5. Other items 132

Notes 156

Appendices 160

Addresses 164

Select bibliography 165

Index 168

Acknowledgements 170

PREFACE

Many important and valuable manuscripts, rare books and artefacts related to Korea have been acquired by donation throughout the long history of the Bodleian Libraries and the museums of the University of Oxford. However, due to an early lack of specialist knowledge in this area, many of these Korean items were largely neglected. The publication of the first volume of *Korean Treasures: Rare Books, Manuscripts and Artefacts in the Bodleian Libraries and Museums of Oxford University* uncovered some of these treasures and presented them for the first time. The book has attracted interest, queries and visits from researchers and institutes from all over the world, including important institutions in Korea such as the Kyujanggak, the National Library of Korea and the National Museum of Korean Contemporary History. In particular, research delegations from the Kyujanggak and the National Museum of Korean Contemporary History have visited and examined some of the items highlighted in *Korean Treasures, Volume 1*. Some of the items have also been exhibited in the Bodleian Libraries as well as loaned to exhibitions in other museums in Europe.

Following the publication of Volume 1, more rare and important manuscripts and artefacts in the Bodleian Libraries and the museums of the University of Oxford have come to light. These prompted the production of this second volume.

The first volume of *Korean Treasures* has five chapters focused on: rare books and manuscripts, ceramics, photographs, scaphe sundials and weapons and other military artefacts. This second volume also has five chapters and highlights other treasures: rare maps, old coins, sources related to the history of Christianity, clothes and accessories, metalwork, water droppers, chests, roof tiles, dolls and weapons.

A major purpose of these presentations of Korean cultural items is to raise the profile of Korean arts and culture, which, though deserving of attention, are occasionally eclipsed by larger collections in the University's museums and libraries.

NOTE TO THE READER

Regarding romanization, the McCune–Reischauer system has been used for Korean, the modified Hepburn system for Japanese and the Pinyin system for Chinese. East Asian personal names are given with family name first, together with dates, where these are known. Names with a different spelling from that dictated by the romanization systems have retained their original spelling as per the personal preference of the individual.

ABBREVIATIONS

Reference numbers for items that may appear in the text carry a location abbreviation as a suffix:

ASH   Ashmolean Museum
BCCL   Bodleian China Centre Library
BOD   Bodleian Library
KSL   Korean Studies Library
PRM   Pitt Rivers Museum
WES   Weston Library (the Special Collections)

Transliterations

Transliterations are Korean, unless indicated with J. for Japanese or C. for Chinese

COLLECTIONS IN THE MUSEUMS OF THE UNIVERSITY OF OXFORD

Ashmolean Museum of Art and Archaeology

The Ashmolean Museum was established in 1683. It is the oldest museum in the UK and one of the oldest in the world. It houses the University's extensive collections of art and antiquities, including many of the Korean objects illustrated in this publication.

Museum of the History of Science

The Museum of the History of Science is housed in the world's oldest surviving purpose-built museum building, originally constructed for the

Ashmolean Museum. It contains one of the finest collections of historical scientific instruments from around the globe. The two Korean scaphe sundials discussed in the first volume are housed and displayed there.

Pitt Rivers Museum

The Pitt Rivers Museum holds one of the world's finest collections on anthropology and archaeology, with objects from every continent and from throughout human history. Premodern Korean weapons and other military artefacts as well as traditional clothing and accessories are housed there. Many are illustrated in this publication, and some of them are on display.

University Museum of Natural History

The University Museum of Natural History houses the University's scientific collections of zoological, entomological, palaeontological and mineral specimens. With 4.5 million specimens it is the largest collection of its type outside the national collections. Since the collection is beyond the scope of this book, none of the collection is included here. Nevertheless, Korean lepidolite and specimens of entomology can be found there.

Admission to these museums is free. For more information concerning these or other University museums, please visit www.museums.ox.ac.uk.

LOCATIONS OF BODLEIAN LIBRARY'S KOREAN COLLECTIONS

Korean Research Collection (both Western and Korean language)

The research collection that was previously housed in the central Bodleian site is now housed in the Book Storage Facility (BSF) in Swindon and may be requested in the reading rooms of the Oriental Institute Library and the China Centre Library.

Korean Teaching Collection (both Western and Korean language)

Material on Korea required for teaching purposes at the Oriental Institute is kept in the Korean Studies Library at the Oriental Institute and the China Centre Library.

Japanese Koreanology

Works in Japanese relating to the study of Korea are made available through the reading rooms of the Oriental Institute Library and the China Centre Library.

Korean Art and Archaeology (both Western and Korean language)

Works relating to Korean art and archaeology are housed in the Eastern Art collection at the Sackler Library.

Korean Manuscripts and Antiquarian Printed Books

These are housed in the Special Collections at the Weston Library.

Korean Maps and Missionary Documents

These are made available in the reading rooms in the Weston Library.

Catalogues

Both Western- and Korean-language works are catalogued on the Oxford Libraries Information System (OLIS).

SOLO (the gateway to the records for the vast collections of the Bodleian Libraries)

SOLO provides original script internet access to sources in Korean as well as Western languages: www.bodleian.ox.ac.uk/bodley.

CHRONOLOGICAL CHART OF EAST ASIAN HISTORY (SIMPLIFIED)

China	Korea		Japan
Qin Dynasty 221–207 BCE	Three Kingdoms Koguryŏ 37 BCE–668 CE (trad. dates)		Yayoi 200 BCE–250 CE
Han Dynasty 206 BCE–220 CE	Paekche 18 BCE–663 CE (trad. dates)		Kofun 250–552
Six Dynasties 222–589	Silla 57 BCE–668 CE (trad. dates)		Yamato 300–710
Tang Dynasty 618–906	Unified Silla 668–936		Nara 710–94
Five Dynasties 907-960			Heian 794–1185
Song Dynasty 960–1126	Koryŏ 918–1392		Kamakura 1185–1333
Yuan Dynasty 1279–1368			
Ming Dynasty 1368–1644	Chosŏn 1392–1910		Muromachi 1336–1568
Qing Dynasty 1644–1911			Momoyama 1568–1600
			Edo 1600–1868
			Meiji 1868–1912
Nationalist Republic 1912–49	Japanese colonial period 1910–45		Taishō 1912–26
			Shōwa 1926–89
People's Republic 1949–	Democratic People's Republic of Korea 1948–	Republic of Korea 1948–	Heisei 1989–

1

MAPS

MAP-MAKING IN KOREA has a long history. The earliest
evidence comes from the Koguryŏ Kingdom (37 BCE–668 CE). A
painting of a city map labelled *Yodong-sŏng* 遼東城 (Liaodong city) has
been found on the wall of a tomb near Sunch'ŏn, about 50 kilometres
north of P'yŏngyang. The first literary evidence also comes from
Koguryŏ, when a map of its territory entitled *Pongyŏk-do* 封域圖
(Map of the infeudated region) was presented to the Tang court. These
early Chinese notices are also reported in early Korean histories such
as *Samguk sagi.*[1] However, none of these have survived. The earliest
surviving map made by Koreans dates to 1402. Although the original
is no longer extant, a copy produced between 1479 and 1485 is held
in the Ōmiya Library, Ryūkoku University Academic Information
Center in Kyoto. It is entitled *Honil kangni yŏktae kukto chido* 混一彊
理歷代國都地圖 (Map of integrated lands and regions of historical
countries and capitals), or known by its abbreviation as *Kangnido*. It is
the earliest surviving dated example of an East Asian map of the world,
predating all Chinese and Japanese examples, the first cartographic
representation of Chosŏn Korea, and the earliest Asian map to show
Europe.[2] *Kangnido* drew on 14th-century Chinese maps, enhanced
using sources available in Korea. The depiction of Japan was based
on a Japanese map brought to Korea in 1402.[3] The *Kangnido* has clear
delineations of Africa and the Arabian Peninsula and a reasonable
shape for Europe. Incidentally, the oldest known printed map of Japan

is a Korean product published in Sin Sukchu's *Haedong chegukki* 海東諸國紀 (*Chronicle of the Countries in the Eastern Sea*) of 1471.[4]

After 1600 the Koreans began to have more contact with the Western world through meetings with European missionaries in Beijing, and information about the West began to influence Korean cartography. Korean diplomats and members of the embassies came back with news and books from the Chinese capital. In 1603 they brought back to Korea Matteo Ricci's world map of 1602, the *Kunyu wanguo quantu* 坤輿萬國全圖 (Complete terrestrial map of all countries). In 1604, they brought Ricci's 1603 edition of *Liangyi xuanlan tu* 兩儀玄覽圖 (Map of a deep and penetrating view of the heavens and the earth). The *Liangyi xuanlan tu* is now housed in the Soongsil University Museum[5] and is one of only a few copies in existence. Imports continued. For example, European books, maps and manufactures were taken to Korea by the envoy Chŏng Tuwŏn in 1631, valued at 300 or 400 ounces of silver. This included the well-known *Zhifang waiji* 職方外紀 (*Unofficial Accounts of Foreign Countries*) of 1623 by Giulio Aleni (1582–1649), together with a separate five-sheet set of accompanying maps entitled *Wanguo quantu* 萬國全圖 (Complete maps of all countries). Also included were books by Ricci and others on astronomy and mathematics, a telescope with an instruction manual, star maps of both the Northern and Southern Hemispheres, a European cannon with an instruction manual, an alarm clock and many other items.[6] Perhaps the two most influential maps are Ricci's *Kunyu wanguo quantu*, which was reproduced in 1708 on the Korean king's orders, and Aleni's *Wanguo quantu*, reproduced around 1791. These are the only two Jesuit maps that were officially reproduced.[7] European cartographic knowledge spread from Korea to Japan, where copies of these maps were also made, like the *c.* 1480 copy of the 1402 *Kangnido*, which had reached Japan as booty from the East Asian War of 1592–98 and was used before Japanese geographic information had been influenced by Portuguese and Dutch missionaries. Interestingly, while the Koreans received and incorporated information on Japan, there was very little movement of general cartographic ideas from Japan to Korea.[8]

THE BODLEIAN WORLD MAP

While Western cartography and influence continued to find their way into Korea from Beijing, there were other new trends in scholarship that encouraged a fresh interest in science and evidential research. Geography, among other disciplines, came to be fashionable among many scholars. It is against this background that the Bodleian Library came to possess a world map entitled *Yŏnggo yanggye Yodong chŏndo* 寧古兩界遼東全圖 (A complete map of the old Hamgyŏng, Kangwŏn, and P'yŏng'an Provinces, and Liaodong). This type of map is known as *Chiguǔiyong chuhyǒngdo* 地球儀用舟形圖 (Globe gores). The *Yǒnggo yanggye Yodong chǒndo* world map, although important, is less known either inside or outside Korea. It is a finely drawn coloured map containing a set of twelve globe gores projected on a single flat sheet (north at the top), measuring approximately 28 x 71 cm. The Bodleian world map was based on Adam Schall's map, *Diqiu shi'erchang yuanxing-tu* 地球十二長圓形圖 (A terrestrial globe with twelve gores),[9] with additional content from the *Wanguo quantu* of Giulio Aleni.[10] Also added are mythical place names derived from the *Shanhaijing* 山海經 (The classic of mountains and seas), such as the Guiguodao 鬼國島 (Ghost country island), Gouguo 狗國 (Dog country), Nurenguo 女人國 (Women's country), Airenguo 矮人國 (Dwarf country), Yechaguo or Yakshaguo 夜叉國 (Ferocious people country), Yimuguo 一目國 (One-eyed people country) and others.

Although it was made in the 18th century, the intention seems to be the preservation of the old map rather than the represention of the geographical reality of the contemporary world, which was then ruled by the Qing Empire. China in this map is basically China of the Ming period, which had two capital cities (Beijing and Nanjing) and thirteen provinces. This seems clear because *Da Ming yi tong* 大明一統 (The united realm of the Great Ming) is also written on the map. Korean loyalties to the Ming lingered long after its disappearance, even while China was ruled by the Qing Empire. Ming military aid to Korea against the Japanese invasions in the 1590s nurtured strong pro-Ming sentiments. Koreans had long considered the Manchus as just another northern barbarian tribal group, and the establishment of Qing rule over Chinese territory came with two invasions of Korea (1627 and 1636–37), during which the Qing publicly humiliated the Korean king and took dozens of hostages from the royal family and other leading Korean families. The result was nationwide anti-Manchu hostility. One expression of the lingering pro-Ming sentiment can be seen in maps: when creating maps of China, Koreans often showed the Ming capitals and Ming provincial organization rather than those of the Qing.[11]

The Bodleian map, in addition to providing details about the world, also gives information about local culture and history, such as these comments regarding Yinggedi 鸚哥地 (Land of the Parrots), Huodi 火地 (Land of Fire), and Lukeguo 路客國 (Land of the savage and cunning). It is not known where the creator obtained his information, but it is probable that some of the information came from Ricci's 1602 *Kunyu wanguo quantu*.[14] For example, Ricci wrote the following about the Land of the Parrots: 'Land of the Parrots – this land has many parrots and is therefore named as such' (鸚哥地 此地多有鸚鵡之鳥故因名地), compared to 'This land breeds numerous parrots and is therefore named as such.'

Another example is Ricci's comment about Lukeguo: 'In this place the fragrant spice plants come in many varieties, but the people are savage and cunning, and we cannot trade with them' (此地香椒多端，但人蠻掮 不 可同交易), as compared to the Bodleian map's statement that 'This place produces chixiang 赤香 (red sandalwood), but the people are savage and cunning, and up to now we have been unable to trade with them.'

In conclusion, the Bodleian map enhanced Schall's world maps by adding information and detail from the creator's own knowledge as well as from Aleni's map and probably from Ricci's map in order to make this map more interesting and useful. He also presented his world map more comprehensively by using colour to distinguish seas, land masses, mountains and rivers, and by using circles and rectangles to make important places stand out. That this map was prepared around the middle of the 18th century also shows that Korean scholars were well aware of what was going on in the outside world. They knew of Ferdinand Magellan's expedition of 1519–20 and of other expeditions, such as the one supported by King Charles of Spain; they knew of cities important to Europeans, such as Rome and Jerusalem.

The Bodleian map also has strong Korean characteristics. Korean Confucian scholars prepared these maps to assist them in their historical studies and in their government posts. They made little distinction between history and geography and fitted their knowledge into familiar frameworks, with stress put on the importance of hierarchical relations between places. The role of hierarchy will be examined below in the discussion of the Bodleian's Korean world atlas. The scholars were skilled calligraphers, writing place names and drawing simple but realistic mountains and rivers with their brushes, but less attention was paid to the precision and scale of the map. This type of projection with globe gores was made to be folded around a sphere and to form a globe, but the creator seems unconcerned with this concept; he simply created the map without bothering too much about the exact size of each of the twelve globe gores, and they are today difficult to fold neatly around a sphere. The Korean scholars appreciated the beauty of the maps, and the maps are works of art as well as useful tools.

Author of the map

There are only two copies of this map known to exist and one has been lost, leaving only the Bodleian copy. Another copy of this map was owned by Imanishi Ryū, and that map was credited to An Chŏng-bok 安鼎 福 (1712–1791, pen name Sunam 順菴), by a modern scholar, Akioka Takejirō, who was able to examine the Imanishi map and includes an illustration in his study [15]. Akioka has asserted that An Chŏng-bok composed the map, because the title 寧古兩界遼東全圖 was written on the back of the Imanishi map. On the envelope that held the Imanishi map was also written the title of the map and the author's name 寧古兩界 遼東全圖 順菴安先生手寫本 (handwritten by Sunam – which was An's pen name). An was a disciple of Yi Ik 李瀷 (pen name Sŏngho 星湖)and a historian. An was introduced to Western learning (sŏhak 西學) through Yi Ik. From his correspondence with Yi Ik, we know that An Chŏng-bok read many Western books, including works by Matteo Ricci, and that An tried to grasp the essence of Western learning. Dabbling in studies of sŏhak was a cultural fashion among the intellectuals of the time.[16] An Chŏng-bok is famous for his historical studies; he authored the important work *Tongsa Kangmok* 東史綱目 (*Outline and Digest of Korean History*) in 1778, which presents a full chronological treatment of Korean history from Tan'gun檀君, the mythical first ancestor of the Korean people, through to the end of the Koryŏ Kingdom (late 14th century CE).

The importance of this map

There are only three examples of this type of map with gores known to have existed in the whole of East Asia during the 18th century:

1 C. *Diqiu shi'erchang yuanxingtu* 地球十二長圓形圖 (地球儀用舟型 世界地圖) by the Jesuit Johann Adam Schall von Bell (1592–1666), published in Volume 5 of *Hun tian yi shuo* 渾天儀説 (1628 or 1636).
2 J. *Chikyū giyō funegata sekai chizu* 地球儀用舟型世界地圖 by Yasui Santetsu 安井算哲 (1590–1652).[17]
3 *Yŏnggo yanggye Yodong chŏndo* (*Chiguǔiyong chuhyŏngdo*) 寧古兩界 遼東全圖 (地球儀用舟型圖) in the Bodleian Libraries.

The rarity of the Bodleian map therefore marks it as very important in the history of the development of East Asian maps, but there is more to its rarity. As noted above, there was another copy of the Bodleian map known to have been owned by Imanishi Ryū 今西龍 (1875–1932), who was a professor at Keijō Daigaku 京城帝國大學 in Seoul during the Japanese colonial period. It is not known how this copy came into his possession. After his death, his collection was donated to Tenri University's 天理大學 library as the Imanishi Ryū Bunkō 今西龍文庫 but no one has seen the map since 1932.

    In 1991, when the National Library of Korea made a photocopy of the Imanishi collection, they confirmed that there was no map with the title *Yŏng koyanggye Yodong chŏndo* (the same as the Bodleian map) there. Tenri University stated that the Imanishi collection does not include all of Imanishi's books and papers, but only a part, and the map is not in their collection. The search then led to the town of Ikeda, where Imanishi was born. A grandson of Imanishi, Professor Bunryū Imanishi, was contacted – a nuclear physicist who had retired from the Institute for Nuclear Study, University Tokyo. He confirmed that the family does not have the map and no one could remember whether or not his father (Haruaki Imanishi, Professor of Tenri University, 1957–72) donated the map to the Tenri University Library. Professor Bunryū Imanishi also sent enquiries to the pupils of his grandfather and father to see if they knew where the map was, but to no avail. So it does seem that the map has gone missing. Fortunately, a picture was taken of the map at Keijō Daigaku by Dr Nakamura Hiroshi 中村拓 (an acquaintance of Akioka Takejirō), who, on his way from China in March and April of 1932 (Showa 7), visited Imanishi to see this map. His photo appeared in an article by Akioka about Imanishi's map in the journal *Rekishi chiri* 歷史 地理 in 1933, where Akioka attributes the map to An Chŏng-bok.[18]

The whereabouts of the other maps are also unknown. The original model, Adam Schall von Bell's map, is only known from its publication in Volume 5 of *Hun tian yi shuo*. An image of Yasui Santetsu's map with text is published as a fold-out frontispiece to an 1899 issue of *Rekishi chiri*,[19] in which the map is said to be preserved at the Grassi Museum in Leipzig, Germany. When the curator was contacted,[20] the reply was that there was no trace of the map in their collections or in the archives. In fact, he replied that he had received quite a few enquiries about this map, but he thought it may have been lost during 'the time of war' (World War II). This would make the Bodleian map not only the only surviving copy in the world but also the only one of this kind of map created in Asia that survives anywhere.

KOREAN ATLASES

Korean atlases were used in the early Chosŏn period and continued to be produced until the 20th century. Koreans assembled atlases much more commonly than did the Chinese or the Japanese. These atlases became uniquely Korean cartographic products. Many are in manuscript form and variously coloured, and some were printed from woodblocks.

Among these atlases, there are differences in title, size, colour, technical skill and binding, but the arrangement of the maps and the content are somewhat standardized: a *Chŏnha-do* 天下圖 map of the world, maps of China, maps of each of the eight Korean provinces, followed by maps of Japan and the Ryūkyū Islands (now Okinawa). Sometimes there are variations in the order of the maps and there may be additional maps of Seoul, P'yŏngyang and Mukden.[21] The atlases are usually not dated, although most of those now in existence are from the 17th to 19th centuries. The atlases often contain supplementary geographical information, such as lists of magistracies and noteworthy places.[22] The Bodleian Library has a rather special atlas that includes many unusual maps not found in other Korean world atlases. Each map in this atlas contains a lot of information, such as numbers of magistrates, population and households, directions, dates, history and even sometimes poems.

The Bodleian's Korean world atlas

Many of the atlases have the title of *Yŏjido* 輿地圖, but the Bodleian's atlas has the unusual title of *Sahae chibang sŭnggae chi do chŏn* 四海地方勝槩之圖 全(Map of the world and regional sceneries – complete) (COREAN.D.2).

The atlas comprises a hand-drawn set of twenty folded and coloured maps (twelve main maps plus eight maps of the Korean provinces). It measures 17 x 28 cm and was made of traditional Korean materials. All the maps are mounted in such a way that they can be folded out quite simply to aid viewing. The maps (pages 20–43) are:

Sahae chido 四海地圖 (Map of the four seas)
Chungwŏn sipsamsŏng chido 中原十三省之圖 (Map of thirteen Chinese provinces)
Pukkyŏngsŏng-do 北京城圖 (Map of Beijing)
Muisan kugok chido 武夷山九曲之圖 (Map of Mount Wuyi)
(*Kiyu Chuja si* 記有朱子詩 [with a poem by Zhu Xi])
Kŭmnŭng sŭnggae chido 金陵勝槩之圖 (Map of the scenery of Nanjing)
Chosŏn chʼongnamdo 朝鮮揔覽圖 (Complete map of Chosŏn)
Hanyangsŏng-do 漢陽城圖 (Map of Hanyang [Seoul])
Kyŏnggi-do 京畿道 (Kyŏnggi Province)
Chʼungchʼŏng-do 忠清道 (Chʼungchʼŏng Province)
Chŏlla-do 金羅道 (Chŏlla Province)
Kyŏngsang-do 慶尚道 (Kyŏngsang Province)
Hwanghae-do 黃海道 (Hwanghae Province)
Pʼyŏngʼan-do 平安道 (Pʼyŏngʼan Province)
Kangwŏn-do 江原道 (Kangwŏn Province)
Hamgyŏng-do 咸鏡道 (Hamgyŏng Province)
Anbyŏn Sŏgwang-sa 安边釋王寺 (Map of Sŏgwang Temple)
Yŏnggotʼap chŏn-do 寧古塔全圖 (Complete map of Ningʼan or Ningguta in Manchuria)
Ilbon chido 日本地圖 (Map of Japan)
Yuguguk chido 琉球國地圖 (Map of Ryūkyū)
Sŏnggyŏng yŏji chŏn-do 盛京輿地全圖 (Complete map of Shengjing or Shenyang)

The dating of the Bodleian world atlas

Most similar atlases are not dated, but nine of the twenty maps in the Bodleian's atlas have the date *kapcha inyŏn* 甲子式年, indicating the Chinese cyclical calendar plus two years. The calendar repeats itself in sixty-year cycles. The year *kapcha* (1744) plus two years would indicate 1746 or, sixty years later, 1806. There are three reasons why the atlas was probably completed in 1746:

1. The total population in Korea is recorded in the atlas as 7,184,894. The *Hogu ch'ongsu* 戶口叢數 (*Aggregate Population Statistics*), published in 1789, gives the total population of Korea as follows: 1741 records 7,192,848 and 1744 records 7,209,213. The *Chosŏn wangjo sillok* 朝鮮王朝實錄 (*Annals of the Chosŏn Dynasty*) reports 7,513,792 for 1801 and 7,563,403 for 1807. The atlas's record is closer to the 1744 *Hogu ch'ongsu* record, suggesting that it was produced nearer that date.
2. The place names Musan 茂山 and Tanch'ŏn 端川 appeared in 1684 and 1720 respectively. Both are marked in the *Hamgyŏng-do* map, because they appeared before the compilation of this atlas. However, the place name Changjin 長津 appeared in 1787, and it does not feature in this map, suggesting it appeared after the map's compilation.
3. In 1767, Anŭm 安陰 was renamed Anŭi 安義 and Sanŭm 山陰 was renamed Sanch'ŏng 山淸 (all in Kyŏngsang Province). In 1776 Isan 理山 in P'yŏng'an Province was renamed Ch'osan 楚山. These places were renamed after 1746. Later names do appear on the atlas, but these were all evidently corrected or updated.

For all of these reasons, it appears that the atlas was produced closer to 1746 than 1806.

The uniqueness of this atlas

Quite a few Korean world atlases have survived. They are mostly, if not all, undated, but the Bodleian's atlas is dated. Typically, as above, they consist of between ten and thirteen maps which include a world map, a map of China, a map of Chosŏn, maps of the eight provinces of Korea, a map of Japan and a map of Okinawa. Vary rarely is a map of Seoul included, and even rarer do we see the inclusion of maps of Beijing and Nanjing. The Bodleian atlas includes all of these as well as maps of Mount Wuyi and Sŏgwang Temple. Moreover, these were produced as paintings, which is unusual in a world atlas. Mount Wuyi is accompanied by a poem, and the depiction of Sŏgwang Temple includes an explanatory note on why the temple was built. Other unusual features of this atlas are the additions of Shengjing, the Manchu capital in Manchuria and the town of Ning'an or Ningguta in Manchuria.

The maps on pages 30–37 depict the eight provinces of Korea. Not only is there a map for each province, but we are also given information on the number of officials, their titles, the sites of their offices, distance from the provincial seat to the capital, the numbers of households and the population for each province. The official titles appearing in the maps of the eight provinces all refer to various types of county magistrates and are placed inside the cartouches that display the name of the county. The numbers of 'officials' 官 noted does not correspond to the number of counties or cartouches indicating a magistracy. Each province is divided for administrative convenience into a left 左道 and right 右道 section with different coloured cartouches for the county names in each section. Along the edge of each province map are notes indicating which provinces border to the north, south, east and west, or whether the sea borders that province.

The provenance of the world map and the world atlas

Both the Korean world map and the world atlas were donated to the Bodleian Library at the same time, around the end of the 19th century by Bishop Mark Napier Trollope (1862–1930). Bishop Trollope is discussed in more detail in Chapter 2.

CONCLUSION

Although able to borrow easily from Sinic culture, peninsular peoples developed distinct cultural and political identities. When Koreans borrowed from China, they often adapted those imports to local needs and conditions, and these adaptations frequently resulted in new inventions and discoveries. The Bodleian's Korean world map exemplifies this very well, as does the Bodleian Korean world atlas, which developed into something uniquely Korean. These Korean maps have vivid colours, realistic mountain forms and beautiful calligraphy, and are indeed prized artistic objects as well as useful tools for scholarly study and governmental administration.

Following page:

Yŏnggo yanggye Yodong chŏndo 寧古兩界遼東全圖
(A complete map of the old Hamgyŏng, Kangwŏn, and P'yŏng'an Provinces and Liaodong)
18th century, approx. 28 x 71 cm
[BOD] MS. B1 (510)

The map contains a number of curious items. There are five places marked within red rectanglar cartouches, implying that these are the five most important places on earth: Chosŏn 朝鮮 (Korea), Pukkyŏng 北京 (Beijing), Namgyŏng 南京 (Nanjing), Yŏkdŏk-a 如德亞 (Judea or Israel) and Rama 羅瑪 (Rome). While places and countries are more or less correctly positioned in the Northern Hemisphere, in the Southern Hemisphere, as in other Western maps of the same period, there is a large landmass now known as the continent of Australia. The name Mokwa namniga 墨瓦臘泥加 (Latin: Terra Australis Incognita, 'unknown land of the South'[12]) is written across the Southern Hemisphere on Schall's and Aleni's maps, while Anamniga 亞臘泥加 is written on the Bodleian map. Both Aleni's and Schall's maps give little or no information on the Southern Hemisphere, while the Bodleian map offers quite a bit of local information about the history and customs at the bottom of ten out of twelve globe gores. From right to left these are:

火地 '[The country of] Huodi (Land of Fire)'
滋蕩無際但有虫燐遍野如火故名火地
'This land is vast and expansive, but there are bioluminescent insects everywhere, like flying embers, and therefore [this place] is called the Land of Fire.' (Huodi is Tierra del Fuego – Spanish for 'Land of Fire' – an archipelago off the southernmost tip of the South American mainland.)[13]

Information at the centre of the Southern Hemisphere reads:
以西把尒(爾)亞國王合
強力之臣墨九蘭
海舶周遍四海不見
得者大地滋蕩無涯
崖際山川蛮俗不可得以
考詳而以墨瓦蘭之求得
故因名墨瓦臘泥加一名
瑪熱辣尼加云

'[Ferdinand] Magellan 墨九蘭, in his capacity as a minister of the King of Spain 西把爾亞, King Charles 國王合強力, sailed all around the four seas. There was a great land, vast and without end, which had not been seen, where its borders were mountains and rivers and its savage customs had not yet been examined in detail. But, because Magellan discovered it we thus name it after him, Mowalanijia 墨瓦臘泥加 (Mowagenijia), alternate name Marelanijia 瑪熱辣尼加.'

Other information includes:
伯亜祚 '[The country of] Boyazuo'
此地人至者絶少未審其土俗何如
'People who have been here are extremely few, and its customs have not been investigated.'

力肚 '[The country of] Lidu'
此則廣問無所産
'This place has been widely investigated, but it does not produce anything.'

路客國 '[The country of] Lukeguo'
此地産赤香但人蛮猾迄不可交易
'This place produces 赤香 [sandalwood?], but the people are savage and cunning, and up to now we have been unable to trade with them.'

鸚哥地 '[The country of] Yinggedi (Land of the Parrots or Australia)'
此地産鸚哥極多故以此爲名
'This land breeds numerous parrots and is therefore named as such.'

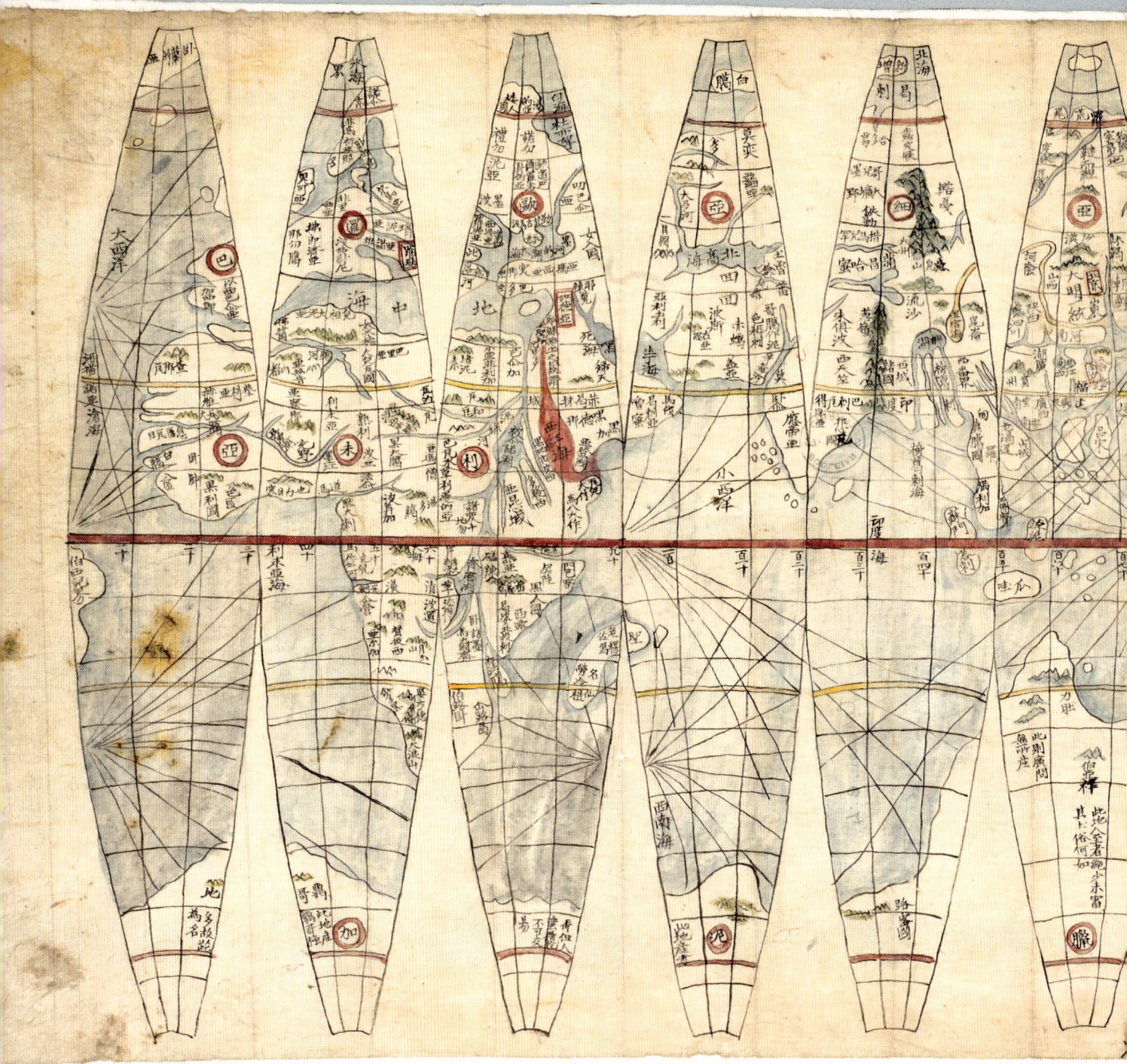

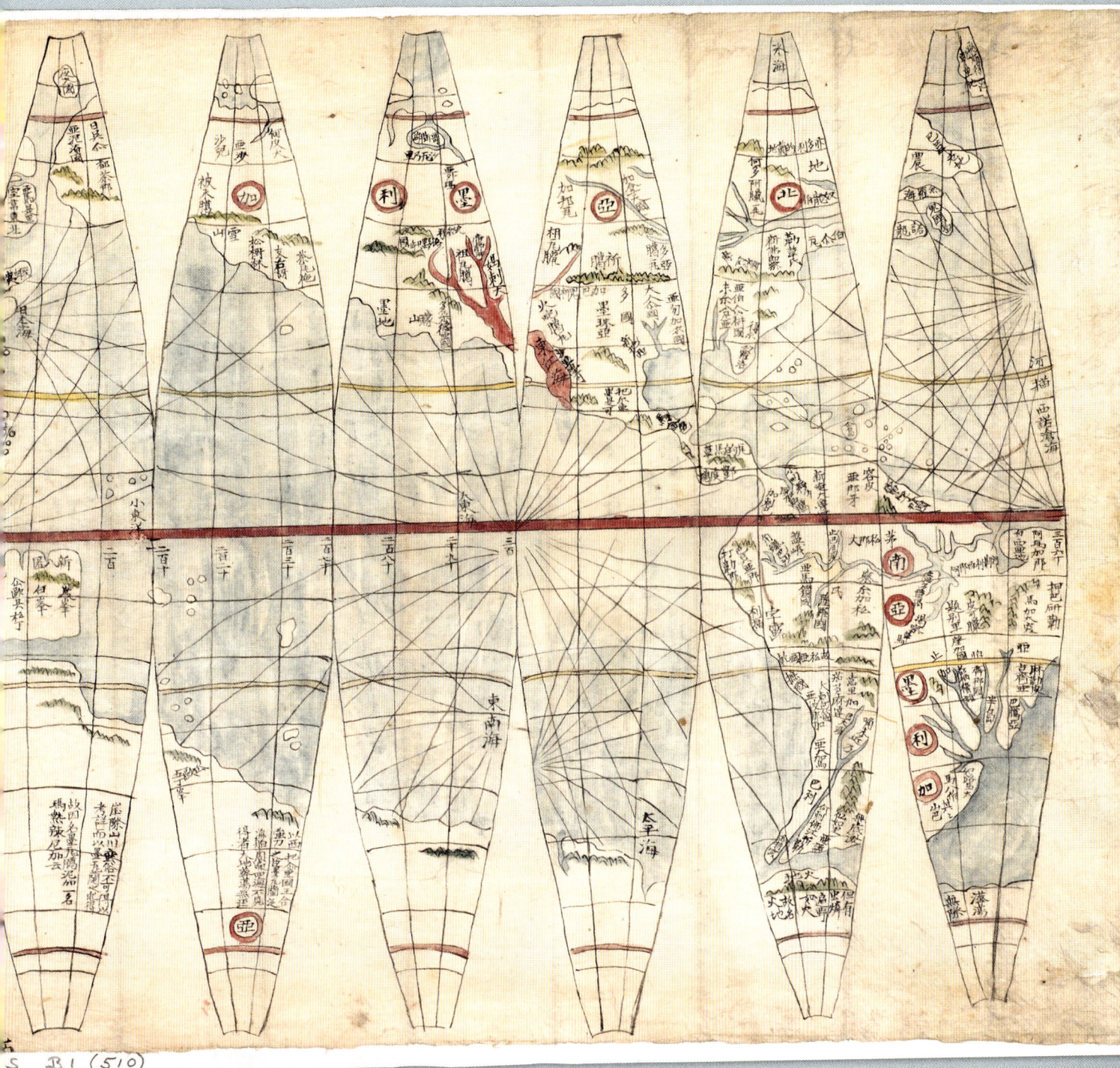

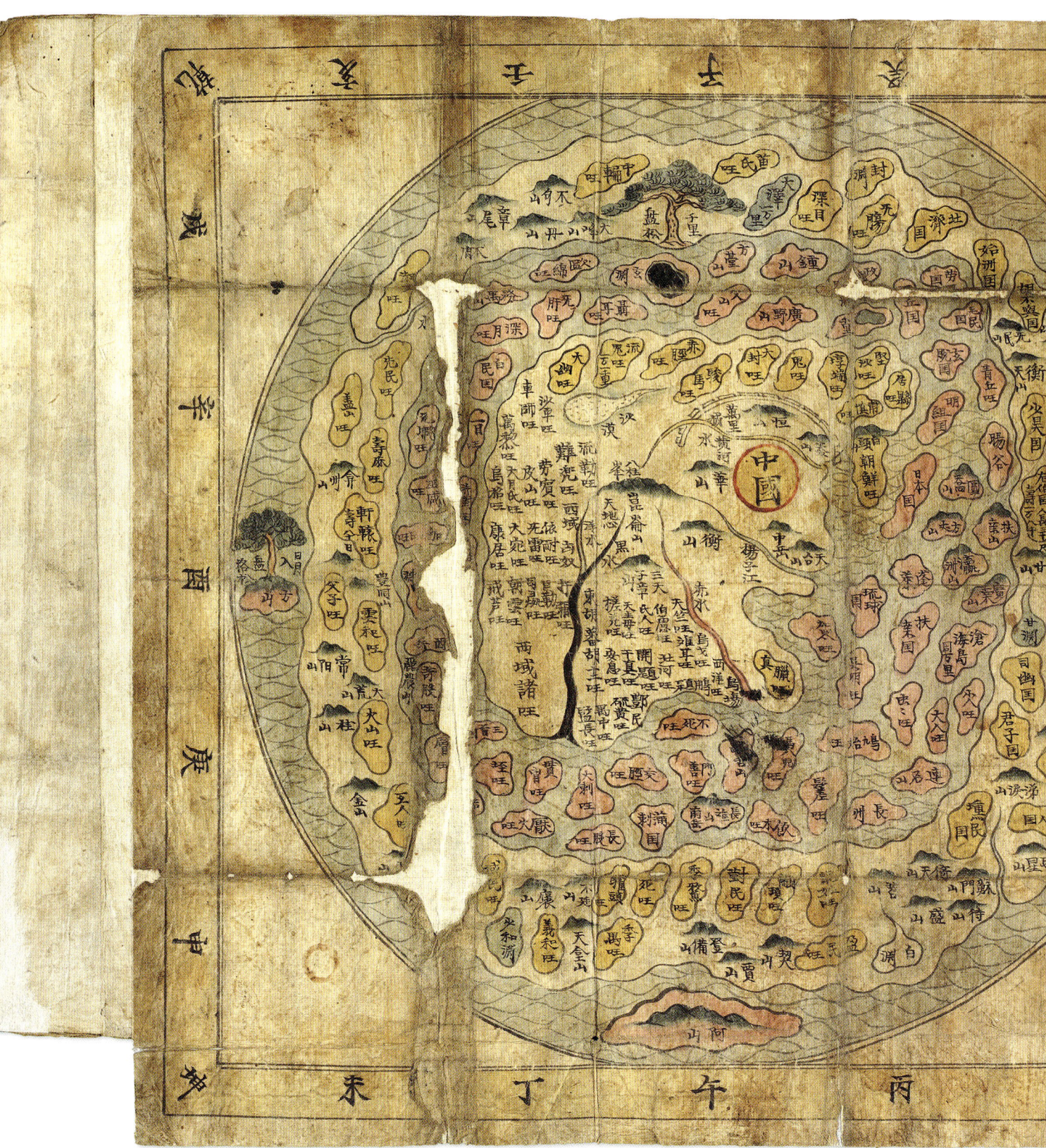

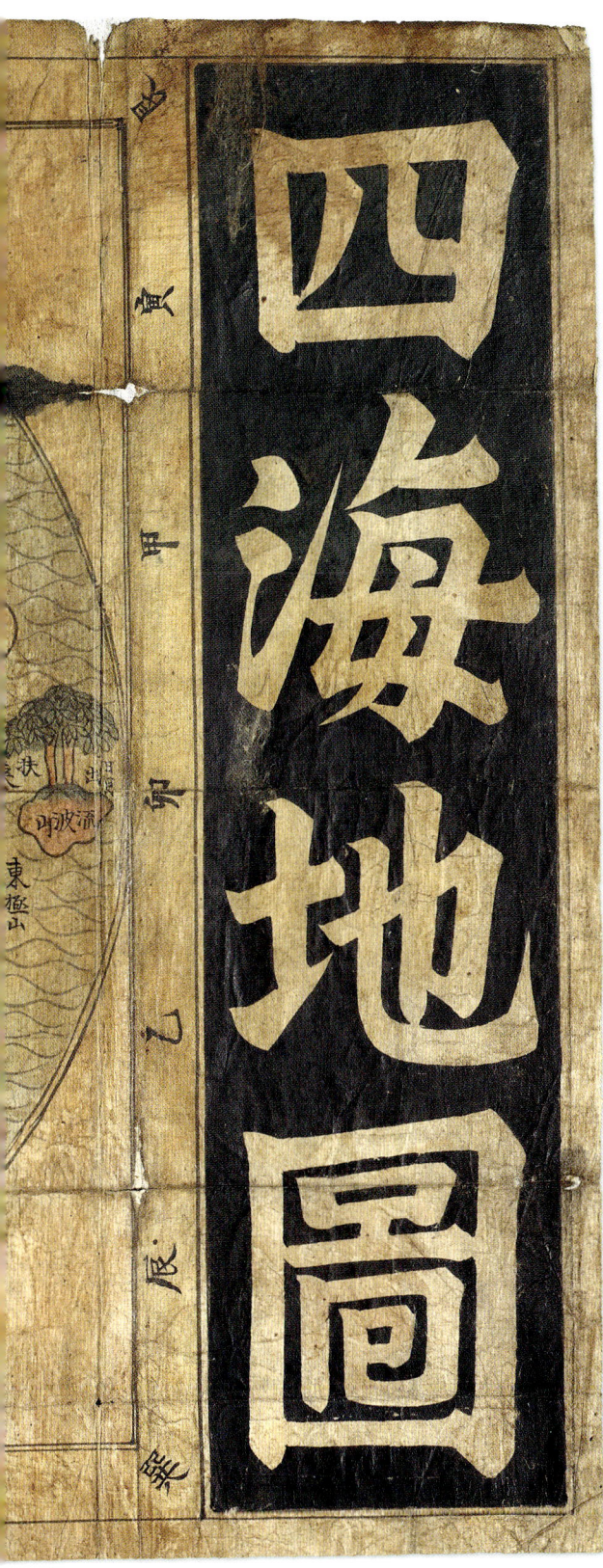

Sahae chido 四海地圖
(Map of the four seas or Map of the world)
1746 (?), 40 x 31 cm
[BOD] Corean.d.2

Chosŏn period atlases typically begin with a map of *Sahae chido* 四海地圖 (The four seas or the whole world, anciently supposed to surround China). This kind of map is commonly known as *Ch'ŏnhado* 天下圖 (Map of the world) or a wheel map and is oriented with north at the top of the map. As is common, in the Bodleian atlas, China is the centre of the map. There is no indication of any cities, provinces or anything apart from the Great Wall Wanlicheng 萬里城, the two major rivers Huang he 黃河 and Yangzi jiang 揚子江, as well as the Five Great Mountains: Tai Shan 泰山 (East), Hua Shan 華山 (West), Heng Shan 衡山 (South), Heng Shan 恒山 (North) and Zhong Shan 中山 (Centre) or Song Shan 嵩山, and a few other mountains. There is no mention of Vietnam, but only Zhenla 真臘 (Kampuchea or Cambodia), which is included to the south. Korea, Japan and Ryūkyū are in their relatively correct positions. In addition, many mythical place names appear on the map. These were derived from Chinese classics such as the *Shanhai jing* 山海經 (*Classic of Mountains and Seas*). The main continent in which China occupies the centre is surrounded by an enclosing ring of sea containing some sixty names of the island countries, including Japan and the Ryūkyūs, while all of the other names are fictional. This sea ring is surrounded by an outer ring of land that contains some forty names of countries. Beyond the outer land ring is another sea ring but there are no names, places or islands in this zone except symbolic trees drawn on islands in the eastern and western parts of the map. These trees are sometimes drawn on the land ring itself, as the northern tree always is. The tree on the east side marks the place where the sun and moon rise, and the tree on the west side marks where they set. The northern tree is a '1,000-*li* coil pine tree' 千里盤松, adjacent to a 'great 10,000-*li* pond' 大澤一万里 – that is, 10,000 *li* in circumference (1 *li* = *c.* 450 metres). The edge of the page is unusually decorated with the ten heavenly stems: 甲乙丙丁戊 己庚辛壬癸.

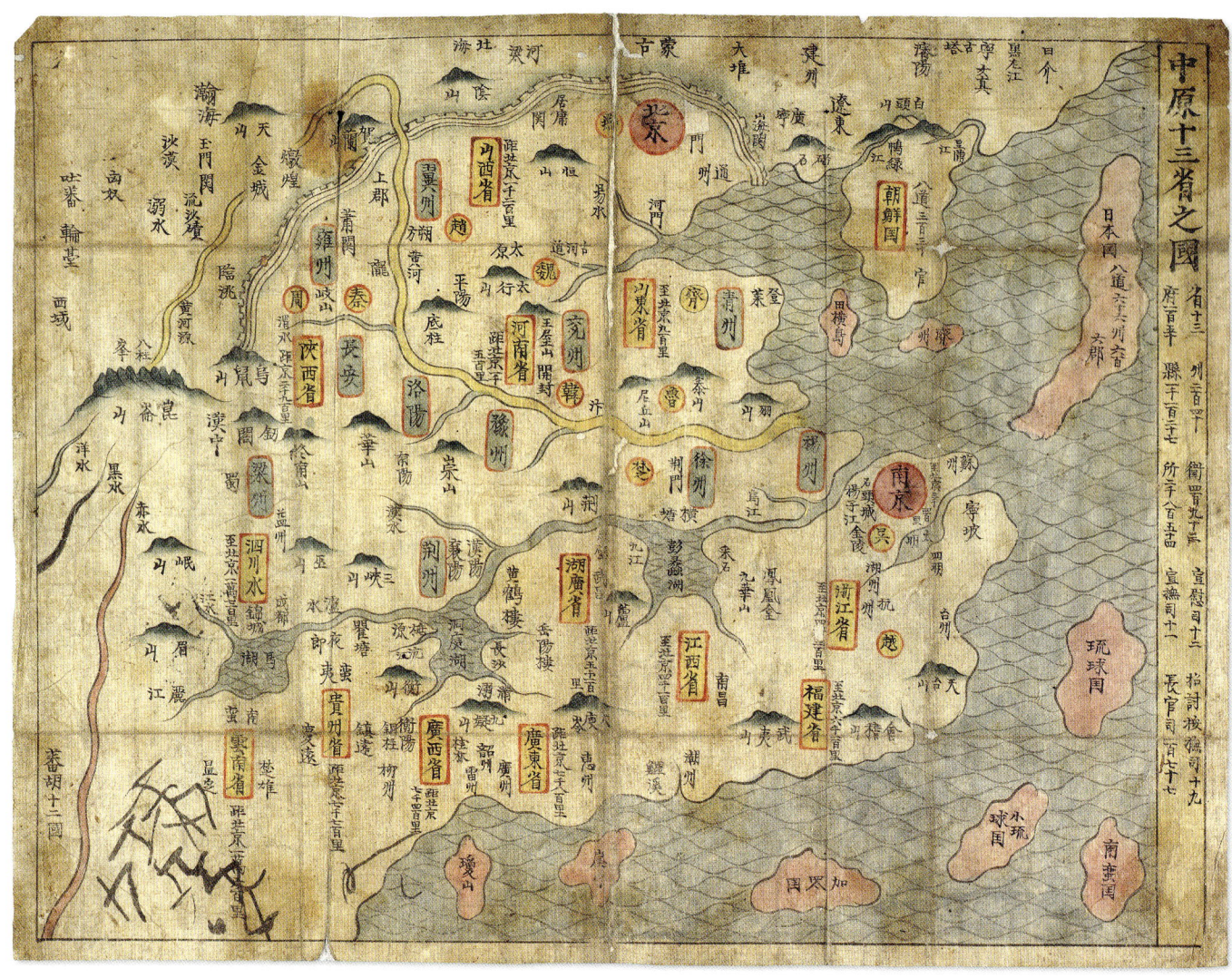

Chungwŏn sipsamsŏng chi-do 中原十三省之圖
(Map of thirteen Chinese provinces)

Mid-18th century, 40 x 31 cm

[BOD] Corean.d.2

The map of the thirteen provinces of China depicts the Great Wall from Niaoshushan 鳥鼠山 in the west to Shanhaiguan 山海關 in the east, along with major rivers and mountains. The names of the thirteen provinces are all highlighted in yellow within a red rectangle or cartouche. Interestingly, although Chosŏn was only one of China's many tributary states, the author gave it a higher position than that of other tributaries by portraying it in the same way as the Chinese provinces, highlighted in yellow within a red rectangle.

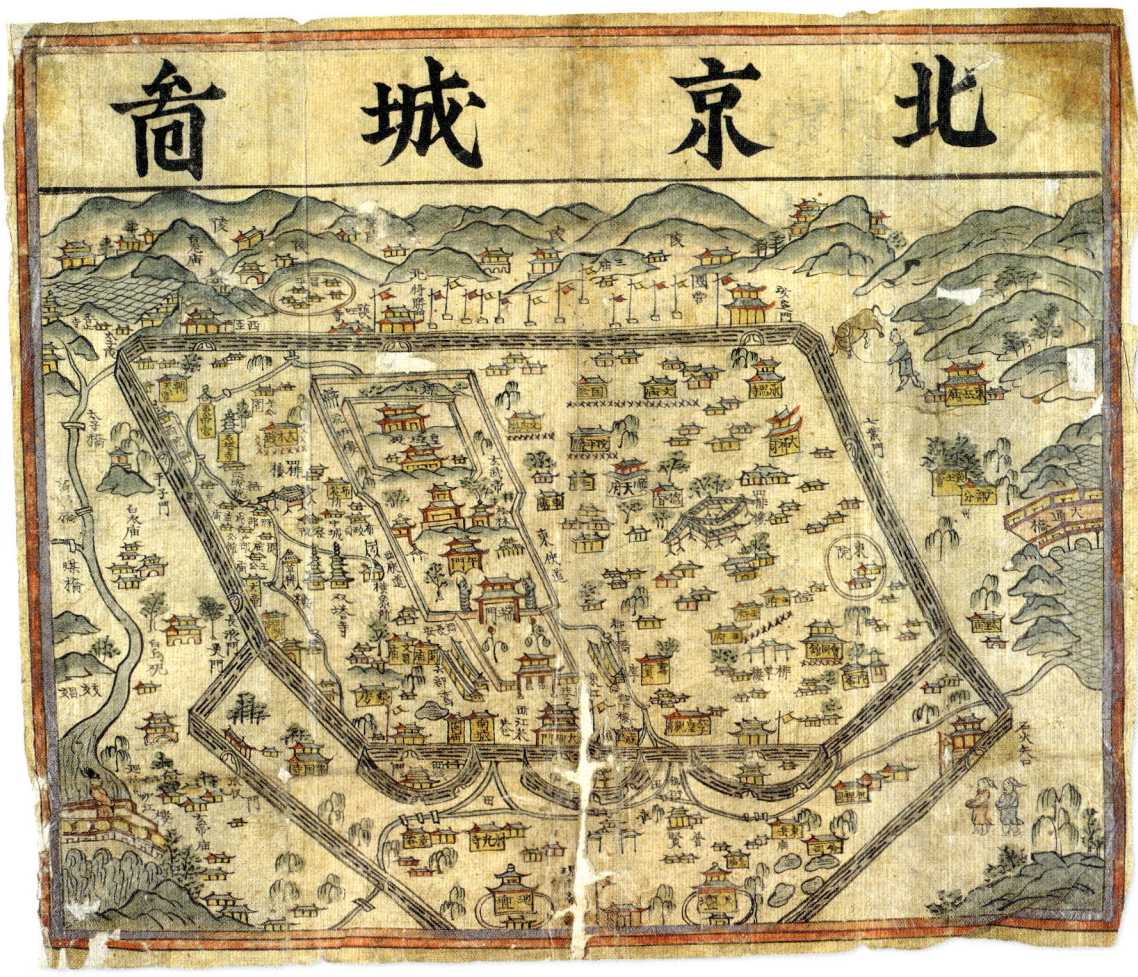

**_Pukkyŏngsŏng-do_ 北京城圖
(Map of Beijing)**

Mid-18th century, 34 x 28 cm

[BOD] Corean.d.2

At the centre is the palace within its enclosure. A city wall
surrounds the palace and the various buildings outside it. There
is a further city wall on the south side enclosing the entrances
to the inner city. The local expression _sijiu cheng_ 四九城 (four
gates within the palace and nine gates along the city wall) is well
illustrated. The Tiantan 天壇 (Temple of Heaven) and the Ditan
地壇 (Temple of Earth) that are depicted on the south side of the
map are still extant today, as are the royal tombs, _Shi San Ling_
十三陵, in the north, outside the city.

Muisan kugok chido 武夷山九曲之圖
(Map of Mount Wuyi)
(*Kiyu Chuja si* 記有朱子詩 [with a poem by Zhu Xi])
Mid-18th century, 40 x 31 cm

[BOD] Corean.d.2

The nine-bend river of Mount Wuyi is presented here, and the map also offers details and names of the surrounding mountains and buildings, including the Wen Gong shu yuan 文公書院 (Zhu Xi's Academy). This painting is accompanied by Zhu Zi's 朱子 (Zhu Xi 朱熹) poem 'Jiu qu zhao ge' 九曲棹歌 (Boat song for the nine bends). The C. Wuyi Mountains are located between Wuyishan City, Nanping prefecture in north-west Fujian Province and Wuyishan Town, Shangrao city in north-east Jiangxi Province. Since 1999 the mountains have been listed as a UNESCO World Heritage Site, for having cultural, scenic and biodiversity value.

It appears that the author of this atlas was a Confucian scholar, as indicated by the fact that he quoted Zhu Xi's poem and illustrated the Wuyi Mountains. Zhu Xi (1130–1200) was a Song dynasty Confucian scholar who has been called the second most influential thinker in Chinese history, after Confucius himself. Zhu Xi lived in Mount Wuyi for many years and built an academy there, which is illustrated in the painting at the fifth bend of the river. Furthermore, the author placed his map of Mount Wuyi at the front of the atlas, after the maps of the world, China and Beijing, and before Nanjing. He is probably thus emphasizing the importance of Confucianism and Zhu Xi in particular. The atlas was produced during the reign of King Yŏngjo 英祖 (1694–1776), who was a deeply Confucian monarch. Confucianism reached a height in Korea in the 18th century.

Zhu Xi's poem
(Jiu qu zhao ge' 九曲棹歌 [Boat song for the nine bends])

武夷山上有仙靈　There are immortals and spirits lodging on Mount Wuyi.

山下寒流曲曲清　Beneath the mountain a cold stream flows curvy and clear.

欲識箇中奇絕處　If you want to know its hidden marvels, sir,

棹歌閑聽兩三聲　Please listen in your idleness to two or three boat songs.

一曲溪邊上釣船　By the first curve of the stream please ride on my fishing boat,

幔亭峰影蘸晴川　The reflection of Curtained Pavilion Peak tinges a sunlit river.

虹橋一斷無消息　No message has come since the Rainbow Bridge was broken;

萬壑千巖鎖翠煙　A myriad of gullies and thousands of cliffs lock in emerald mists.

二曲亭亭玉女峰　By the second curve stands the graceful Jade Maid Peak,

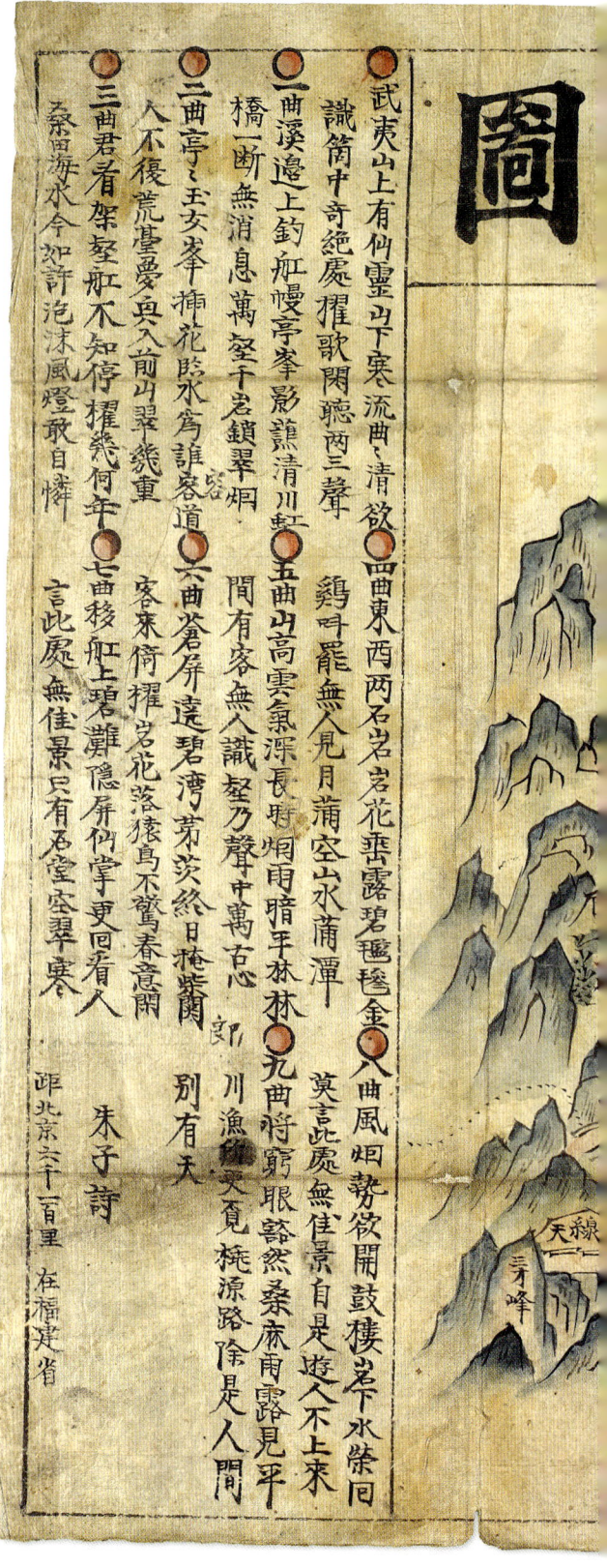

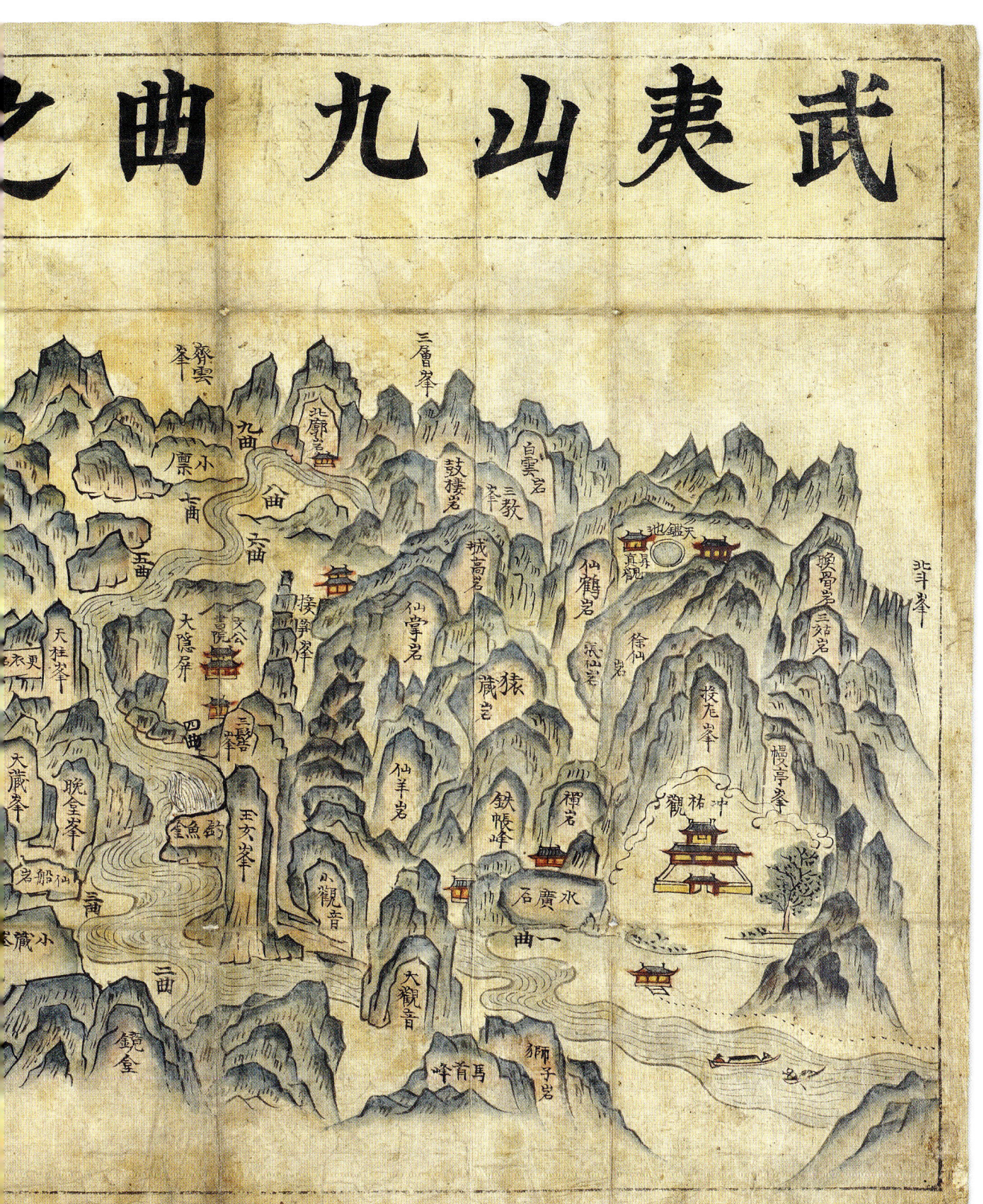

插花臨水為誰容　Wearing blossoms by the water – for whom does she adorn herself?

道人不復陽台夢　The Man of the Way no longer dreams the Sun Terrace dream;

興入前山翠幾重　Ride your spirits to enter the forward mountains, the layered green!

三曲君看架壑船　By the third curve, sir, behold the boats high above the cliff;

不知停櫂幾何年　No one knows for how many years their oars have been at rest.

桑田海水今如許　Mulberry fields have turned into an ocean, now so vast –

泡沫風燈敢自憐　Amid floating foam and lamps in the wind, dare we pity ourselves?

四曲東西兩石巖　By the fourth curve stand two rocky cliffs to the east and to the west,

巖花垂露碧ГГ　Dewy blossoms on the cliffs stoop and glitter amid the lush green.

金雞叫罷無人見　The golden rooster has finished its crowing, but no one is there to see;

月滿空山水滿潭　Moonlight fills the empty mountain, and water brims the deep.

五曲山高雲氣深　By the fifth curve stands a mountain high, where clouds densely gather,

長時煙雨暗平林　Where in long seasons the misty rain darkens low-rising woods.

林間有客無人識　In the woods lives a sojourner whom no one knows,

欸乃聲中萬古心　Who in the creaking song of oars lodges his mind in eternal antiquity.

六曲蒼屏遶碧灣　By the sixth curve, the Dark Screen Peak embraces an emerald bay;

茅茨終日掩柴關　Where a thatched hut closes its brushwood door through the long day.

客來倚櫂巖花落　When the guest arrives by oar, blossoms are falling from the cliff;

猿鳥不驚春意閑　Gibbons and birds are not startled, the spring mood is at ease.

七曲移船上碧灘　By the seventh curve, tow the boat to the emerald shoal,

隱屏仙掌更回看　And turn around to see the Screen of Reclusion and the Divine Palm.

人言此處無佳景　People say this place lacks fine scenery:

只有石堂空翠寒　There is only an empty stone hall in verdant chill.

八曲風煙勢欲開　By the eighth curve the wind is to break the mists;

鼓樓巖下水縈洄　Beneath the Cliff of Drum Tower, the water eddies.

莫言此處無佳景　Please do not say this place lacks fine scenery;

自是遊人不上來　It is only that no visitor has yet ventured this far.

九曲將窮眼豁然　By the end of the ninth curve, one's vision suddenly broadens,

桑麻雨露見平川　Many flat fields of mulberries and hemp spread in rain and dew.

漁郎更覓桃源路　If the fisherman seeks again a road to the Peach Blossom Spring –

除是人間別有天　[Here it is,] beside the realm of man, under another sky!

朱子詩　　　　Zhu Zi's poem

距北京六千一百里 在福建省

In Fujian province, distance to Beijing is 6,100 li.

(translation by Yang Zhiyi)

In the poem, the boat travels along the nine-curve stream revealing hidden marvels at the turn of each bend, a utopia to be realized, which inspired many later visitors to Mount Wuyi to write similar poems in response.

Kŭmnŭng sŭnggae chi-do 金陵勝槩之圖
(Map of the scenery of Nanjing)

Mid-18th century, 36 x 28 cm

[BOD] Corean.d.2

Jinling 金陵 (literally 'Gold Mausoleum') is one of the earlier names for Nanjing. The city has had a number of other names. The name Jinling has been used since the Warring States period (475–221 BCE) in the Zhou dynasty, and it became a Chinese national capital from as early as 317 CE during the Jin dynasty (265–420). The name Nanjing was officially given to the city during the Ming dynasty by that dynasty's first emperor, Zhu Yuanzhang 朱元璋 (Hongwu Emperor), who overthrew the Yuan dynasty. He renamed the city (which had been called Yingtian), rebuilt it, and made it his dynastic capital in 1368. He used 200,000 labourers over twenty-one years to construct a 48-kilometre-long city wall around Yingtian and to build a palace complex and government halls. Hongwu's city wall remains in good condition and has been well preserved, being among the most extensive surviving city walls in China.[23]

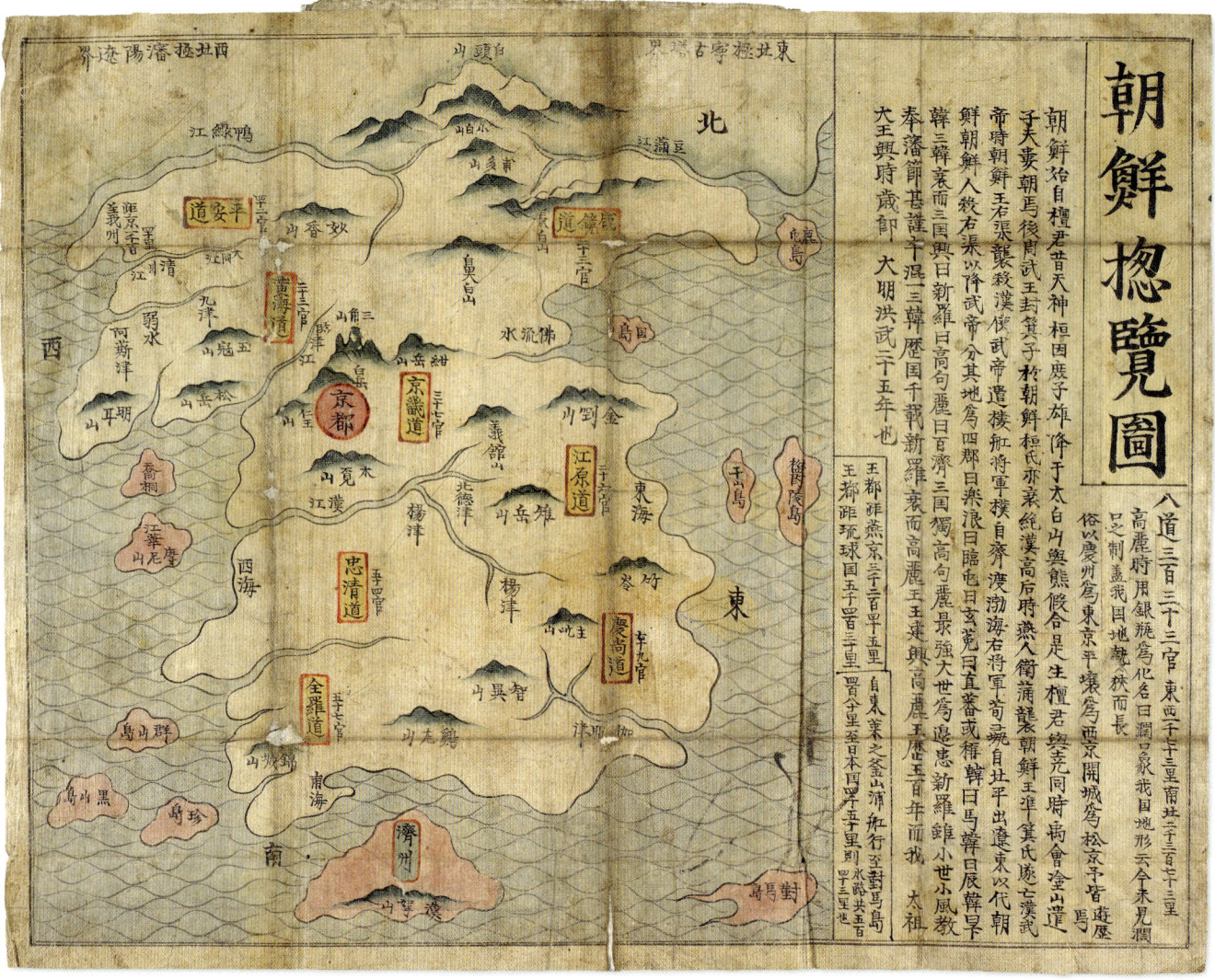

Chosŏn ch'ongnamdo 朝鮮摠覽圖
(Complete Map of Chosŏn)
Mid-18th century, 40 x 31 cm

[BOD] Corean.d.2

The text begins by offering general information: for example, the number of officials in the eight provinces is 323; the distance from east to west is 1,713 *li* and from south to north 2,373 *li*. It then gives a brief history of Korea, starting from Tan'gun 檀君 to 1392 and ends with details of the distances to other places:

Distance from the capital city 王都 to Beijing 燕京 is 3,245 *li*
Distance from the capital city to Ryūkyū 琉球 is 5,430 *li*
Distance from Tongnae 東萊 (Pusan 釜山) to Tsushima 對馬島 is 480 *li* and to Japan 4,050 *li*, including a sea journey of 543 *li*.

The eight province names are highlighted in yellow within red rectangles. The capital city of Hanyang 京都 (Seoul) is highlighted in pink within a red circle. The map also tells us the number of officials stationed in each province:

Kyŏnggi-do 京畿道 37
Ch'ungch'ŏng-do 忠清道 54
Chŏlla-do 全羅道 57
Kyŏngsang-do 慶尚道 79
Hwanghae-do 黃海道 23
P'yŏng'an-do 平安道 42
Kangwŏn-do 江原道 26
Hamgyŏng-do 咸鏡道 23

Hanyangsŏng-do 漢陽城圖
(Map of Hanyang [Seoul])
1746, 40 x 31 cm

[BOD] Corean.d.2

Hanyang is one of many names for Seoul. The city is depicted surrounded by mountains, and on the eastern and southern sides is the Han River 漢江. The number of households within the city is given as 28,298, and the population as 202,147, with a notation of the date: *kapcha inyŏn* 甲子式年 (the *kapcha* year plus two years), or 1746.

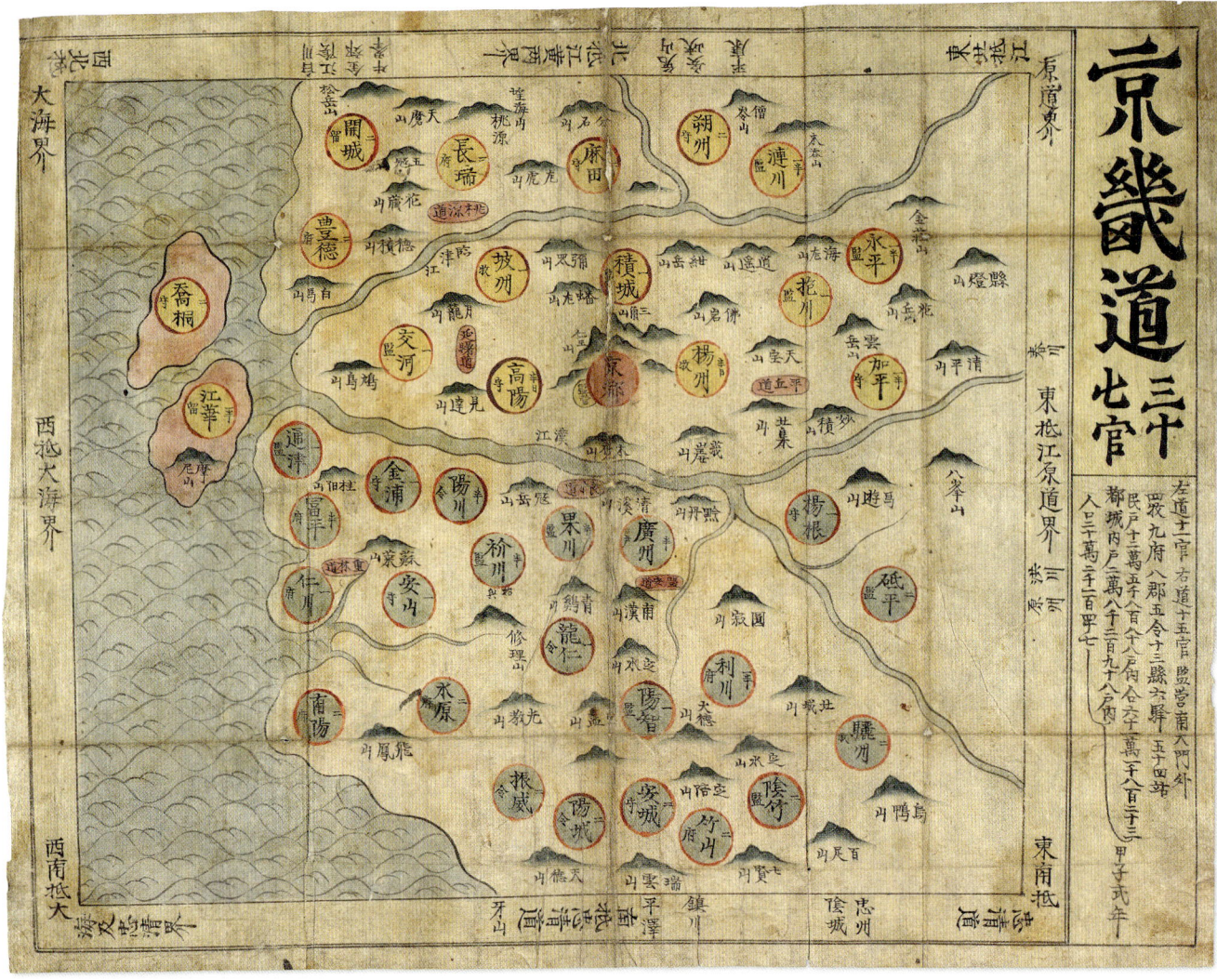

Kyŏnggi-do 京畿道
(Kyŏnggi Province)
1746, 40 x 31 cm
[BOD] Corean.d.2

This map tells us that: 'Eleven magistracies were in the left of
the province and fifteen magistracies in the right. Kyŏnggi has
125,888 households and a population of 601,823. Inside the city,
there are 28,298 households with a population of 202,147.'

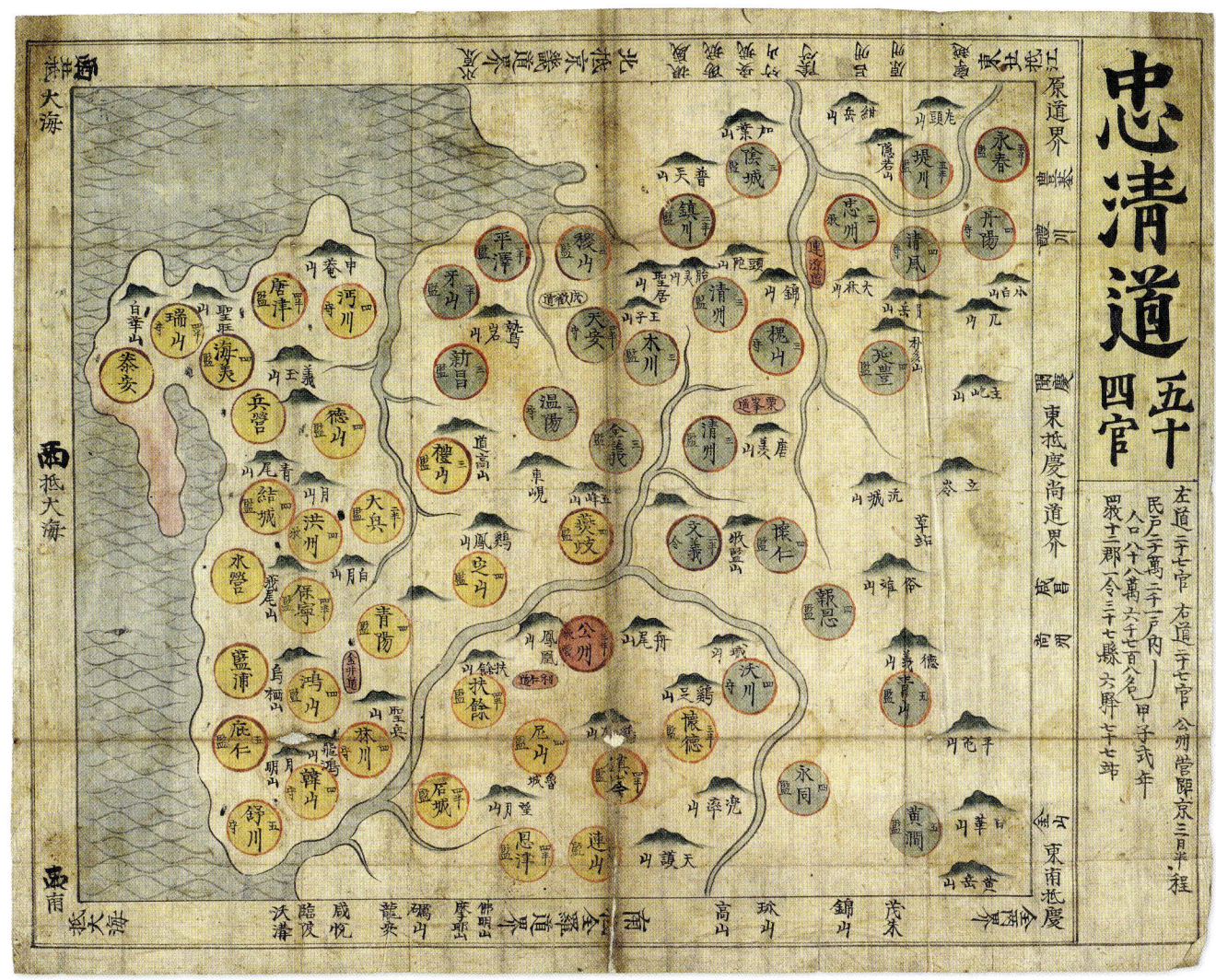

Ch'ungch'ŏng-do 忠清道
(Ch'ungch'ŏng Province)
1746, 40 x 31 cm

[BOD] Corean.d.2

This map tells us: 'Twenty-seven magistracies are located on
the left, and twenty-seven in the right part of the province. The
distance from the provincial seat in Kongju 公州 to the capital is
three days. Ch'ungch'ŏng Province had 202,001 households and
a population of 886,708.'

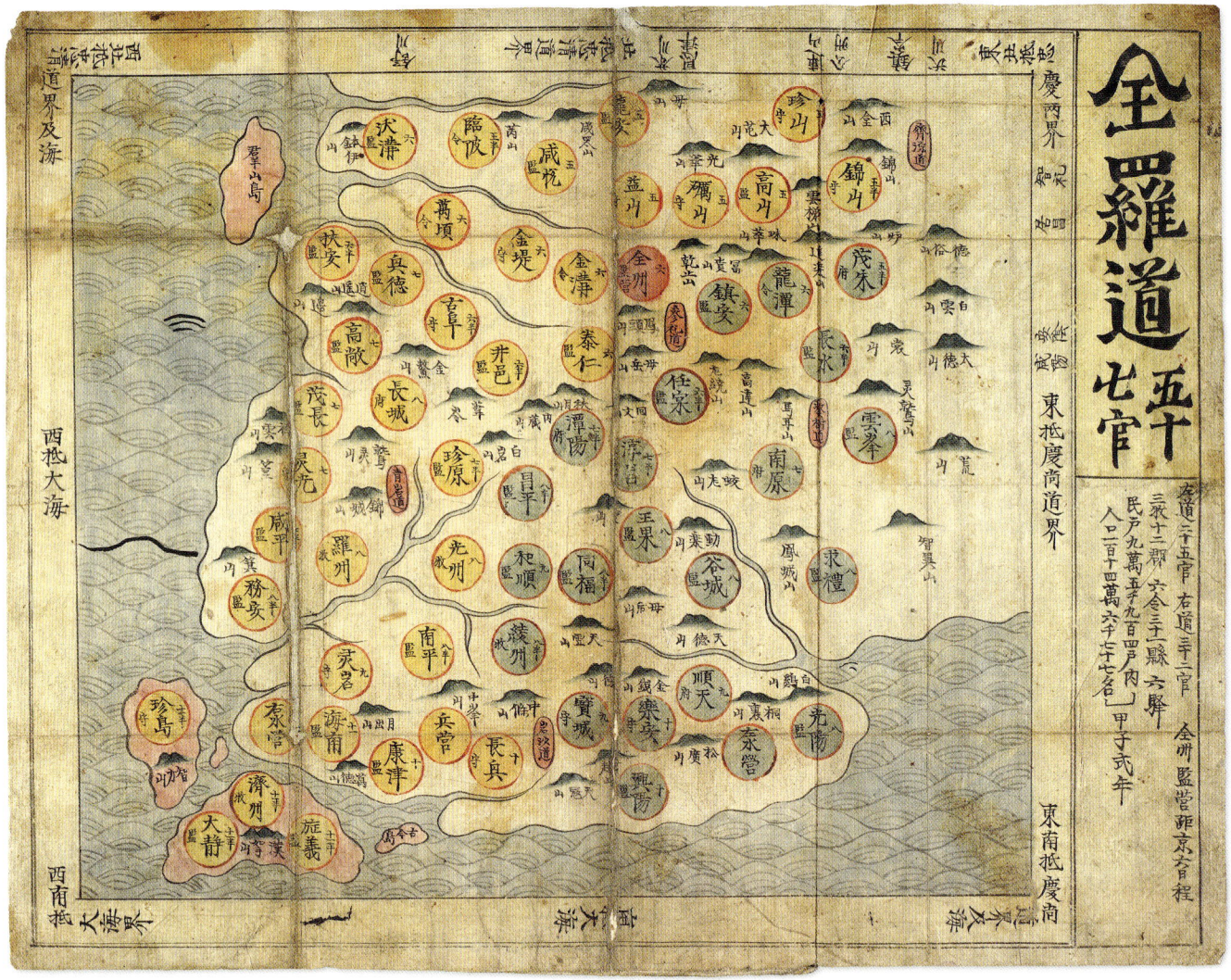

Chŏlla-do 金羅道
(Chŏlla Province)
1746, 40 x 31 cm

[BOD] Corean.d.2

This map tells us: 'There are twenty-five magistracies on the left of the province and thirty-two magistracies on the right. The distance from the provincial seat in Chŏnju 全州 to the capital is a six-day journey. Chŏlla Province has 95,904 households and a population of 1,146,077.'

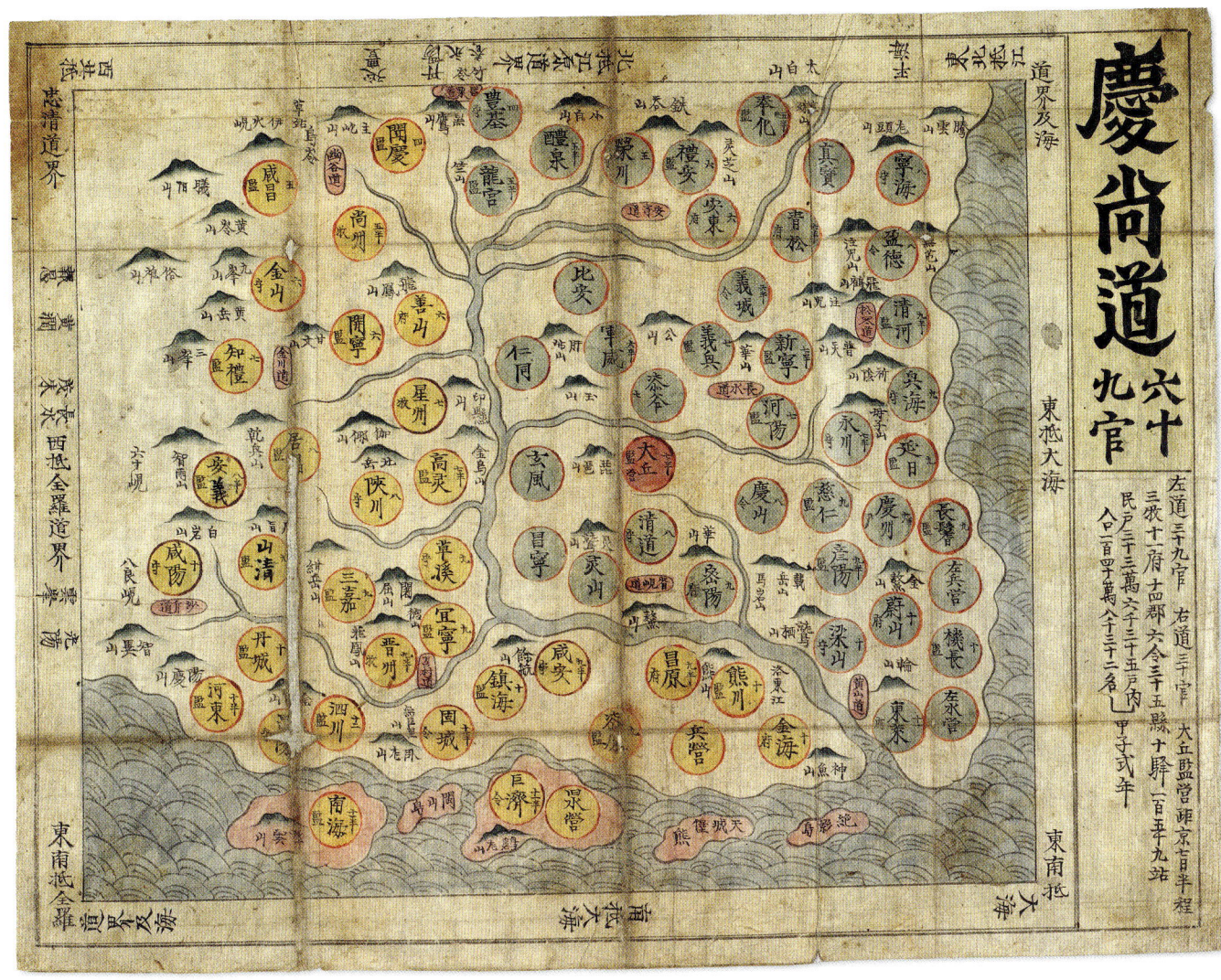

***Kyŏngsang-do* 慶尚道**
(Kyŏngsang Province)

1746, 40 x 31 cm

[BOD] Corean.d.2

This map tells us: 'Thirty-nine magistracies are on the left of the province and thirty magistracies on the right. The distance from the provincial seat in Taegu 大丘 to the capital is a trip of seven and a half days. Kyŏngsan Province has 336,035 households and a population of 1,408,032.'

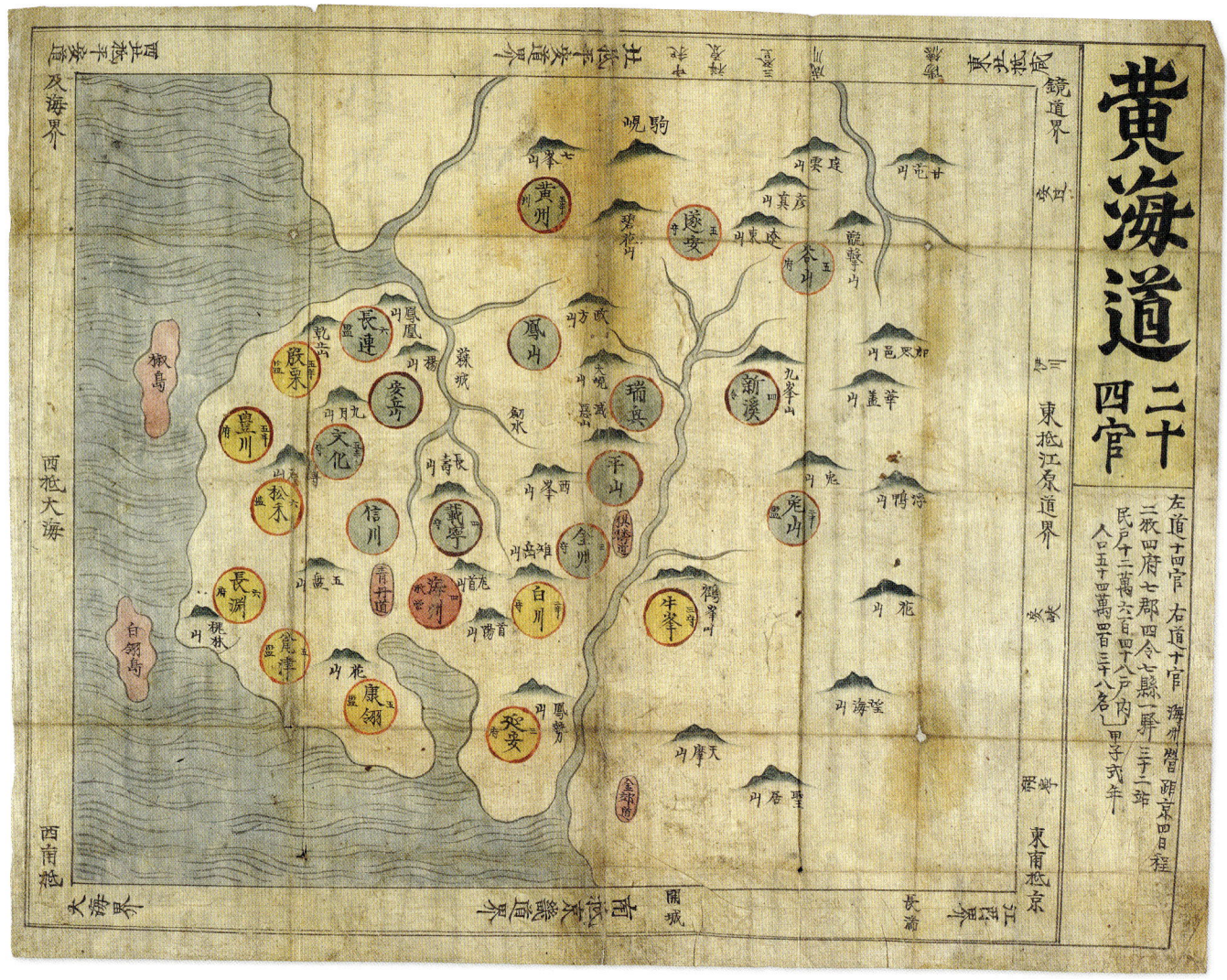

Hwanghae-do 黃海道
(Hwanghae Province)
1746, 40 x 31 cm

[BOD] Corean.d.2

This map tells us: 'Fourteen magistracies are located on the left of the province and nine on the right. The distance from the provincial seat in Haeju 海州 to the capital is a four-day trip. Hwanghae Province has 120,648 households and a population of 540,438.'

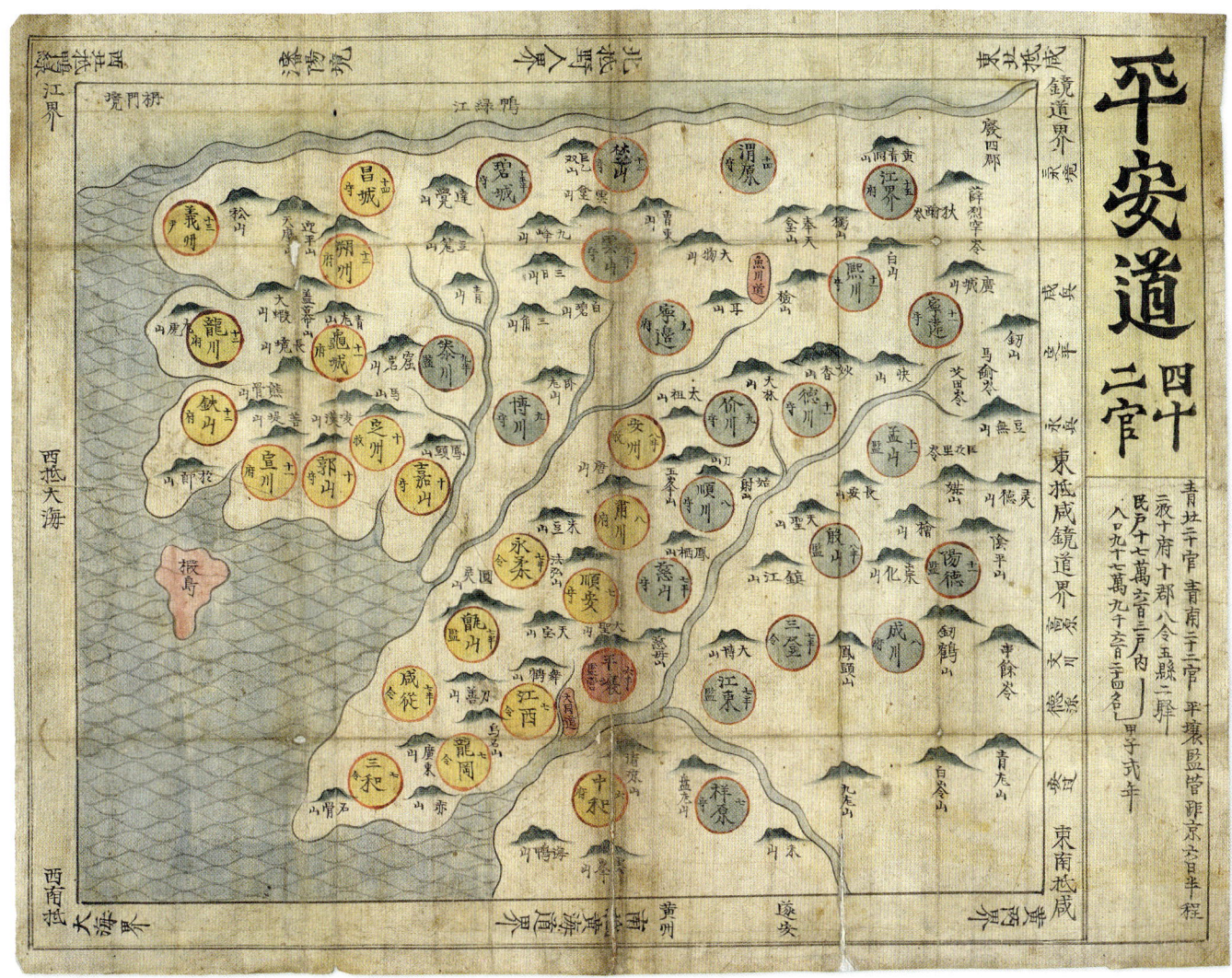

P'yŏng'an-do 平安道
(P'yŏng'an Province)
1746, 40 x 31 cm
[BOD] Corean.d.2

This map tells us: 'Twenty-four magistracies are located in the
northern part of the province 青北 and twenty-two magistracies
are in the southern part of the province 青南. The distance from
the provincial seat in P'yŏngyang 平壤 to the capital is six and
a half days. P'yŏng'an Province has 170,603 households and a
population of 979,624.'

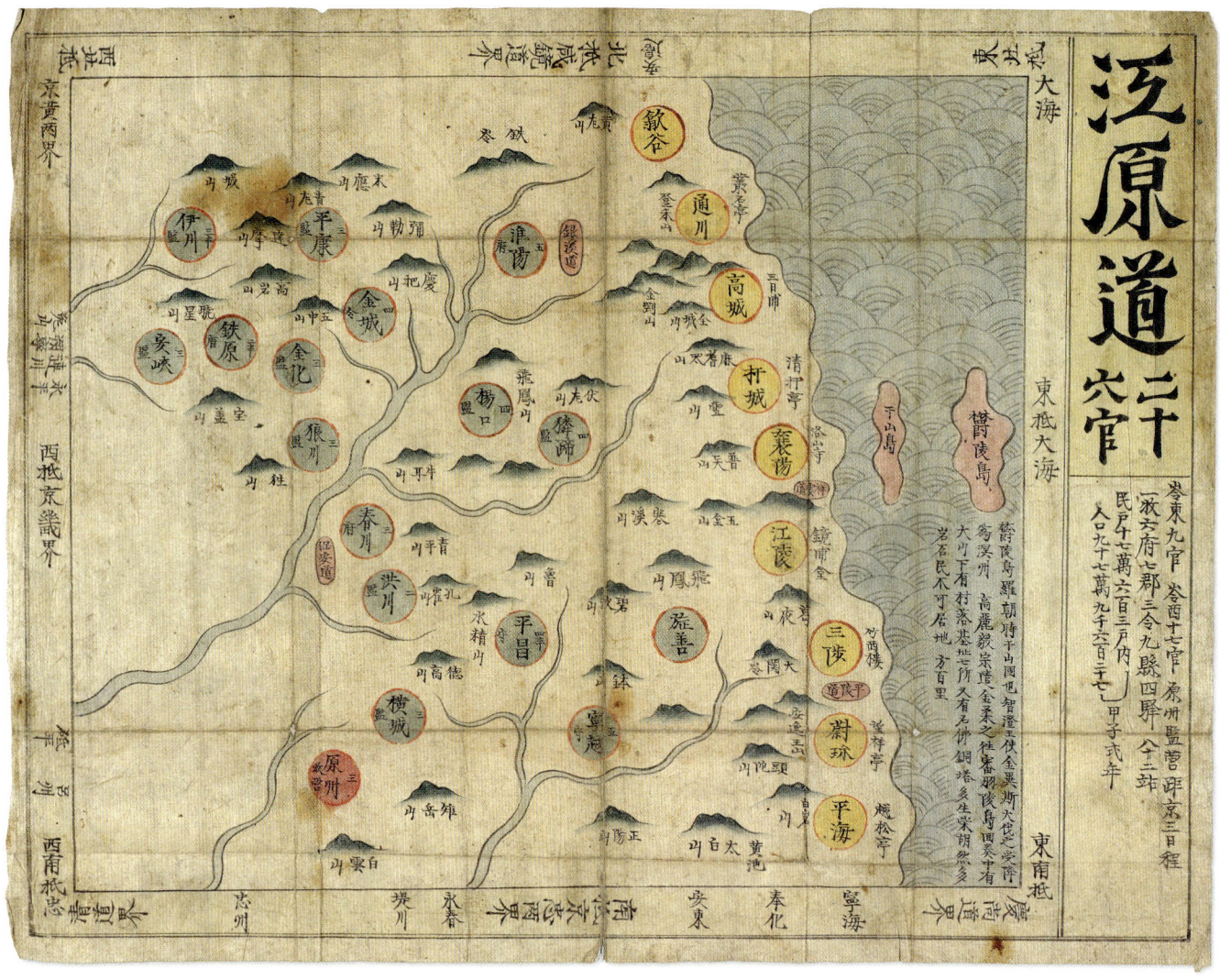

Kangwŏn-do 江原道
(Kangwŏn Province)

1746, 40 x 31 cm

[BOD] Corean.d.2

This map tells us: 'Nine magistracies are located in the eastern part of the province 嶺東 and seventeen magistracies in the southern part of the province 嶺南. The distance from the provincial seat in Wŏnju 原州 to the capital is a three-day trip. Kangwŏn Province has 170,603 households and a population of 979,627.'

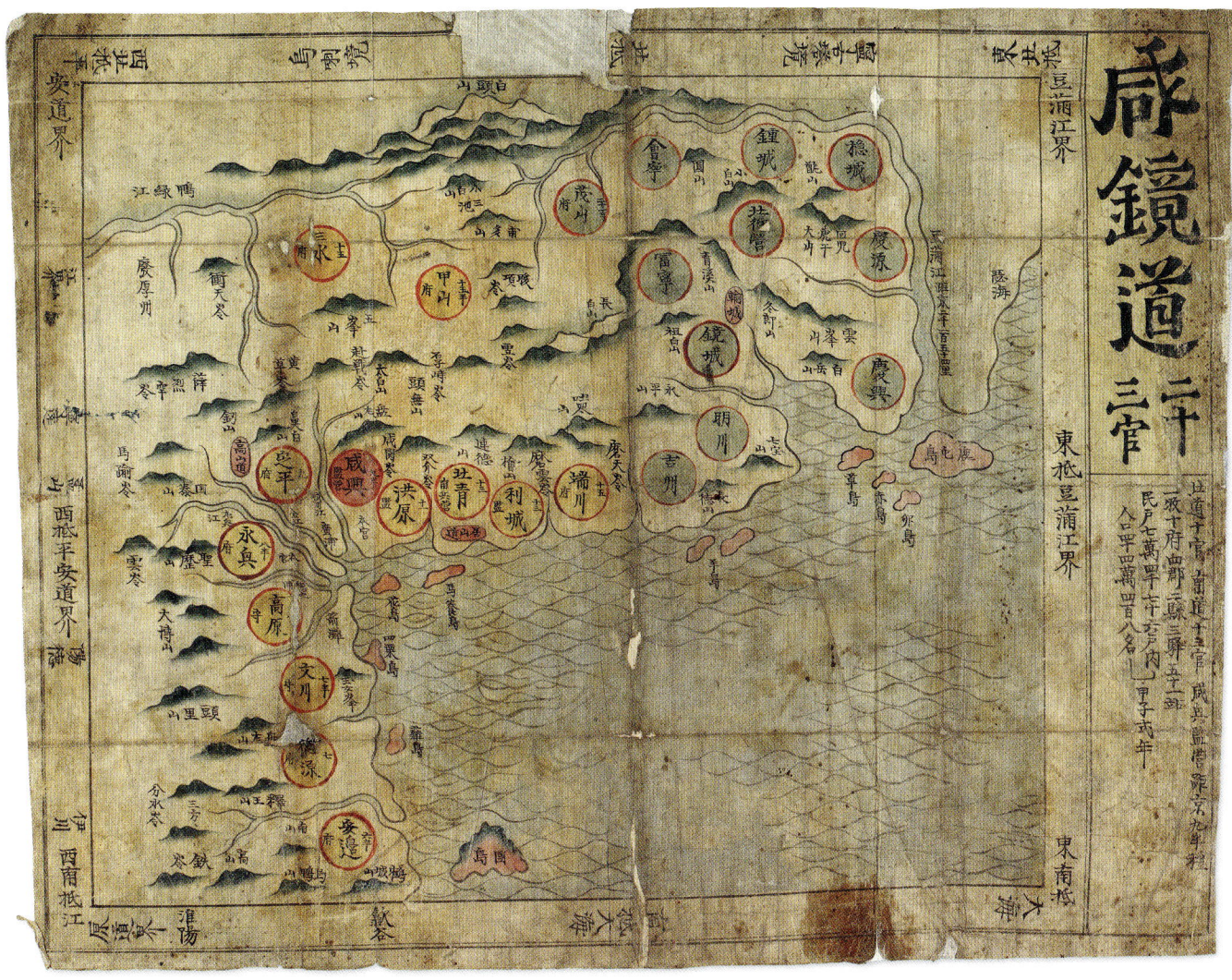

Hamgyŏng-do 咸鏡道
(Hamgyŏng Province)

1746, 39 x 31 cm

[BOD] Corean.d.2

This map tells us: 'Ten magistracies are located in the north and thirty magistracies in the south of the province. The distance from the provincial seat in Hamhŭng 咸興 to the capital is a nine-day trip. Hamgyŏng Province has 74,076 households and a population of 440,408.'

書僧屬鄭夢周等名板
藏在寺尚宛然前臨溪上有龍
飛興慶二樓甚軒敞

雪峯山釋王寺記

我 太祖康獻大王洪武十七年辛禑十年甲子歲自金馬來寓鶴城結草爲屋爲人性度寬弘行止非凡
里人以寬厚大人稱 祖一夕假寐夢見萬家鷄一時鳴又聞千家砧一時鳴又入破屋中負三椽而出
又見落花落鏡忽驚寤不知夢兆之吉凶譪〻傍有一老婆欲向說夢問驗婆止之曰丈人安知
大丈夫方來事此西去四十里雪峯山土窟中有異僧遁世逃名食松被葛言行非凡但形貌㿜然故
目爲黑頭陁者坐不動今九年矣宜可問及 祖即布衣藜杖尋土窟見僧坐禮而進曰草屋塵人欲決
疑事願慈悲垂答僧擧頭曰何事耶 祖曰昨夜夢見萬家鷄一時鳴又聞千家砧亦一時鳴又見
落花落鏡又身入破屋負三椽而出此古夢將何驗也僧改容曰此皆將作君王之夢也非常夢也曰
萬家鷄聲者賀高貴位也千家砧聲者報御近當也花落何無實落鏡豈無聲負三椽者乃王
字也花鏡亦佷王業之夢也僧又擧頭熟視曰公有滿面君王態也公今日事愼不出於口此庀地
建一刹名曰釋王寺至住〻〻又曰大事不可速成限三年設五百聖齋禱祈則聖僧必助王業耳公若不
信吾教則非徒事不成禍必滅身望須十分謹之 祖退庸執師禮曰敬受教矣願和尚慈悲助
我大事僧點頭唯唯 祖一年內建釋王寺畢又三年內設五百齋畢鄉人皆不知所以也至洪武戊辰辛禑
十四年使 太祖爲都統使攻遼東四月初 祖統軍于義州五月中渡鴨綠江及至威化島 祖擧義回
軍也至洪武二十五年壬申七月十六日 祖即位于松京壽昌宮即尋雪峯土窟僧封王師此無
學也於是無學出爲 太祖還先墓定王都吁草屋中起君王土窟中作王師其大因緣偉哉
其解夢日乃釋王之始也其即位日乃釋王之終也然則釋王釋王乃先祖化家爲國之最
初願刹也宜歷聖之敬護也然爲緜歷傳記中爲兵火被蕩惜哉余今日適過此不忍
泯蹟敍筆略記釋王寺之始終爾

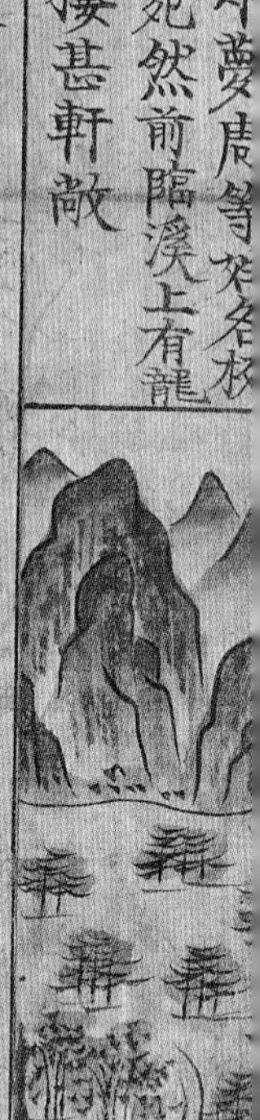

Anbyŏn Sŏgwang-sa 安边釋王寺
(Map of Sŏgwang Temple)
Mid-18th century, 40 cm x 31 cm
[BOD] Corean.d.2

Sŏgwang-sa is a Buddhist temple located in Sŏlbong-ri in Kosan County, Kangwŏn Province, the Democratic People's Republic of Korea. Once one of Korea's largest Buddhist temples, the complex was mostly destroyed by bombing in 1951 and today lies in ruins. Although the author was a Confucian scholar, he seems to have had a deep interest in Buddhism and the temple. He presents the Sŏgwang Temple map with a long explanation about the history of how the temple was named.

Here is a brief summary: one day when T'aejo 太祖 was having a nap, in his dream he heard the crowing of roosters from 10,000 households and heard the sound of cloth-washing stones from 1,000 households. He entered a dilapidated house, carried out three rafters and saw flowers fall into a mirror. Right at that moment he suddenly awoke and wondered whether this dream was auspicious or not. He then went west for 40 *li* and came to Mount Sŏlbong 雪峰. There he found a cave where a monk lived in seclusion. He told the monk his dream and the monk explained to him that it was a sign that he would one day become a king: 'The crowing of roosters from 10,000 households celebrates the high and noble position; the sound of cloth-washing stones from 1,000 households indicates the king will soon come to the throne. The person carrying the three rafters (which makes up the Chinese character for king 王) will be the king.' The monk then looked at his face and told him that he had the face of a king. However, he must not tell anyone about this, and it would be best to build a temple here and name it Sŏgwang. The monk added that T'aejo should not rush into becoming a king but allow himself three years from the building of the temple, which would help him towards becoming a king. Within a year, T'aejo completed the temple and lavishly filled it with sutras, sculptures of the Buddha and other related items. The people living in the surroundings did not know why the temple was built there. And indeed, T'aejo ascended the throne on the 16th day of the seventh month of Hongwu 25 (1392) at the Such'ang Palace 壽昌 in Songgyŏng 松京 (Kaesŏng 開城).

Yŏnggot'ap chŏn-do 寧古塔 全圖
(Complete map of Ning'an or Ningguta in Manchuria)
Mid-18th century, 40 x 40 cm

[BOD] Corean.d.2

During the early Qing dynasty, the town of Ning'an 寧安, known then under the Manchu name Ningguta (transcribed into Chinese as 寧古塔), was one of the most important towns in Manchuria beyond the 'Willow Palisade'. The name Ningguta literally means 'six' in the Manchu language, because it was once guarded by six grandsons of Möngke Temür 猛哥帖木儿.

Ning'an is a city located approximately 20 kilometres south-west of Mudanjiang 牡丹江, in Heilongjiang 黑龍江 Province. It is on the Mudanjiang River (formerly known as the Hurka River), which flows north, eventually flowing into the Sungari River 阿什河 near Sanxing 三姓. Ning'an is now a county-level city and a part of the prefecture-level city of Mudanjiang.[24] On the map can be seen two red lines that track the routes into China departing from Ŭiju 義州 to the west of Paektusan 白頭山 and crossing the Amnokgang River 鴨綠江 (Yalu River) and from Hŭinyŏng 會寧 to the east of Paektusan and crossing the Tuman River 豆滿江.

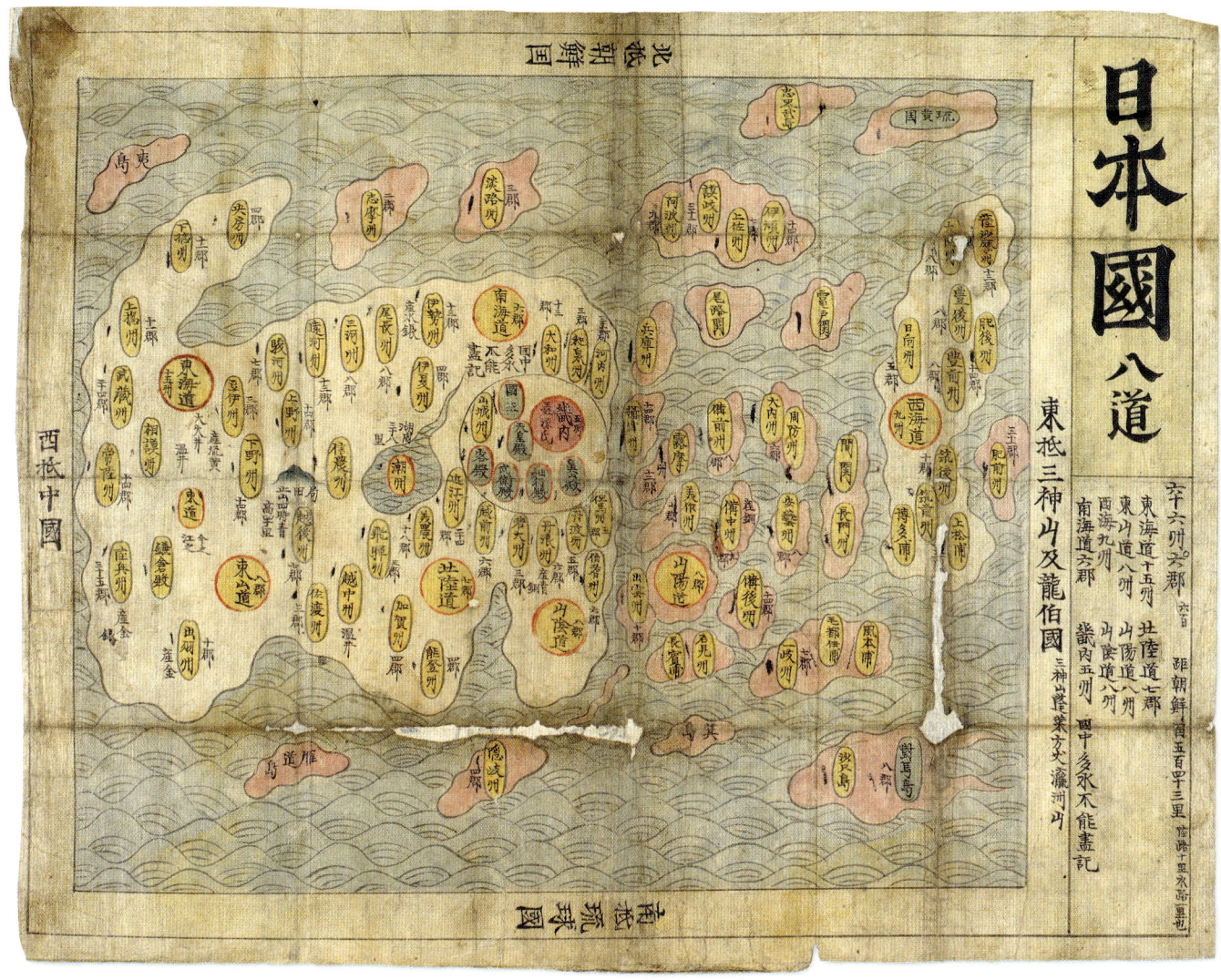

Ilbon chido 日本地圖
(Map of Japan)
Mid-18th century, 40 x 31 cm

[BOD] Corean.d.2

In Korean world atlases, Chinese places usually come first, followed by Korea, and then Japan, showing the relative hierarchy of the world order in the minds of Korean scholars. This map differs from all others in that the view is from the Korean peninsula looking south, which would place south at the top, but the top is labelled north, as in the other maps. Although the right-hand side is labelled east, it is actually western Japan. Korea is said to be to the north from this map, while the island of Tsushima 對馬 is placed on the southern side of the map, far from the approach to Korea. In short, the orientation is correct if one is looking from the peninsula to the south and west, but the labels appear to be backwards. The information on the map consists of a general administrative description with place names. Japan has eight provinces 八道, sixty-six administrative divisions 州, and six districts 郡. It is 543 *li* from Korea, and ten land *li* is equivalent to one sea *li*. The eight provinces consist of: the Tōkaidō 東海道 (with fifteen administrative divisions), the Tōsandō 東山道 (with eight administrative divisions), the Saikaidō 西海道 (with nine administrative divisions), the Nankaidō 南海道 (with six districts), the Kinai 畿內 (with five administrative districts), the San'indō 山陰道 (with eight administrative divisions), the San'yōdō 山陽道 (with eight administrative divisions) and the Hokurikudō 北陸道 (with seven districts). The map explains that there are many rivers in the country, which cannot all be listed.

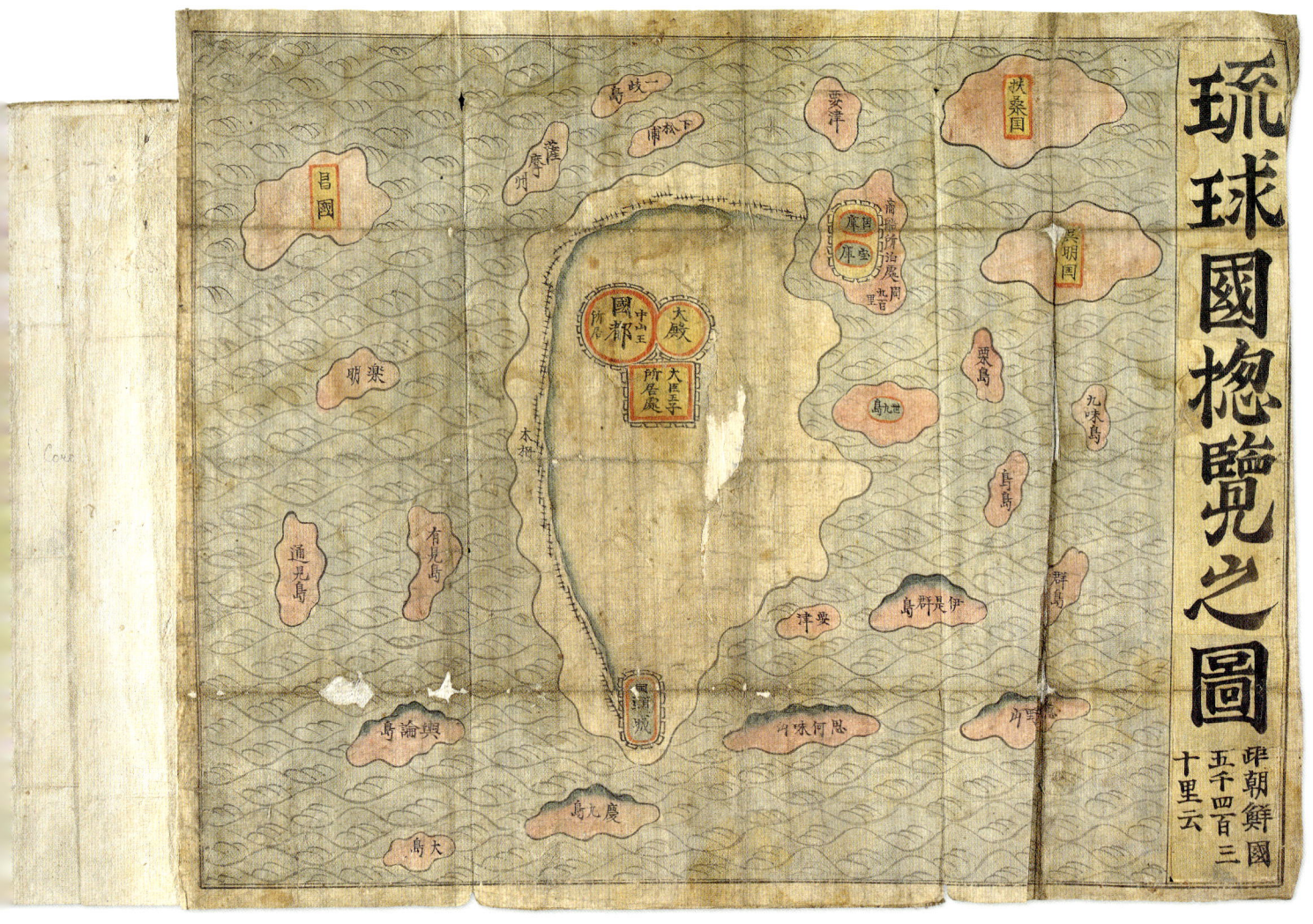

Yuguguk chido 琉球國地圖
(Map of Ryūkyū)
Mid-18th century, 40 x 31 cm

[BOD] Corean.d.2

The Ryūkyū Kingdom 琉球國 (Okinawa) was an independent kingdom that ruled most of the Ryūkyū Islands from the 15th to the 19th centuries. It was invaded in 1609 by the Satsuma domain and made a vassal. When the domains were dissolved after the Meiji Restoration, Ryūkyū was annexed by the new Japanese state in 1879 and renamed Okinawa. In Korean world atlases, the Ryūkyū Kingdom has always been placed at the end, after Japan. The author seemed not to have much knowledge of the Ryūkyū Kingdom, because very little information is offered, except for the statement that the distance to Korea is said to be 5,430 *li*.

Sŏnggyŏng yŏji chŏn-do 盛京輿地全圖
(Complete Map of Shengjing or Shenyang)
Mid-18th century, 40 x 31 cm

[BOD] Corean.d.2

The map depicts the extent of the Shengjing 盛京 territory in the Qing dynasty. The Manchu leader Nurhaci 努爾哈赤 captured Shenyang 沈陽 in 1625 and moved his government apparatus to the city, or Simiyan hoton, as it is called in the Manchu language. The official name was changed to Shengjing 盛京 ('rising capital') or Mukden (in Manchu) in 1634. 'Mukden' comes from the Manchu word *mukdembi*, meaning 'to rise', and this intent is reflected in the Han Chinese name. Nurhaci ordered the Imperial Palace to be constructed in 1626, symbolizing the

city's emerging status as the Jurchen political centre. The palace featured more than 300 ostentatiously decorated rooms and twenty gardens as a symbol of power and grandeur. After the fall of the Ming dynasty and the routing of the Shun army in the Battle of Shanhai Pass 山海關 on the following day, the Manchus successfully entered the Shanhai Pass in 1644 to establish the Qing dynasty and relocated their capital to Beijing. Shenyang retained considerable importance as the secondary capital and the spiritual home of the Qing dynasty.[25] It is very unusual for a Korean world atlas to include Shengjing (Shenyang), but its location at the very end probably indicates that the Korean author was still loyal to the Ming even though China was then ruled by the Qing Empire.

2

COINS, AMULETS AND CHATELAINES

EARLY KOREAN COINS before the 17th century were few in number and are very rare. From 1633 onwards, bronze coins were produced with only one obverse type and that type prevailed until modern times. What makes Korean coins valuable as historical objects are the systematic varieties of inscriptions on the reverse that indicate mints and even furnaces. Unlike Chinese or Japanese coins, Korean coins do not have official reign titles, so dating is difficult. Amulets or charms were produced as well and were intended to bring good luck and ward off evil. These were carried by a variety of people during the Chosŏn dynasty. They were made of silver, bronze, white or yellow brass and sometimes enamelled with red, yellow and blue colours. The chatelaines are key charms or large amulets to which smaller charms, coins or coloured ribbons were attached. They were given to brides on their wedding day and were kept hanging in the house after the wedding. Korean amulets are considered to be well made and more attractive than those produced in China and Japan.

COINS

The Ashmolean Museum of Art and Archaeology has one of the most important collections of East Asian coins in Europe. It has more than 20,000 coins, with 15,000 Chinese coins, 1,600 Japanese coins and 3,066 Korean coins.[1] This is the largest known collection of Korean coins in the United Kingdom and perhaps in Europe. The British Museum has 2,474

Korean coins and charms,[2] and the Fitzwilliam Museum has 1,435 Korean coins.[3] The Manchester Museum at the University of Manchester is the only other known collection, containing seventy-two coins.[4] In recent years, the Fitzwilliam collection[5] and the British Museum collections have been catalogued, and digital images have been put online (fully for the Fitzwilliam and partially for the British Museum). In December 2016, cataloguing of the Ashmolean collection images and data was also completed and put online.[6] The Ashmolean collection appears to include a slightly larger number of scarce or unusual coins than the Fitzwilliam Museum or the British Museum, but these specifics have yet to be clearly determined. The Korean examples below are from the Ashmolean Museum and are all identified by the Heberden Coin Room (HCR) number, fully searchable on the Ashmolean Museum website under East Asian coins (http://hcr.ashmus.ox.ac.uk/coin).

The Korean coins include early pieces from the 11th century and excellent examples of the 1423-minted *Chosŏn t'ongbo* 朝鮮通寶, as well as a comprehensive collection of *sangp'yŏng t'ongbo* 常平通寶 coinage from later centuries. The Korean coin collection was mostly donated by C.T. Gardner (1842–1914), who was the first Western numismatist specializing in Korean coinage. He served as British consul for many years in China before being appointed to Korea in 1884, where he built up this fine collection, including two examples of every monetary type, rare coins and Korea's first modern milled coinage issued in 1882. There are also some coins from the famous collection of Kutsuki Masatsuna 朽木昌綱 (1750–1802). Parts of his collection of East Asian coins were sold to the British Museum and the Ashmolean Museum in the 1880s.[7]

According to Korean historical records, iron coins were issued around 996 CE, and indeed iron coins without inscription have been found in tombs near Kaesŏng 開城. During the years 996–1009, copper coins were issued with inscriptions on the obverse of *Kŏnwŏn chungbo* 乾元 重寶 (C. *Qianyuan zhongbao*) after the Tang dynasty reign of Qianyuan (758–60). On the reverse, the coins have additional characters that read *Tongguk* 東國 (Eastern Kingdom or Korea). During the period 998–1009, another coin was produced with the inscription of *Kaewŏn t'ongbo* 開元 通寶 (Circulating treasure of the *kaewŏn* year), which is identical to the coins cast during the reign of the Tang Emperor Gao Zu 高祖 (r. 618–26). In 1097, a mint was established by King Sukjong 肅宗 (r. 1095–1105) and a variety of coins were cast during the years 1097–1107. These include the series carrying the inscriptions *Tongguk* 東國 (Eastern Country), *Haedong* 海東 (Eastern Sea), and *Sam Han* 三韓 (Three States) (pages 52–3).

The reading of the inscriptions is either from top to bottom and right to left: *Tongguk t'ongbo* 東國通寶, *Tongguk chungbo* 東國重寶, *Sam Han t'ongbo* 三韓通寶 and *Sam Han chungbo* 三韓重寶, (pages 52 and 53) or clockwise, starting from the top – top, right, bottom, left – as in the example of *Haedong t'ongbo* 海東通寶 and *Haedong chungbo* 海東重寶 (page 52). The coins issued in the 10th and 11th centuries were never popular, and when counterfeiting became widespread, public dissatisfaction increased. In the early 12th century, Korea ceased issuing copper coins or used coins imported from Song China, and they did not appear again until the 15th century. Mulberry paper money or *chŏhwa* 楮貨 was also issued from 1391 and into the early Chosŏn period, but no examples survive.

Also, in 1101, large silver coins known as *tae-ŭnbyŏng* 大銀瓶 (vase coins), in the shape of the land of Koryŏ, were issued. These were first made with twelve *yang* 兩 of silver (approx. 450 grams) and two *yang* 兩 of copper (approx. 75 grams) to weigh 525 grams, which is close to one *kŭn*

Major government and military mints before the modern period

Number	Mint mark at top of the reverse	Issuing agency	English translation
1	抄	Chŏngch'och'ŏng 精抄廳	Elite Military Bureau
2	摠 or 㧾	Ch'ongyungch'ŏng 摠戎廳	Command of the Northern Approaches
3	戶	Hojo 戶曹	Ministry of Taxation
4	訓	Hullyŏn togam 訓鍊都監	Military Training Command
5	工	Kongjo 工曹	Ministry of Works
6	兵	Pyŏngjo 兵曹	Ministry of War
7	賑	Chinhyulch'ŏng 賑恤廳	Relief Bureau
8	備	Pibyŏnsa 備邊司	Border Defence Council
9	營	Ŏyŏngch'ŏng 御營廳	Capital Guard Unit
10	武	Mubisa 武備司	Military Supply Office
11	武	Muwiyŏng 武衛營	Palace Guards Garrison
12	禁	Kŭmwiyŏng 禁衛營	Capital Garrison
13	向	Yanghyangch'ŏng 粮餉廳	Bureau of Food Supply
14	宣	Sŏnhyech'ŏng 宣惠廳	Rice and Cloth Bureau for the Uniform Land Tax Law (*Taedongbŏp*)
15	均	Kyunyŏkch'ŏng 均役廳	Office of Equal Service
16	經	Kyŏngnich'ŏng 經理廳	Government Bureau of Pukhan Mountain Fortress
17	典	Chŏnhwan'guk 典圜局	Bureau of Mintage
18	昌	Ch'angdŏkkung 昌德宮	Ch'angdŏk Palace
19	守	Suŏch'ŏng 守禦廳	Bureau for the Defence of Namhan Mountain Fortress
20	京	Kyŏnggi kamyŏng 京畿監營	Kyŏnggi Provincial Office
21	京水	Kyŏnggi suyŏng 京畿水營	Kyŏnggi Provincial Naval Command
22	沁	Kanghwa kwalliyŏng 江華管理營	Kanghwa (Kyŏnggi Province) City Military Office
23	松	Kaesŏng kwalliyŏng 開城管理營	Kaesŏng (Kyŏnggi Province) City Military Office

斤 (approx. 600 grams). We have no extant examples of the large silver vase coins.[8] They were said to be used mainly for large transactions and as ceremonials gifts and rewards or even bribes.[9] Because they were too large and inconvenient, by 1350 they had gone out of circulation.[10] More convenient *swaeŭn* 碎銀 (fragmentary or 'crushed' silver) coins were used from 1287, although we have no extant specimens.[11] Smaller silver vase coins known as *so-ŭnbyŏng* 小銀瓶 were also made from 1331, but again we do not have any extant examples.[12] Examples of both fragmentary silver and the small silver vase coin can be seen in the Bank of Korea Money Museum 한국은행 화폐박물관, although their authenticity has yet be verified. The small vase was probably made of *chŏngdong* 靑銅 (bronze), but the debasement of silver vase coins became common.[13]

24	開	Kaesŏng kwalliyŏng 開城管理營	Kaesŏng (Kyŏnggi Province) City Military Office
25	圻	Kwangju kwalliyŏng 廣州管理營	Kwangju (Kyŏnggi Province) City Military Office
26	水	Suwŏn kwalliyŏng 水原管理營	Suwŏn (Kyŏnggi Province) City Military Office
27	忠	Ch'ungch'ŏng kamyŏng 忠淸監營	Ch'ungch'ŏng Provincial Office
28	平	P'yŏng'an kamyŏng 平安監營	P'yŏng'an Provincial Office
29	平兵	P'yŏng'an pyŏngyŏng 平安兵營	P'yŏng'an Military Command
30	黃	Hwanghae kamyŏng 黃海監營	Hwanghae Provincial Office
31	海	Haeju kwalliyŏng 海州管理營	Haeju (Hwanghae Province) City Military Office
32	尚	Kyŏngsang kamyŏng 慶尚監營	Kyŏngsang Provincial Office
33	尚水	Kyŏngsang suyŏng 慶尚水營	Kyŏngsang Provincial Naval Command
34	尚左	Kyongsang chwayŏng 慶尚左營	Left Kyŏngsang Provincial Naval Command
35	尚右	Kyongsang uyŏng 慶尚右營	Right Kyŏngsang Provincial Naval Command
36	統	T'ongyŏng kwalliyŏng 統營管理營	T'ongyŏng City (Kyŏngsang Province) Military Office
37	昌	Ch'angwŏn kwalliyŏng 昌原管理營	Changwŏn (Kyŏngsang Province) City Military Office
38	江	Kangwŏn kamyŏng 江原監營	Kangwŏn Provincial Office
39	原	Wŏnju kwalliyŏng 原州管理營	Wŏnju (Kangwŏn Province) City Military Office
40	春	Ch'unch'ŏn kwalliyŏng 春川管理營	Ch'unch'ŏn (Kangwŏn Province) City Military Office
41	全	Chŏlla kamyŏng 全羅監營	Chŏlla Provincial Office
42	全兵	Chŏlla pyŏngyŏng 全羅兵營	Chŏlla Military Command
43	全左	Chŏlla chwayŏng 全羅左營	Left Chŏlla Provincial Naval Command
44	全右	Chŏlla uyŏng 全羅右營	Right Chŏlla Provincial Naval Command
45	咸	Hamgyŏng kamyŏng 咸鏡監營	Hamgyŏng Provincial Office
46	咸北	Hamgyŏng pugyŏng 咸鏡北營	North Hamgyŏng Provincial Office
47	咸南	Hamgyŏng namyŏng 咸鏡南營	South Hamgyŏng Provincial Office
48	利	Iwŏn kwalliyŏng 利原管理營	Iwŏn (Hamgyŏng Province) City Military Office
49	問	Sajongsa 司饛寺	Sajongsa

It was not until the advent of the Chosŏn dynasty in 1392 that copper coins were minted for wide circulation. The first coinage was issued in 1423 and was inscribed *Chosŏn t'ongbo* 朝鮮通寶. Chosŏn is the name of an ancient Korean state that may have existed from before 200 BCE. The name was selected by the Ming emperor for the state that arose in 1392 and fell in 1910.

The *Chosŏn t'ongbo* was the first coin issued by the Chosŏn dynasty, but due to its inferior weight and quality the exchange rate fell below its intrinsic value and production was stopped. In 1464, money in the shape of an arrowhead was introduced by King Sejo 世祖 (r. 1455–68). It was known as *chŏnp'ye* 箭幣 (arrowhead coin) and could be used as money during times of peace and as an arrowhead during times of war. It was not well received, but two examples were excavated in 1975.[14] These attempts at coinage generally failed because of the Korean government's lack of commitment to producing adequate supplies to meet demand. Rice and cloth remained the most popularly accepted forms of currency and were accepted for tax payments.

In 1625 Korea again issued the *Chosŏn t'ongbo* 朝鮮通寶 with a different calligraphic style and Japanese copper, but it was not until the year 1633 that the most common Korean coin was first cast. King Injo 仁祖 (r.1623–1649) ordered the *sangp'yŏngch'ŏng* 常平廳 (Ever-Normal Bureau), the government's famine relief office, to mint coins. The coins carried the office name 常平 and 'universal currency' 通寶 on the obverse side, making the inscription *sangp'yŏng t'ongbo* 常平通寶. This obverse inscription 常平通寶 became the standard legend on all Korean coins until the 1890s. Although laws were also promulgated to enforce the use of the coins, the political upheavals of the 1620s (a royal coup in 1623 and the first Manchu invasion in 1627) and the 1630s (the second Manchu invasion in 1636) stymied efforts to produce coins which were widely used.

Further attempts at coin production and circulation were made in the early 1650s, and although some success was achieved in Hwanghae 黃海 and P'yŏng'an 平安 provinces, and even the capital Hansŏng 漢城, or Hanyang 漢陽 (Seoul), this attempt also failed because of limited production.[15] The minor success that was achieved in the corridor from Seoul through to the Chinese border in the north-west was probably a result of the higher commercialization of this region through its trade with China. Success of both coin production and coin acceptance is usually dated from 1678 with the promotion of minting, government use of coins and government acceptance of coins for taxation. The major tax reform, the *Taedongbŏp* 大同法 (Taedong tribute tax) was designed to amalgamate taxation of rice, cloth and coins. It was rolled out nationally from 1608 to 1708 (1608 Kyŏnggi Province; 1623 Kangwŏn Province; 1651 Ch'ungch'ŏng Province; 1658 Chŏlla Province; 1677 Kyŏngsang Province

Small silver vase coin and fragmentary or 'crushed' silver in the Bank of Korea Money Museum

James B. Lewis photographs

and 1708 Hwanghae Province; Hamgyŏng, P'yŏng'an and Cheju were exempted). Supplies of coins may never have been entirely satisfactory, but the use of coins had expanded beyond urban areas and the northwest corridor by the early 1700s. A number of government offices and military units established mints to cast coins. We do have some records but money supply is difficult – perhaps impossible – to determine as coins were never officially withdrawn but were instead used for recasting.

Korean coins cast over the late Chosŏn period (1600–late 19th century) were cast in a round shape with a square hole in the centre. The square hole allowed the mint workers to brace the coins on a wooden stick when polishing off the metal spurs around the edges. The obverse side carried the four-character inscription *sangp'yŏng t'ongbo*. The reverse side carried various inscriptions, but often had a single character at the top as the mint mark. Other marks included numbers and symbols that indicated the series or furnace codes and perhaps other information. As shown below (pages 55–6), numbers may appear as numbers or they may follow the word order of the *Chŏnjamun* 千字文 (*Thousand Character Classic*) with the first word 天 as one; 地 as two, and so on. Characters for the five elements and the eight trigrams from the *Yijing* 易經 (*Book of Changes, c.* late 9th century BCE) might also appear to indicate series or other markers. The extensive marks on the reverse of Korean coins is unusual in East Asia. Chinese and Japanese coins rarely, if ever, carried any mint or series marks, only reign dates, which Korean coins did not bear.

Many coins have additional symbols (dot, circle, crescent, horizontal line, vertical line, trigrams, etc.) on the reverse. It is not known what these symbols indicate, but they probably refer to series, furnace numbers or the time when they were cast.

The *Chŏnjamun*, written by the Chinese scholar Zhou Xingsi 周興嗣 (470–521) of the Six Dynasties period (early 6th century CE) was used to express numbers, because it was widely known, even to the semiliterate. The text was a primer and marks the development of parallelism in Chinese letters. It contains 1,000 characters in 125 couplets with two four-character lines in each couplet in parallel verse and rhymed sequence.[16] The following are the first sixteen characters of the *Thousand Character Classic*:

天地玄黄, 宇宙洪荒
日月盈昃, 辰宿列張

The five elements or five phases *o-haeng* 五行 – *mok* 木 wood, *hwa* 火 fire, *t'o* 土 earth, *kŭm* 金 metal and *su* 水 water – describe interactions and relationships between phenomena. They appeared in the early Han dynasty and entered Korea and became widespread as an adjunct to neo-Confucian metaphysical ideas.[17] They are still used as a reference in some forms of martial arts and Chinese medicine.

The eight trigrams *p'algwae* 八卦 date from the Confucian classic *Zuo Zhuan* 左傳 (*c.* 4th century BCE). Each trigram consists of three parallel lines, either whole or broken in the middle and are the components of the hexagrams found in the *Yijing*. The trigrams often appear as an auspicious decoration, and are on the South Korean national flag.[18] The two examples on page 56 (right-hand side) carry the fourth trigram, *zhen* 震, which means thunder, among other things.

During the 1880s, miscellaneous Chinese characters appeared on the reverse side of *sangp'yŏng t'ongbo* coins. These characters appear to be yet another system to refer to a specific furnace or series:

Character	Korean	English translation
元	*wŏn*	first
全	*chŏn*	whole
文	*mun*	literature
生	*saeng*	produce
天	*ch'ŏn*	heaven
光	*kwang*	light
正	*chŏng*	upright
大	*tae*	great
工	*kong*	job
千	*ch'ŏn*	thousand
吉	*kil*	auspicious

Some of the coins in the collection were painted. The painted pieces tend to be of high quality and may have been used as 'mother' coins for moulds. There are also examples of defective coins in the collection. It was inevitable that errors occurred during the production process, and some coins managed to slip through the control inspection and entered circulation. There are also coins with indentations and holes punched all the way through them. The indentations are visible only from one side, sometimes in groups of two and three and are obviously intentional markings. Coins bearing these marks were all cast in the period 1742–53. Most of them are from mints in or near Seoul. The purpose of these markings is unknown.

In 1882, silver coins in three denominations were minted. On the face of these coins appeared a new title for Korea – *taedong* 大東, or the Great Eastern [Kingdom] – and on the reverse the character *ho* 戶 (treasury). These were Korea's first modern coins. The square hole in the centre of each coin was filled and replaced with a circle of blue enamel on the reverse. These coins were hoarded or smuggled out of the country for their metal content. The cost of silver increased, production became impractical, and minting was stopped within a year.

From 1886, a series of coins were struck that included gilded tin coins, tin coins coated with silver and copper coins. Because of a shortage of gold and silver, as well as operating costs, the Bureau of Minting did not produce these in bulk and the coins did not go into circulation.[19] In 1893, a series of silver and copper coins were struck by machinery, some of which was bought in from Germany and some from Japan. These are said to have adopted the modern silver standard in imitation of the Japanese currency system.[20] These coins have ouyat blossoms, the royal crest of the Korean Empire on the top of the obverse and a double dragon design on the reverse.

After Japan defeated Russia in the 1904 Russo-Japanese War, the Japanese government imposed a Protectorate Treaty over Korea in which Korea accepted Japanese counsel in major state affairs. The Korean government was also forced to sign the 'Agreement on Currency Control and Management' with the Daiichi Bank, which then began to issue new kinds of currency from the Imperial Japanese Mint (est. 1871) in Osaka.[21] The Daiichi Bank coins have a phoenix design on the obverse and an ouyat blossom at the top of the reverse.

Coins inscribed *tongguk* 東國

Tongguk t'ongbo 東國通寶
998–1097. Diameter 2.41 cm, weight 3.13 g. Bronze
[ASH] HCR30377 (© Ashmolean Museum, University of Oxford)

Tongguk t'ongbo 東國通寶
998–1097. Diameter 2.4 cm, weight 2.8 g. Bronze
[ASH] HCR30378 (© Ashmolean Museum, University of Oxford)

Tongguk chungbo 東國重寶
998–1097. Diameter 2.57 cm, weight 3.97 g. Bronze
[ASH] HCR30381 (© Ashmolean Museum, University of Oxford)

Coins inscribed *haedong* 海東

Haedong t'ongbo 海東通寶
1097–1105. Diameter 2.47 cm, weight 3.12 g. Brass
[ASH] HCR30347 (© Ashmolean Museum, University of Oxford)

Haedong t'ongbo 海東通寶
1097–1105. Diameter 2.53 cm, weight 4.17 g. Bronze
[ASH] HCR30341 (© Ashmolean Museum, University of Oxford)

Haedong chungbo 海東重寶
1097–1105. Diameter 2.43 cm, weight 3.48 g. Bronze
[ASH] HCR30359 (© Ashmolean Museum, University of Oxford)

Coins inscribed *Sam Han* 三韓

Sam Han t'ongbo 三韓通寶
1097–1105. Diameter 2.33 cm, weight 3.35 g. Bronze
[ASH] HCR30365 (© Ashmolean Museum, University of Oxford)

Sam Han chungbo 三韓重寶
1097–1105. Diameter 2.48 cm, weight 3.48 g. Bronze
[ASH] HCR30373 (© Ashmolean Museum, University of Oxford)

Coins inscribed *Chosŏn t'ongbo* 朝鮮通寶 and *Sangp'yŏng t'ongbo* 常平通寶

Chosŏn t'ongbo 朝鮮通寶
1423–45. Diameter 2.41 cm, weight 3.18 g. Bronze
[ASH] HCR30139 (© Ashmolean Museum, University of Oxford)

Sangp'yŏng t'ongbo 常平通寶
1633–78? Diameter 2.23 cm, weight 4.67 g. Brass
[ASH] HCR29816 (© Ashmolean Museum, University of Oxford)

Examples of *sangp'yŏng t'ongbo* 常平通寶 coins with different mint marks

Mint mark: 平 *p'yŏng*
(No. 28 in list)
1679–1742. Diameter
3.05 cm, weight 5.9 g. Brass

[ASH] HCR30530 (© Ashmolean Museum,
University of Oxford)

Mint mark: 開 *kae*
(No. 24 in list)
1679–1752. Diameter
2.83 cm, weight 6.55 g. Brass

[ASH] HCR30046 (© Ashmolean Museum,
University of Oxford)

Mint mark: 工 *kong*
(No. 5 in the list)
1685–1752. Diameter
3.5 cm, weight 6.91 g. Brass

[ASH] HCR28040 (© Ashmolean Museum,
University of Oxford)

Mint mark: 備 *pi*
(No. 8 in list)
1742. Diameter 2.5 cm,
weight 3.54 g. Brass

[ASH] HCR28971 (© Ashmolean Museum,
University of Oxford)

Mint mark: 營 *yŏng*
(No. 9 in list)
1742–52. Diameter 2.92 cm,
weight 4.78 g. Brass

[ASH] HCR29343 (© Ashmolean Museum,
University of Oxford)

Mint mark: 禁 *kŭm*
(No. 12 in list)
1742. Diameter 2.33 cm,
weight 4.3 g. Brass

[ASH] HCR29573 (© Ashmolean
Museum, University of Oxford)

Mint mark: 賑 *chin*
(No. 7 in list)
1742. Diameter 2.4 cm,
weight 4.47 g. Brass

[ASH] HCR30207 (© Ashmolean
Museum, University of Oxford)

Mint mark: 尚 *sang*
(No. 32 in list)
1742–52. Diameter
2.92 cm, weight 4.68 g.
Brass

[ASH] HCR30287 (© Ashmolean
Museum, University of Oxford)

Mint mark: 江 *kang*
(No. 38 in list)
1742–52. Diameter
3.09 cm, weight 7.42 g.
Brass

[ASH] HCR30410 (© Ashmolean
Museum, University of Oxford)

Mint mark: 咸 *ham*
(No. 45 in list)
1742–52. Diameter
3.02 cm, weight 5.4 g.
Brass

[ASH] HCR30493 (© Ashmolean
Museum, University of Oxford)

Mint mark: 海 *hae*
(No. 31 in list)
1742–52. Diameter
3.01 cm, weight 5.56 g.
Brass

[ASH] HCR30617 (© Ashmolean
Museum, University of Oxford)

Mint mark: 訓 *hun*
(No. 4 in list)
1752. Diameter 2.73 cm,
weight 4.27 g. Brass

[ASH] HCR28186 (© Ashmolean
Museum, University of Oxford)

Examples of *sangp'yŏng t'ongbo* 常平通寶 coins with additional symbols

Mint mark: 營 *yŏng*
(No. 9 in list) sun (circle)
No. 5 (五)
1742. Diameter 2.48 cm,
weight 4.25 g. Brass
[ASH] HCR29282 (© Ashmolean Museum,
University of Oxford)

Mint mark: 營 *yŏng*
(No. 9 in list) moon (crescent)
No. 2 (二)
1742. Diameter 2.46 cm,
weight 3.99 g. Brass
[ASH] HCR29296 (© Ashmolean Museum,
University of Oxford)

Mint mark: 圻 *ki*
(No. 25 in list) star (dot)
No. 2 (二)
1742–52. Diameter 3 cm,
weight 7.8 g. Brass
[ASH] HCR30742 (© Ashmolean Museum,
University of Oxford)

Examples of *sangp'yŏng t'ongbo* 常平通寶 coins with *Thousand Character Classic* characters used as numbers

天 *ch'ŏn* (1) heaven
1742-1752. Diameter
3.03 cm, weight 6.36 g. Brass
[ASH] HCR28581 (© Ashmolean Museum,
University of Oxford)

地 *chi* (2) earth
1742-1752. Diameter
3.08 cm, weight 6.19 g. Brass
[ASH] HCR29204 (© Ashmolean Museum,
University of Oxford)

宙 *hwang* (6) infinite time
1742-1752. Diameter
3.09 cm, weight 6.61 g. Brass
[ASH] HCR29213 (© Ashmolean Museum,
University of Oxford)

黃 *hwang* (4) yellow
1742–52. Diameter 3.3 cm,
weight 6.1 g. Brass
[ASH] HCR30279 (© Ashmolean Museum,
University of Oxford)

月 *wŏl* (10) moon
1742–52. Diameter 3.09 cm,
weight 5.75 g. Brass
[ASH] HCR30504 (© Ashmolean Museum,
University of Oxford)

宇 *u* (5) space
1832. Diameter 2.68 cm,
weight 4.21 g. Brass
[ASH] HCR27937 (© Ashmolean Museum,
University of Oxford)

Examples of *sangp'yŏng t'ongbo* 常平通寶 coins with the five elements probably to indicate series

木 *mok* (wood)
1752. Diameter 2.64 cm,
weight 5 g. Brass
[ASH] HCR29418 (© Ashmolean Museum,
University of Oxford)

火 *hwa* (fire)
1752. Diameter 2.76 cm,
weight 5.38 g. Brass
[ASH] HCR29439 (© Ashmolean Museum,
University of Oxford)

金 *kŭm* (metal)
1752. Diameter 2.63 cm,
weight 5.39 g. Brass
[ASH] HCR29484 (© Ashmolean Museum,
University of Oxford)

水 *su* (water)
1752. Diameter 2.59 cm,
weight 4.77 g. Brass
[ASH] HCR29503 (© Ashmolean Museum,
University of Oxford)

土 *t'o* (earth)
1752. Diameter 2.65 cm,
weight 4.89 g. Brass
[ASH] HCR29464 (© Ashmolean Museum,
University of Oxford)

Examples of *sangp'yŏng t'ongbo* 常平通寶 coins with trigrams to suggest good fortune or to indicate series

☳ (*Zhèn* 震)
Mint mark: 統 *t'ong* (No. 28 in list)
1742–52. Diameter 3.07 cm, weight
6.23 g. Brass
[ASH] HCR28370 (© Ashmolean Museum, University of Oxford)

☳ (*Zhèn* 震)
Mint mark: 統 *t'ong* (No. 28 in list)
1742–52. Diameter 3.03 cm, weight
6.98 g. Brass
[ASH] HCR28310 (© Ashmolean Museum, University of Oxford)

Examples of *sangp'yŏng t'ongbo* 常平通寶 coins with miscellaneous Chinese characters to indicate series

元 *wŏn*
1832. Diameter 2.38 cm,
weight 4.86 g. Brass

[ASH] HCR29854 (© Ashmolean Museum,
University of Oxford)

全 *chŏn*
1832. Diameter 2.54 cm,
weight 4.08 g. Brass

[ASH] HCR28160 (© Ashmolean Museum,
University of Oxford)

文 *mun*
1832. Diameter 2.32 cm,
weight 4.13 g. Brass

[ASH] HCR28791 (© Ashmolean Museum,
University of Oxford)

生 *saeng*
1832. Diameter 2.45 cm,
weight 4.29 g. Brass

[ASH] HCR29923 (© Ashmolean Museum,
University of Oxford)

天 *ch'ŏn*
1836. Diameter 2.42 cm,
weight 3.52 g. Brass

[ASH] HCR28556 (© Ashmolean Museum,
University of Oxford)

光 *kwang*
1852. Diameter 2.43 cm,
weight 3.72 g. Brass

[ASH] HCR28764 (© Ashmolean Museum,
University of Oxford)

Examples of painted *sangp'yŏng t'ongbo* 常平通寶 coins

1679–95. Diameter 3.2 cm, weight 6.5 g. Brass

[ASH] HCR30226 (© Ashmolean Museum, University of Oxford)

1742–52. Diameter 2.97 cm, weight 7.04 g. Brass

[ASH] HCR29329 (© Ashmolean Museum, University of Oxford)

1752. Diameter 2.57 cm, weight 4.48 g. Brass

[ASH] HCR29406 (© Ashmolean Museum, University of Oxford)

1752. Diameter 2.85 cm, weight 4.7 g. Brass

[ASH] HCR28197 (© Ashmolean Museum, University of Oxford)

Examples of defective *sangp'yŏng t'ongbo* 常平通寶 coins

A rare casting defect shows two characters from
the obverse upside-down on the reverse
1752. Diameter 2.58 cm, weight 4.8 g. Brass

[ASH] HCR29413 (© Ashmolean Museum, University of Oxford)

A common defect is a double impression of characters
1752. Diameter 2.65 cm, weight 5.95 g. Brass

[ASH] HCR29465 (© Ashmolean Museum, University of Oxford)

Another rare error is a mixture of the obverse
on the reverse
1830. Diameter 2.57 cm, weight 3.57 g. Brass

[ASH] HCR28453 (© Ashmolean Museum, University of Oxford)

The obverse in this sample is blank
1883. Diameter 3.76 cm, weight 5.03 g. Brass

[ASH] HCR28036 (© Ashmolean Museum, University of Oxford)

The obverse and the reverse are the same, except
that the obverse retains the character *po* 寶
1752. Diameter 2.66 cm, weight 8.73 g. Brass

[ASH] HCR29404 (© Ashmolean Museum, University of Oxford)

Examples of *sangp'yŏng t'ongbo* 常平通寶 coins with indentations or holes

One indentation on the
bottom rim of the reverse
1742. Diameter 2.32 cm,
weight 4.46 g. Brass

[ASH] HCR29284 (© Ashmolean Museum,
University of Oxford)

One indentation on the
right rim of the reverse
1742–52. Diameter 3.03 cm,
weight 6.98 g. Brass

[ASH] HCR28310 (© Ashmolean Museum,
University of Oxford)

Three indentations on
the top rim of the reverse
1742–52. Diameter 3.13 cm,
weight 6.82 g. Brass

[ASH] HCR30506 (© Ashmolean Museum,
University of Oxford)

One indentation on the left
rim of the reverse
1752. Diameter 2.8 cm,
weight 4.45 g. Brass

[ASH] HCR28296 (© Ashmolean Museum,
University of Oxford)

Four holes drilled through
the coin evenly at the
corners of the square hole
1742–52. Diameter 2.95 cm,
weight 7.82 g. Brass

[ASH] HCR29330 (© Ashmolean Museum,
University of Oxford)

Four holes drilled through
evenly on top, bottom, right
and left on the rim
1806. Diameter 2.61 cm,
weight 3.68 g. Brass

[ASH] HCR30176 (© Ashmolean Museum,
University of Oxford)

One hole randomly drilled
through the coin
1742–52. Diameter 3.01 cm,
weight 8.91 g. Brass

[ASH] HCR30489 (© Ashmolean Museum,
University of Oxford)

One hole randomly drilled
through the coin on the rim
1757. Diameter 2.91 cm,
weight 4.56 g. Brass

[ASH] HCR27721 (© Ashmolean Museum,
University of Oxford)

Examples of modern Taedong 大東 coins

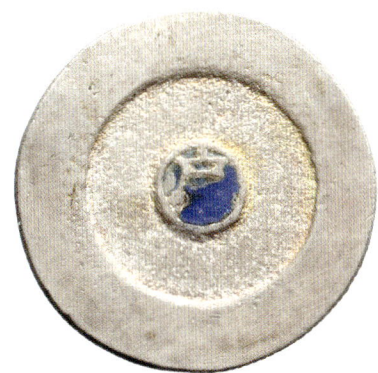

Mint mark: *Hojo* 戶曹 호조
taedong il-chŏn 大東一錢
ho 户
1882. Diameter 2.16 cm,
weight 3.78 g. Silver
[ASH] HCR30352 (© Ashmolean Museum,
University of Oxford)

Mint mark: *Hojo* 戶曹 호조
taedong i-chŏn 大東二錢
ho 户
1882. Diameter 2.78 cm,
weight 6.54 g. Silver
[ASH] HCR30354 (© Ashmolean Museum,
University of Oxford)

Mint mark: *Hojo* 戶曹 호조
taedong sam-chŏn 大東三錢
ho 户
1882. Diameter 3.35 cm,
weight 10.64 g. Silver
[ASH] HCR30355 (© Ashmolean Museum,
University of Oxford)

Examples of struck coins

A modern struck coin
Obverse: 大朝鮮開國四百九十七
年, 십문, 10 *MUN* (497th year of the
founding of Great Chosŏn, *sip mun*, 10
MUN). Reverse: 十文 (*sip mun*)
1888. Diameter 2.79 cm, weight 7.14 g,
Copper
[ASH] HCR30390 (© Ashmolean Museum,
University of Oxford)

A struck coin (nickel?)
Obverse: 朝鮮, 開國五百二年, 두돈오푼, ¼ *YANG* (Chosŏn, 502nd year of the founding, *tu chŏn o p'un*, ¼ *YANG*) Reverse: 二戔五分 (2 *chŏn* 5 *pun*)
1893. Diameter 2.09 cm, weight 4.68 g. Nickel (?)

[ASH] HCR30389 (© Ashmolean Museum, University of Oxford)

A struck copper coin
Obverse: 大朝鮮, 開國五百五年, 오푼, 5 *FUN* (Great Chosŏn, 505th year of its founding, 5 *p'un*, 5 *FUN*) Reverse: 五分 (5 *pun*)
1896. Diameter 2.79 cm, weight 7.1 g. Copper

[ASH] HCR30391 (© Ashmolean Museum, University of Oxford)

A struck brass coin
Obverse: 大朝鮮, 開國五百一年, 한푼, 1 *FUN* (Great Chosŏn, 501st year of its founding, 1 *p'un*, 1 *FUN*) Reverse: 一分 (1 *pun*)
1892. Diameter 2.35 cm, weight 3.45 g. Brass

[ASH] HCR30387 (© Ashmolean Museum, University of Oxford)

Struck copper Daiichi Bank coin
Obverse: 大韓, 光武十年, 반 전, ½
CHON (Great [Empire of] Korea, tenth
year of Kwangmu (1906), *pan chŏn*, ½
CHON) Reverse: 半錢 (*panjŏn*)
Mint mark: Osaka, 1906. Diameter
2.2 cm, weight 3.58 g. Copper (?)
[ASH] HCR30396 (© Ashmolean Museum, University of Oxford)

Struck nickel (?) Daiichi Bank coin
Obverse: 大韓, 光武十一年, 오전,
5 *CHON* (Great [Empire of] Korea,
eleventh year of Kwangmu (1907),
5 *chŏn*, 5 *CHON*) Reverse: 五錢 (5 *chŏn*)
Mint mark: Osaka, 1907. Diameter
2.12 cm, weight 4.59 g. Nickel (?)
[ASH] HCR30394 (© Ashmolean Museum, University of Oxford)

Struck copper (?) Daiichi Bank coin
Obverse: 大韓, 隆熙三年, 일 전, 1 CHON
(Great Korea, third year of Yunghŭi
(1909), 1 *chŏn*, 1 CHON) Reverse: 一錢
(1 *chŏn*)
Mint mark: Osaka, 1909. Diameter
2.38 cm, weight 4.19 g. Copper (?)
[ASH] HCR30395 (© Ashmolean Museum, University of Oxford)

AMULETS

The Ashmolean Museum also has a collection of amulets: items that were carried on one's person to bring good fortune and ward off evil. The Korean amulets were cast by the regular coinage mints in Kyŏnggi Province between 1600 and the end of the 19th century.[22] The amulets have a great variety of shapes: round, octagonal, irregular or in the shape of animals or other motifs and designs. Decorations include bats, birds, butterflies, bees and flowers, as well as auspicious and mythical creatures and figures. Their inscriptions are in Chinese characters. In addition to common auspicious words such as longevity 壽, wealth 富 and happiness 福, some inscriptions are also taken from the Confucian classics or from Daoist incantations. H.A. Ramsden has commented that Korean amulets are 'generally well made and more attractive than those of the Chinese and also the Japanese'.[23]

Amulet: two bees facing each other with a square hole in the middle.
Obverse: 五子出身 C. *Wu zi chu shen* (Five sons pass the civil service examination and have careers). Reverse: 百年同樂 C. *Bai nian tong le* (Rejoice together for 100 years)
19th century. Diameter 2.82 cm, weight 8.47 g. Scalloped openwork, brass cast
[ASH] HCR28875. (© Ashmolean Museum, University of Oxford)

Bees suggest industry and thrift. The phrase 五子出身 or 五子登科 (May your five sons pass the civil service examinations) is frequently seen on amulets. It refers to Dou Yanshan 竇燕山

(also known as Dou Yujun 竇禹钧) (872–954), who lived in the Five Dynasties period (907–960). At the age of thirty, he was still without a son. In a dream, his late grandfather advised him to engage in charitable deeds as soon as possible or he would soon die and be childless. Dou Yanshan did take on charitable deeds, and ten years later his grandfather appeared again in his dreams and told him that the Underworld Office had decided to extend his life for three dozen years and grant him five sons, each of whom would enjoy honour and renown.[24] He became famous for the doting attention he paid to the education of his children.

Amulet: two bats facing each other with a square hole in the middle.
Obverse: 壽福康寧 C. *Shou fu kang ning* (longevity, happiness, health and peace).
Reverse: 富貴多男 C. *Fu gui duo nan* (wealth, honour and numerous sons).
19th century. Diameter 3.59 cm, weight 10.62 g. Brass cast

The character for bat 蝠 has the pronunciation *pok*, which is a homonym with 福 *pok* (blessing or happiness), an auspicious symbol frequently used in decorative arts.

Amulet: octagonal with inscriptions.
Obverse: 孝悌忠信 禮義廉恥 – four Confucian injunctions: *hyo* 孝 (filial piety), *che* 悌 (respect for one's older brother), *ch'ung* 忠 (loyalty to one's monarch) and *sin* 信 (sincerity towards one's male friends) and four Confucian virtues: *ye* 禮 (propriety), *ŭi* 義 (righteousness), *yŏm* 廉 (integrity) and *ch'i* 恥 (sense of shame). Reverse: 富貴福祿 百子千孫 – *pu* 富 (wealth), *kwi* 貴 (honour), *pok* 福 (happiness), *rok* 祿 (good material fortune), *paekcha* 百子 (100 sons), *ch'ŏnson* 千孫 (1,000 grandsons).
19th century. Diameter 34.6 cm, weight 18.39 g. Brass cast

Amulet: *sangp'yŏng t'ongbo* 常平通寶 coins joined together
Mint mark: 春川管理營 Ch'unch'ŏn kwalliyŏng (No. 40 in list)
Five-*mun* coins. 1888? Diameter 6.72 cm, weight 14.12 g. Brass cast

[ASH] HCR30735 (© Ashmolean Museum, University of Oxford)

Amulet: inscriptions taken from Confucian classics.

Obverse: 窈窕 C. *Yao tiao* (gentle and graceful) Reverse: 淑女 C. *Shu nu* (a fair maiden)

19th century. Diameter 2.48 cm, weight 3.75 g. Brass cast

[ASH] HCR28882 (© Ashmolean Museum, University of Oxford)

The study of Confucian classics *Saso̊-samgyo̊ng* 四書三經 (*Four Books and Three Classics*[25]) formed the larger part of the Korean education curriculum for boys. Phrases from the classics were much used on charms. The phrase here, 窈窕淑女 (Gentle and graceful is the girl) is taken from the second line of the first song from *Shi Jing* 詩經 (*Book of Odes*). It is followed by 君子好逑 (A fit wife for the gentleman).[26]

Amulet: inscriptions from the Daoist 道教 (Togyo) canon.

Obverse: 斬邪治鬼 C. *Zhan xie zhi gui* (To cut off evil and suppress demons). Reverse: eight trigrams.

Date unknown. Diameter 2.12 cm, weight 7.08 g. Brass cast

[ASH] HCR30065 (© Ashmolean Museum, University of Oxford)

The eight trigrams on the reverse are symbols used in Daoist cosmology to represent the fundamental principles of reality. This is a popular inscription on Daoist talismans, but this talisman may be quite unusual as Daoism never flourished in Korea to the extent it did in China; the neo-Confucian Korean state held it in suspicion.

乾 Qián	兌 Duì	離 Lí	震 Zhèn	巽 Xùn	坎 Kǎn	艮 Gèn	坤 Kūn
☰	☱	☲	☳	☴	☵	☶	☷

Samples of amulets with symbolic conceptions of longevity and love

Amulet: conceptions of longevity and love.
Obverse: 嘉友 C. *Jia you* (Good friend). Reverse: 香
信 C. *Xiang xin* (Fragrant trust).
19th century. Diameter 2.52 cm, weight 4.67 g.
Brass cast

[ASH] HCR28873 (© Ashmolean Museum, University of Oxford)

Two butterflies 蝴蝶 (K. *hojŏp* or *nabi* and *nabi*, C.
hudie). The butterfly symbolizes longevity, because
the second character is a homophone of *die* 耋
(seventy or eighty years old).[27] The design of a pair
of butterflies also originates from the story of the
butterfly lovers Liang Shanbo and Zhu Yingtai 梁山
伯與祝英台, one of China's great folktales. Zhu
disguised herself as a man in order to attend school
to study; there she met Liang, and they became
good friends. Years later, when Zhu revealed to Liang
that she was a woman, they fell in love. However,
Zhu's parents had already arranged her marriage to
someone else. Liang was so sad that he died from a
broken heart and Zhu threw herself into his grave to
join him. They emerged as a pair of butterflies and
flew away together.

**Amulet: round, openwork with a looped hole
for hanging.**
Obverse: 河 C. *He* (River) and a fish leaping out of
water. Reverse: 海 C. *Hai* (Sea) and a fish jumping.
19th century. Diameter 4.02 cm, weight 13.39 g.
Brass cast

[ASH] HCR28885 (© Ashmolean Museum, University of Oxford)

The inscriptions are in the cartouche in front of
the fish's mouth. Fish (魚, K. *ŏ*, C. *yu*) in Chinese
is a homophone with the Chinese *yu* 餘 (K. *yŏ*),
meaning surplus and abundance. Carp (C. *li* 鯉 K.
ri) is a homophone for *li* 利 (K. *ri*), meaning profit.
When shown with a lotus (C. *lian* 蓮, K. *ryŏn* or *yŏn*),
as it is here, it suggests the homonym *lian* 連 (K.
ryŏn or *yŏn*), meaning 'continuous'. In short, the
meaning is 'Year after year live in abundance'.

CHATELAINES

Chatelaines or key pendants *yŏlsoep'ye* 열쇠폐 are large amulet pieces
to which charms, coins and sometimes coloured ribbons were attached.
These were normally given to brides on their wedding day. There are fine
examples of chatelaines in the Pitt Rivers Museum.

**Chatelaine: key pendant – circular
bronze plaque.**

The inscription within the inner circle
reads: Obverse: 吾君萬年 C. *Wu jun wan
nian* (Our lord 10,000 years). Reverse: 壽
富多男 C. *Shou fu duo nan* (Longevity,
wealth, many sons).
Length 20.5 cm, weight 162 g. Bronze
and pigment.

[PRM] 1892.18.2 (© Pitt Rivers Museum, University of Oxford.
Donated by William Richard Carles, May 1892)

The characters 君 and 男 are missing
respectively from the obverse and
reverse. Within the next circle there are
deer, birds and trees. The outer circle
has ten charms with various forms and
designs. Between the designs are small
rings through which keys and ribbons
would be hung.

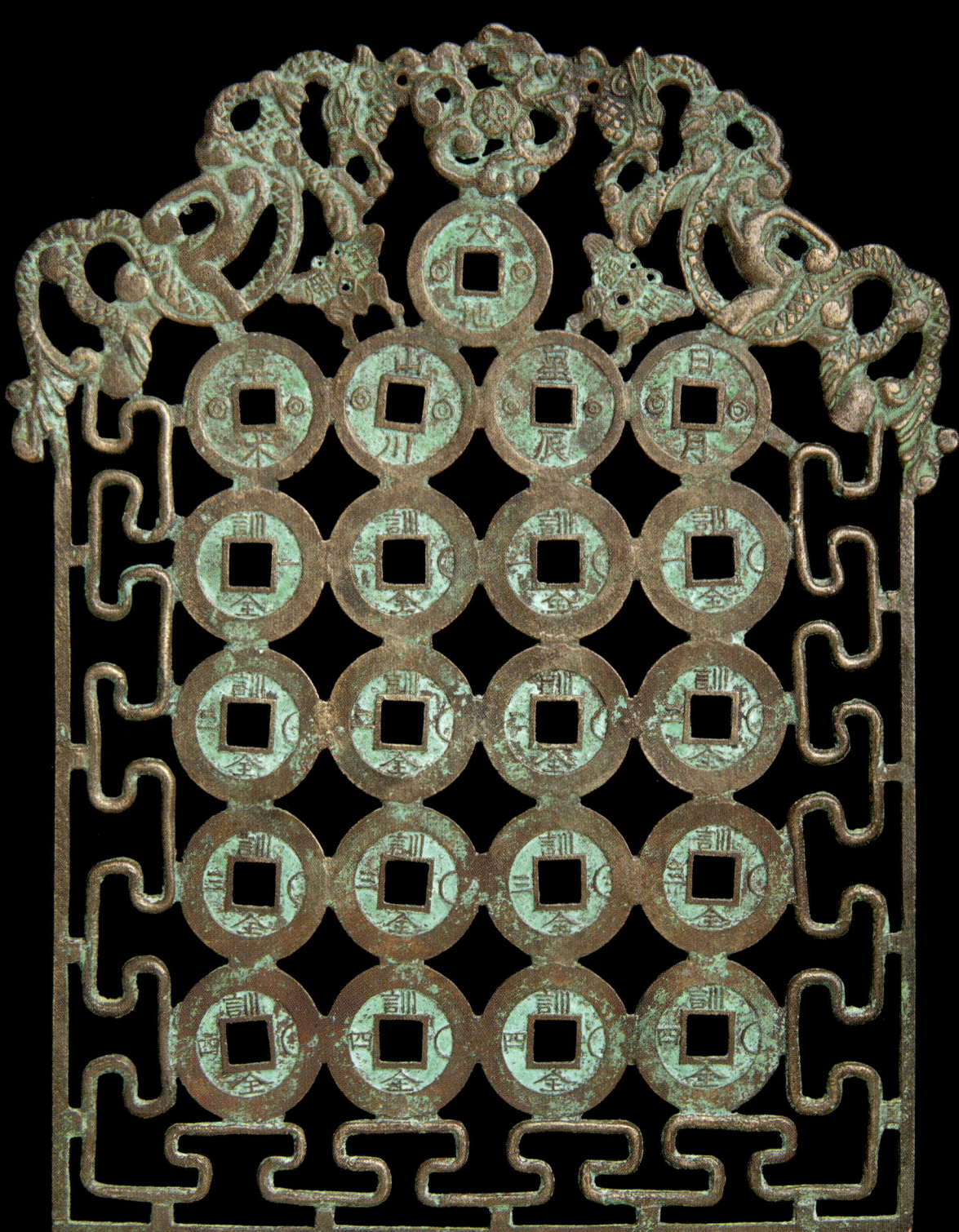

Chatelaine: various charms and pendants in a frame, two dragons on top

Date unknown. Width x height 14.2 x 19.5 cm, weight 240.8 g. Brass cast

[ASH] HCR30741 (© Ashmolean Museum, University of Oxford)

There are five round charms at the top flanked by two butterflies and followed by sixteen *sangp'yŏng t'ongbo* coins in a square frame with a Greek key design on three sides. On the very top are two dragons.

Chatelaine: key pendant of cast brass with figures in relief

Obverse: Crane on top, and bat on the bottom with a stylized longevity 壽 character at the centre. Reverse: 壽福康寧富貴多男 Six blessings (longevity, happiness, health and peace, wealth, honour and numerous sons) within a scalloped border surrounded by seven circles. Yin–yang symbol at the centre.

Length 8.6 cm, weight 67 g. Brass.

[PRM] 1938.30.4 (© Pitt Rivers Museum, University of Oxford)

**Chatelaine: key pendant – a bronze plaque with five
small holes on the bottom edge, with a raised design.**
Obverse: 聖壽 C. *Sheng shou* (The age of a sage, or
patriarch). Reverse: 千歲 C. *Qian sui* (1,000 years)
Length 17.8 cm, weight 345 g. Bronze.

[PRM] 1899.10.1 (© Pitt Rivers Museum, University of Oxford, presented by W.G. Aston Esq.)

These items were common presents for a bride. The
evergreen trees symbolize a good old age. Traditionally the
hare lives in the moon and pounds the drugs from which
the elixir of immortality is made in a mortar.

Chatelaine: key pendant — in the shape of a purse.
Obverse: 方相氏 C. *Fangxiang shi* (the Chinese exorcist) is on the top, and a stylized 壽 C. *Shou* (longevity) character is at the centre, surrounded by five bats. Reverse: 方相氏 C. *Fangxiang shi* (the Chinese exorcist) is on the top, and at the centre, a dragon is flying among clouds, together with ten birds. There are also the characters for the six blessings. Max. diameter approx. 47 cm, weight 1.10 kg. Brass, ribbon textile and pigment.
[PRM] 1902.5.1 (© Pitt Rivers Museum, University of Oxford, donated by William Mayhew, January 1902)

3

CHRISTIANITY IN KOREA

THE IMPORTANCE OF Christianity in Korea is clear from the relative numbers of Christians in the population. About 2 per cent of the Japanese population claim to be Christian. The Chinese Christian population is about 10 per cent (excluding Hong Kong with about 13 per cent and Macau and Taiwan at about 6 per cent each). Almost 9 per cent of Vietnamese are Christian. Some 36 per cent of the South Korean population profess Christianity. Only the Philippines (90 per cent) and Timor-Leste (87 per cent) have larger Christian populations.[1]

The history of Christianity in Korea can be divided into three periods. The first is the initial encounter in the 1590s, which left nearly no trace.[2] The second is the actual beginning of missionary activity, at first entirely Catholic, from the 1780s to the late 19th century. The third is from the introduction of Protestantism in the late 19th century up to the present.[3] There are no holdings in the Bodleian Library from the first two periods, but the Library does have rich holdings from the Protestant period spanning the late 19th century into the middle of the 20th century. These holdings are almost entirely from the Anglican Church. This chapter introduces the Anglican materials produced during the third period after outlining the general historical context.

BEFORE THE 19TH CENTURY

Spanish Jesuits were actively proselytizing in Japan from 1549, and over the ensuing decades up to 1592 the missionaries in Japan heard about

Korea and dreamt of bringing their mission there, although St. Francis Xavier does not mention Korea.[4] In the maelstrom of the East Asian War or the Japanese invasion of Korea (1592–98) the first Jesuits crossed to Korea. Gregorio de Céspedes (1551–?), a Spanish Jesuit, had been in Japan from 1577 and was ordained a Jesuit priest in 1592. From 1593, he was chosen to provide pastoral care to Christians involved in the invasion and went to Korea with a brother Jesuit born in Japan called Hankan Leon. They arrived in the fortress belonging to Konishi Yukinaga 小西行長 (1555?–1600, baptized Augustine) late in 1593. Konishi is the most famous of the Christian *daimyō* in Korea, but there were others: Sō Yoshitoshi 宗義智 (1568–1615), lord of Tsushima, baptized Darius; Kuroda Yoshitaka 黒田孝高 (1546–1604), baptized Simeon Josui and his son Kuroda Nagamasa 黒田長政 (1568–1623).[5] Originally from Himeji domain, Nagamasa went on to receive Chikuzen (Fukuoka) domain in northern Kyūshū from Tokugawa Ieyasu after the Battle of Sekigahara in 1600. Céspedes and his companion scarcely encountered any Koreans and returned to Japan in the spring of 1595. The occasional Jesuit followed,[6] but without any effect. Although some historians point to this early encounter with Christianity,[7] the current consensus in South Korea on the history of Catholicism dates the widespread practice of the faith from the late 18th century. No functioning church survived in Korea following the Japanese invasion, nor do we have any records of surreptitious Christian communities before the late 18th century, as we do for Japan.

By the late 18th century, a number of Confucian intellectuals in Korea had come to recognize certain social changes that appeared alarming. In particular, they were disturbed by the expansion of commerce, the increasing social mobility that it produced, and the apparent lack of domestic prosperity – in contrast to what they saw in China at the time. Their political world was riven with factions and proposing government policy was difficult.

Although King Yŏngjo 英祖 (1694–1776, r. 1724–76) and his successor, King Chŏngjo 正祖 (1752–1800, r. 1776-1800), had placated the worst of the factional wars by creating a system of rotating offices, struggles continued, in which the winning faction would often take over government posts and severely punish the losing faction, sometimes with exile and sometimes with execution. King Chŏngjo nurtured innovative intellectuals such as Chŏng Yakyong 丁若鏞 (1762–1836), and many of these men had visited Qing China as members of Korean embassies. In China, they had been stirred by the new turn towards Evidential Learning. The practitioners of Evidential Learning dismissed the Song-period commentaries in favour of a return to a closer scrutiny of ancient, canonical Confucian texts, reputedly those from the late Zhou and before the rise of the Qin. The school of Evidential Learning developed what we might recognize as philological and hermeneutical methods to examine allegedly ancient texts. In the course of their research, they discovered that canonical texts had their own histories and that most of the so-called Confucian classics dated from the Han dynasty.

Into that heady atmosphere of intellectual iconoclasm and economic prosperity in 18th-century China went some of the best young minds of Korea. They returned with a desire to practise these new methods and to look at their own society with fresh eyes. While they promoted the methods of Evidential Learning, they also acquired an interest in new technologies and in the purveyors of new technology in China, the Catholic missionaries. Many of these Korean scholars were associated with the so-called Southerner (南人 Nam'in) faction, part of the political opposition at the time. Initially drawn to the more accurate calendars, timepieces and maps they utilized, Korean intellectuals found the Christian faith of the fathers an interesting new approach in their pursuit of knowledge of the Dao, the ultimate purpose of all scholarship for them.[8] Some Koreans visiting Beijing on official embassies found themselves attracted by the religious elements of Christianity and converted. The most famous of the converts was Yi Sǔnghun 李承薰 (1756–1801). His father had been secretary to the annual tributary envoy to the Qing royal court, and Yi Sǔnghun was attached to the 1783 envoy on the wishes of the Southerner faction, who were then favoured at court under King Chǒngjo. Members of the Southerner faction requested that Yi Sǔnghun bring back Western books and whatever else he could find related to mathematics, astronomy, geography and literature. They also asked him to approach the Iberian Jesuits for instruction in their religion, and through those contacts he became the first Korean known to be baptized. The baptism took place early in 1784, at the North Church in Beijing, and he took the Christian name Peter.[9] Within ten years of Yi's return to Korea, some 4,000 Koreans of both sexes had been converted to Christianity.[10]

The history of the fledging Church is well known. A group of intellectuals met in a private home in the modern area of Myǒngdong in Seoul to discuss the religion. Within this group was Chǒng Yakyong, favoured by King Chǒngjo and a leader of the Southerner faction. Other Confucian scholars associated with the Southerner faction gathered to read Christian catechisms and discuss the doctrines; and in many ways their interest and even acceptance of the religion has been lauded as an instance of a self-generated Christian community. It was only after another ten years that ordained missionaries arrived from China to further consolidate the fledgling Church. The intellectual interest indicates the advanced literate state of the society and the naturally inquisitive nature of the scholars of the Southerner faction. Their interest lay primarily in whether Catholicism had something new and enlightening to reveal about the Dao and the pursuit of the Dao.

In the febrile atmosphere of court politics, any interest in what might be construed as heterodoxy created vulnerabilities for political rivals to exploit.[11] A small persecution was launched in 1791 and then a much larger persecution from 1801, followed by others over the course of the 19th century. The persecutions originated in the question of whether a Christian convert was allowed to practise ancestral rites. In the 18th century the papacy had declared that ancestral rites were heresy, pitting Christian doctrine in opposition to Confucian practice. That conflict between the new Western religion and Confucian tradition became a public issue in the autumn of 1791 when two Confucian scholars, Yun Chich'ung 尹持忠 (1759–1791, baptized Paul) and Kwŏn Sang'yŏn 權尙然 (1751–1791, baptized Jacob), suspended their ancestral worship and took it a step further by burning their ancestral tablets and burying the ashes in the garden.[12] The Korean government considered it illegal to ignore or denigrate ancestral rites and could not overlook what the two *yangban* 兩班 (scholar-official) had done. Filial piety was considered not just a socially useful practice but was synonymous with loyalty to the state. To reject ancestral rites was political treason.

The two criminals belonged to the Southerner faction, even though certain members of the faction, such as Chŏng Yakyong, were favourites of the king. King Chŏngjo did not extend the persecution, and there were no further attempts by court officials to intensify it. This suggests that the 1791 persecution was largely a reaction to an ideological threat provoked by criminal actions. Of course, the treason was motivated by a heterodox belief in Christianity, and that naturally led to greater hostility towards the religion, particularly by those in the upper classes who were loyal to Confucian traditions[13] or who saw belief in Christianity as a vulnerability in their political rivals. When King Chŏngjo suddenly died in 1800, more widespread persecutions began.

The persecution that began from early 1801 was largely politically motivated; religion was a pretext for factional struggle at court, but the allegation was treason. In 1801 a convert by the name of Hwang Sayŏng 黃嗣永 (1775–1801, baptized Alexis) sent a letter brushed on silk to the Bishop of Beijing recounting the suffering of Korean Christians. Hwang Sayŏng's 1801 'Silk Letter' explained the factional struggle that launched the persecution, named and described the circumstances of the Christian victims and apostates, and also asked for French military assistance to protect Korean Christians.[14]

If the 'Silk Letter' had just identified martyrs and practising Christians, we would probably know very little about it, because there were other similar missives, but Hwang Sayŏng went on to propose a far more serious course of action to the bishop in Beijing. First he proposes that the bishop attempt to enlist official Chinese intervention in Korea to punish the Korean king for his misdeeds (using his own calendar and minting his own coins), but then Hwang asks that the bishop request the French Far East Fleet to intervene on behalf of Korean Catholics. He argues that Korea has been at peace for centuries and has no credible military power: 'At the first sign of trouble, the Korean army will disintegrate.'[15] He requests several hundred warships and 50,000–60,000 troops. He proposes that they deliver a demand to the Korean king to tolerate Catholicism or suffer attack. When the 'Silk Letter' was intercepted by authorities and came to the attention of the government, it provided clear proof that Catholicism was indeed a treasonous teaching, and the 1801 persecution was launched.[16]

In later decades, Korean Christians requested that priests be sent. In the 1830s, a Chinese priest and three French priests secretly entered Korea. The number of converts grew to about 9,000.[17] Persecution led to the deaths of many, including the three French missionaries who were beheaded in the eighth lunar month of 1839 at Saenamtŏ 새남터 (or 沙南基 사남기), the execution site on the shores of the Han River in Seoul.[18] The deaths of these foreign missionaries had long-term consequences, because it was the first offensive move by the Korean government towards anybody or anything linked to the Western powers.

Due to the hostility of the Korean government towards Catholicism and the constant threat of persecution, the French missionaries were well aware of the need to appoint local priests who could more easily assist Korean Christians in religious practices. Hence Father Philippe Maubant selected three Korean seminarians in 1836 – Kim Taegŏn 金大建 (1821–1846, baptized Andrew), Ch'oe Pangje 崔方濟 (1820?–1837, baptized Francis) and Ch'oe Yangŏp 崔良業 (1821–1861, baptized Thomas) – and took them to the seminary in Macao, where they were to study for the priesthood. Kim Taegŏn was ordained in 1844 in Shanghai as the first Korean Catholic priest.[19] Attempting to establish new routes via the Yellow Sea to bring in more missionaries, Father Kim was arrested in the fifth lunar month of 1846 by local officials and confessed. The officials found among his possessions a Catholic book and other Christian items, proving his religious identity.[20] The arrest of a Catholic on the frontier of the Korean peninsula was a very sensitive issue for the Korean government, which had received reports from China regarding the first Opium War of 1839–42. The reports accused Westerners of spreading heterodox learning as well as opium.

While Father Kim was under arrest, Korean suspicion towards Western forces turned into alarm when three French naval vessels appeared off the coast in the summer of 1846. This was a show of force by the French government in response to the deaths of the three French missionaries in 1839. In response to this threat by the French navy, court officials, including Prime Minister Kwŏn Ton'in 權敦仁 (1783–1859), argued that the Korean Christians had called forth the French vessels and so those under arrest should be condemned as rebels. King Hŏnjong 憲宗 (1827–1849, r. 1834–49) accepted this demand and ordered the beheading of Father Kim Taegŏn and the public display of his head. Accordingly, in the ninth month of 1846, Father Kim died at the age of twenty-five at the Saenamt'ŏ execution grounds.[21]

All of these incidents prompted persecutions, but worse was to come. The persecution of 1866–71 was a large-scale crackdown that lasted for six years and resulted in over 8,000 martyrs, according to French records. There were an estimated 23,000 Christians in total at the time in Korea, meaning that about one in every three Christians died.[22] This final persecution was deeply tied to imperialist activities by foreign powers and the Korean government's response to perceived threats. Again, it involved high politics.

King Chŏljong 哲宗 (1831–1864, r. 1849–64) died in January 1864 without an heir, and was succeeded by King Kojong 高宗 (1852–1919, r. 1864–1907), the second son of Hŭngsŏn Taewŏn'gun Yi Haŭng 興宣大院君李昰應 (known as the Taewŏn'gun, 1820–1898), who was a direct descendant of King Injo 仁祖 (1595–1649, r. 1623–49). The succession of King Kojong was a result of the Queen Dowager's desire to retain control of the throne within her clan, and Kojong's father (the Taewŏn'gun) was appointed regent. While power within the royal court had been almost entirely in the hands of the Andong Kim family throughout the reign of the previous three kings, the Taewŏn'gun attempted to take over political control and eliminate the old ruling factions that had threatened the sovereign power of the king. It was as part of this process of trying to strengthen the monarchy and stabilize the regime that the Taewŏn'gun took up Christianity as a political target.[23]

The persecution began early in 1866. As the debate within the Korean court began to swirl around whether to open the country to Europeans or completely resist overtures, Bishop Siméon-François Berneux (1814–1866), Vicar Apostolic of Korea, was arrested in the second month of 1866. The Taewŏn'gun's position was isolationist, and his move to arrest the missionaries and persecute the French priests was connected to an attack on his opponents at court. He intended to close Korea to Western powers. It was at this time that nine of the twelve missionaries residing in Korea were executed, including Bishops Berneux and Daveluy. In 1984, they were canonized with 101 others, including Father Kim Taegŏn.[24]

The fate of the missionaries became a matter of national security to the Catholic French authorities. Father Ridel (1830–1884), Father Calais (1833–1884) and Father Féron (1827–1903) fled to China in the summer of 1866. Father Ridel met Admiral Pierre-Gustave Roze (1812–1883), commander of the French Far Eastern Squadron. Father Ridel requested a rescue mission to save the lives of the Korean Christian converts and missionaries. By late September, Admiral Roze had led three French military vessels from China and arrived at Inchǒn, guided by Father Ridel and three Korean Christians to pressure the Korean government and survey the geography.[25] Roze returned in October with six ships. The French campaign lasted six weeks in the autumn of 1866 and was limited to Kanghwa Island, located at the mouth of the Han River, downriver from the capital, Seoul. The expedition led to Korea's first military encounter with a Western power and ended when the French finally retreated in November and took with them an enormous quantity of royal books,[26] along with other national treasures.

The 1866 military campaign was the first by a Western military against Korea in modern times. It was also the first time that French missionaries acted on behalf of their own country and called for military force against the Korean government. The attack and looting of some of the country's most valued treasures led to outrage in the Chosǒn court and only strengthened the persecution. But more and stranger developments were yet to come.

Ernst J. Oppert (1832–1903), a German merchant attempting to establish trade with Korea, set off from Shanghai in May 1868 to dig up the grave of the Taewǒn'gun's father, intending to use the burial goods (perhaps even the buried remains) to negotiate with the Taewǒn'gun for the opening of trade ports. This act had been suggested to Oppert by Father Féron and his Korean followers who had been able to flee the persecution. Oppert and his party landed in Korea and found the tomb but failed to complete their plan and left, pursued by Korean soldiers. Desecration of the grave of the regent's father only confirmed the wisdom of the Taewǒn'gun's isolationist policy, and increased suspicion immediately fell on Korean Christians.

A final incident involved the United States Navy. An American vessel led by Admiral J. Rodgers landed on the shores of P'ung Island 豊島 in Kyǒnggi Province 京畿道 late in May 1871 to enquire after the fate of the General Sherman, a trading vessel that had disappeared in 1866, and to request trade negotiations with the Korean government.[27] The Americans were rebuffed but stayed in the area. When they approached the mouth of the Han River, they were fired on from the shore. Although there was no damage, Admiral Rodgers occupied Kanghwa Island between 10 and 12 June 1871. Contrary to expectations by the Americans that the Korean government would open up trade from fear of further military assault, the Taewŏn'gun announced a total rejection of the West and erected anti-foreign steles 斥和碑 척화비 in various places around the country. The inscriptions read: 'To not fight back on the occasion of a Western invasion is to make peace with Western barbarians, and to assert peace means to betray our country. All our descendants should beware. Written in 1866, established in 1871.'

After two days, the Americans retreated. It was not until 1882 and after extensive Chinese mediation that a treaty was struck between the United States and Korea, the first treaty between the Chosŏn court and any Western power.

SUMMARY OF THE 19TH-CENTURY CONTEXT

The problems presented by Christianity as a heterodox teaching in contradiction to Confucianism were apparently not insurmountable. Some of the best minds in Korea in the late 18th century found Christianity to be complementary to Confucian ethics. But an overwhelming conflict arose when ancestor ritual was forbidden by papal bulls, and this position came to a head for Korean Christians in 1790–91. The destruction of ancestral tablets by two Korean Christians sparked a punitive response from the highest level of the state.

The ensuing persecution, though not severe, brought Christianity to the attention of the Chosŏn court as a political threat which then fatally linked the religion with politics. Political rivals acquired a new arena of contention, a new opportunity for slander and a new weapon to wield. Following the untimely death of King Chŏngjo in 1800, those literati who had dabbled with Christianity or even embraced it now became vulnerable.

The purveyors of Christianity had the misfortune to be associated with invading armies. In the late 16th century, Koreans first encountered Christianity as a belief held by some of the Japanese ransacking their country. Gregorio de Céspedes, the Spanish priest, was a field chaplain of sorts to Konishi Yukinaga's forces. Although he and his colleagues despaired of the destruction, ministered to the abducted Koreans and quickly moved to stop the European trade in Korean slaves, the damage had already been done simply by association. In the late 18th century, there were no armies attacking Korea, but Hwang Sayŏng's 1801 'Silk Letter', brushed by a desperate Christian facing a growing persecution, went too far and pleaded for foreign armies to attack Korea. That act of betrayal made Christianity no longer merely a form of heterodoxy. It became high treason, and over the following decades it was treated as such. By 1866, foreign priests abandoned their apolitical stance and led French forces to Korean shores, thereby confirming the Chosŏn court's worst fears. Further outrages by other imperial powers and greedy merchants from the West only reinforced what was already obvious.

Kang Jae-eun, the well-known Zainichi historian in Japan, argues that the 'Silk Letter' was a critical turning point in Korean perceptions of the West and set Korea on a path different from those followed by Japan and Qing China over the course of the 19th century.[28] This claim remains to be tested and explored with further comparative research, but some things are certain. From 1801 to the 1870s, Catholicism was persecuted, and doctrinal threats faded in the face of a growing identification of Catholicism with European imperialism. Protestantism faced this history when it entered the country just a few years later, but the Protestants were officially tolerated by treaty and benefited from a series of fortuitous circumstances because of their association with medicine and education.

PROTESTANTS ENTER KOREA WITH GREAT SUCCESS FROM THE 1880S

After the Kanghwa Treaty with Japan in 1876 and the treaty with the United States in 1882, everything changed. Horace Newton Allen (1858–1932), a physician with the American diplomatic legation, arrived in September 1884. He was close by when the Kapsin Coup occurred in December 1884. Kim Okkyun 金玉均 (1851–1894), Sŏ Chaep'il 徐載弼 (1864–1951) and others of the Enlightenment Party attacked high officials in the cabinet as they were celebrating the opening of Korea's first post office. Min Yŏngik 閔泳翊 (1860–1914), related to the queen, was stabbed and lay wounded, but Allen went to his aid and saved his life. Having saved a relative of the queen, Allen received the trust of the royal family and was allowed to open a medical school, which eventually graduated the first class of Korean physicians in 1908 and later became Severance Hospital and Yonsei University's Medical School.[29] Esther Park 金點童 (1876?–1910) was the first woman trained in Western medicine, and her example gave Korean women access to a medical education. More missionaries followed, and they focused on three areas: medicine, education and evangelism.[30]

Private missionary schools blossomed for both men and women, Yonsei and Ewha were only the most famous. Yonsei was founded by Horace G. Underwood (1859–1916) in cooperation with Horace Newton Allen. Ewha was founded by Mary F. Scranton (1832–1909) under the patronage of the queen.[31] The missionary schools became hotbeds of Korean patriotism and Western-style liberalism for two reasons. One was that they offered an alternative to Japanese-style education. The second was that since 1910 basic education for Koreans had been in Japanese and was primarily vocational. Only the missionary schools offered higher education. The Japanese did not ignore higher education but sought constantly to impose controls, and the Residency-General (1905–10) declared that all schools needed a permit and could only use authorized textbooks. Despite the controls, the English language and access to information from abroad that was not Japanese meant that higher education came to be identified with Christianity, science, cosmopolitanism and patriotism. As literacy spread among women and the lower classes through the missionaries' active use of the vernacular script, *han'gŭl*, education became more democratized. Direct experience of self-rule was also encouraged by the nature of the structure of the Protestant churches with their councils and elected leaders.

Medicine and education made missionaries very popular among Koreans. The missionaries were widely received and welcomed, as evidenced by anecdotal statements:

> Suddenly the command was issued from somewhere, 'Open wide the gates,' and lo, in stepped the missionary. The doors had remained fast closed till he was ready, but now the hour had come. From that day on the missionary has been the representative Westerner, not the merchantman nor official, but the missionary, the *moksa* [pastor], passing the length and breadth of the land, in the far north, down south, all the way from Seoul to Pusan, to Ŭiju, gazed at by the wondering multitudes.[32]

Converts multiplied, particularly among the educated, literate and social-elite classes. In 1903, the Korean YMCA was founded, and in 1909 there was a widespread evangelical campaign called 'A Million Souls for Christ'. P'yŏngyang came to be called the 'Jerusalem of the East' because of its number of churches. South Korea has recently become the second largest exporter of missionaries after the United States.[33] A significant part of this Protestant history is accessible through the Bodleian Library's collection of archives on the Church of England's mission to Korea.

SOURCES IN OXFORD RELATED TO THE HISTORY OF PROTESTANT CHRISTIANITY IN KOREA

During the period of the opening of Korea – typically in the 1880s when a number of diplomats, traders and foreign experts were present – it tends to be the Western missionaries who have left us the most knowledge about the interaction between modern Korea and the West. Unlike the diplomats, who usually lived in Korea for a short period of time and were restricted to interaction with certain social strata, the missionaries lived in Korea with the support of their institutional organizations over a much longer time. They interacted with and lived among all levels of Korean society, right from the very bottom to the highest level of society. Indeed, in the months after 8 October 1895, when the queen was assassinated by a band of Japanese thugs because of her ongoing opposition to Japan's imperial plans, the terrified king, fearing for his life, insisted that a group of Western missionaries should sleep close to him in the palace each night. A Mrs Underwood had acted as the queen's physician, and after the assassination, she prepared meals for the king, who thought people were trying to poison him. The core members of this group were James S. Gale (1863–1937), Homer B. Hulbert (1863–1949), George Heber Jones (1867–1919), Horace G. Underwood and H.G. Appenzeller (1858–1902). All these men were involved a few years later in the foundation of the Royal Asiatic Society Korea Branch (RASKB) in 1900. Other missionaries who were members of the RASKB from the very start included Horace Newton Allen, Oliver R. Avison (1860–1956) and Mark Napier Trollope (1862–1930).[34] The RASKB published an annual journal, *Transactions*, starting from the year it was founded.[35]

These missionaries were all highly educated and did not restrict themselves to building churches. They were active in establishing schools and hospitals and providing education and medical care. Oxford fortunately received collections, materials and works donated by these missionaries who brought back items after residing in Korea during this period of engagement. These include records of the missionaries' work, translations, correspondence, photographs of schools and hospitals being established and photographs of the daily life of people in Korea. This chapter focuses mostly on the sources documenting the activities of the Anglican Church in Korea between 1891 and the 1960s.[36]

The first arrivals to the Bodleian Library were a group of books from the New Testament translated in the 1880s into the native Korean script, *han'gŭl*, by John Ross (1842–1915).[37] These books were part of the donation from the well-known Orientalist, the Reverend Solomon Caesar Malan (1812–1894), given to the Bodleian Indian Institute Library in 1885. Malan's donation of some 4,000 volumes was the largest gift ever received by the Bodleian Indian Institute Library. Ross's New Testament books are included on the '100 Hangul Heritage' list promulgated by the government of the Republic of Korea as they are the first books of the Bible in *han'gŭl*.[38] As such, they are of priceless linguistic value in documenting the vernacular in the late 19th century.[39] The translated books in the Bodleian collection are: the Gospel of Matthew, Gospel of Mark, Gospel of Luke and Acts, Gospel of John and the New Testament.[40] Other works relating to Korea by John Ross are also available at the Bodleian.[41] All the title pages, except the New Testament, carry the bookplate of the 'The Malan Library'.

Ross was never able to enter Korea, but after the early 1880s the mission field opened up and the Anglican Church took an interest. Bishop Charles John Corfe (1843–1921) was summoned in 1889 by Archbishop Edward White Benson of Canterbury (1829–1896, bishop 1883–96), to become the first bishop in Korea and to found the Anglican diocese in that country. Bishop Corfe travelled through America, where he collected Eli Landis, a young doctor who was to become a significant scholar of Korean culture. They landed at Inch'ŏn in 1890, and in mid-November 1900 the Kanghwa Anglican Cathedral was opened on Kanghwa Island.[42] Bishop Corfe was also responsible for founding the magazine *The Morning Calm*[43] and is attributed as the author of the rare book entitled *Terminations of the Verb* (하다).[44] *Terminations* is the earliest book in English on the study of Korean verbs and the Bodleian copy is the only known surviving copy anywhere in the world.[45]

Bishop Corfe resigned in 1904 and was succeeded by Bishop Arthur Turner (1862–1910). The Japanese Protectorate was established in mid-November 1905. That was a period of crucial political importance for Korea, and many Koreans sought comfort in the Christian churches. The Anglican Church had already spread south from Seoul to Suwŏn, and chapels were constructed in various other parts of the country. The growth was so extensive that Bishop Turner is said to have died of overwork in 1910, his episcopate lasting only five years.[46]

Mark Napier Trollope was born in London and educated at New College, Oxford. He was the first priest to volunteer for Korea in 1890 in response to an appeal from Bishop Corfe for volunteers. He went to Korea in the same year and became the scholar of the mission and one of the foremost authorities on the culture of the country. From 1890 to 1902 he was chaplain to the bishop and the senior missionary for the Society for the Propagation of the Gospel (SPG), and vicar general from 1896 to 1902. The Kanghwa Church (also known as the Church of St Peter and St Paul), built around 1900, was designed by Trollope. The beautiful building harmonizes Korean-style architecture and Western church architecture splendidly and is now regarded as a national treasure.[47] In 1902 he returned to England for a time on account of the ill-health of his father. He went back to Korea as the new bishop in 1910, coinciding with Japan's complete annexation of the country and Trollope's diocese. Despite the annexation, Bishop Trollope was able to expand the Church's activities. To train the local clergy, he established St Michael's Seminary 성미가엘신학원 in 1914, predecessor to Sungkonghoe (Sŏnggonghoe) University 성공회대학교 (聖公會大學校), the Anglican University. He also built the Anglican cathedral, the Church of St Mary the Virgin and St Nicholas, in 1924 in central Seoul, next to the British Embassy compound. It boasts Romanesque architecture and mosaic murals. Bishop Trollope continued to serve in Korea until his sudden death in 1930.[48] He was also president of the RASKB in 1917–19, 1922–25 and 1928–30.

Trollope was also a keen collector of books, and his library of old Korean books numbered 'something round ten thousand volumes, and contains many priceless editions'.[49] Many of the rare and important Korean books and manuscripts in the Bodleian Library were donated by him sporadically between 1896 and 1930. What remains of his library, called the 'Landis Library', now forms part of Yonsei University.[50]

The Bodleian is also fortunate to have a collection of materials known as the Trollope Papers. These include the private correspondence of Bishop Trollope from 1891 to 1929, as well as letters received and sent between 1889 and 1928 from the archives of the United Society for the Propagation of the Gospel (USPG).[51] There are also bound copies of *Morning Calm*, the diocesan newsletter from 1890, as well as photographs related to missionary work. The Trollope Papers include the following:

1 The private correspondence of Bishop Trollope from 1891 to 1929 (housed in two boxes). The bishop wrote on average two to three letters a month over nearly thirty years (shelfmark USPG X620).
2 The D Series contains Copies of Letters Received (CLR) in three volumes (shelfmark CLR 86–88): v.1 (1889–1904), v.2 (1904–13) and v.3 (1913–28). There is an index in v.3.
3 Three volumes of the Copies of Letters Sent (CLS) are letters sent to Korea (shelfmark CLS 66–68): v.1 (1889–1911), v.2 (1911–23) and v.3 (1923–28). There is an index in each of the volumes. There are also special subject reference pages at the beginning.

In addition, there is an index to the USPG archive, with annual reports of the USPG, committee minutes and missionary reports from 1701 to 1970 for various mission fields. Those related to Korea do not appear until the end of the 19th century.

These were all received at Rhodes House in 1986 from the USPG, along with the rest of the USPG archive. Before then it could be consulted by researchers in a reading room at the USPG offices in London. The materials were probably donated to the USPG during the first half of the 20th century. Since the USPG's main purpose was to help the Church in the neediest parts of the world, and not to run a reading room, the USPG thought that researchers would be better served if the archive was placed in a repository with other related collections and relevant secondary material. The society accordingly deposited the majority of the archive from 1701 to *c.* 1970 in Rhodes House. Material later than 1970 is still with the USPG in London, as are the personnel records. The material in Oxford was in the Bodleian Library of Commonwealth and African Studies (BLCAS) at Rhodes House until 2014, when the entire USPG archive, including all the photos, were moved to the Bodleian and are now held in the Weston Library. The catalogues, and the index cards to the photos, are in the David Reading Room on Level 5 of the Weston Library. Correspondence covering the period between 1889 and 1928 records official activities right from the beginning of the establishment of an Anglican organization in Korea – that is, from the first bishop, Corfe – to the third bishop, Trollope.

The most recent notable acquisition is from Monsignor Cecil Richard Rutt (1925–2011). Rutt, educated at Pembroke College, Cambridge, and Kelham Theological College, was ordained a priest in the Church of England in 1952 and sent to Korea as a missionary in 1954. He rose to become the Bishop of Taejŏn (1968–74) with later bishoprics at St Germans (1974–79) in Cornwall and Leicester (1979–90). He converted to Roman Catholicism in 1994 and was ordained a priest in 1995. The Pope honoured him with the title Monsignor in 2010. He served as the president of the Royal Asiatic Society, Korea branch, in 1974. He was awarded an honorary doctorate of literature from the Confucian University, Seoul, in 1974, the Tasan Cultural Award (for writings on Korea) in 1964, and given the Order of Civil Merit, Peony Class (Republic of Korea), also in 1974. The Bodleian Library is fortunate to have received his library in 2008.[52]

Bishop Rutt's donation to the Library is a large collection, which arrived in October 2008. It is composed of about 2,000 items, of which 432 are in Western languages. The collection is the larger part of Bishop Rutt's personal library and offers an impressive scholar's collection, with approximately 35 per cent of the papers on history, 25 per cent on literature; 20 per cent are reference works, and 20 per cent are related to Chinese studies. Although the collection was mostly published in the latter half of the 20th century, it is significant for its inclusion of classical literature, history and reference works on Korean studies. Many of the titles are now out of print and difficult to obtain. Additionally, there are some titles that were published during the Japanese annexation, and there is a small collection of rare books related to early linguistic studies, grammar and textbooks. Also included are some unpublished materials by James Scarth Gale (1863–1937) and rare photos of Gale and his family, among the many other things that Rutt obtained from Gale's family while preparing Gale's biography. There are also photographs of Bishop Rutt taken when he was in Korea, as well as hymn and sermon texts.[53] For works related to Christianity in the Rutt collection, see Appendix 1. For materials by

James Scarth Gale obtained by Rutt from Gale's family while preparing Gale's biography, see Appendix 2.

Rutt's collection of Gale's writings contains important material. As well as Gale's writings and translations, there are some of his letters and photos, and the list of books sent by Gale to the Library of Congress (LOC) on his retirement. Although Gale sent his books to the LOC, the LOC did not make a record of the gift and the LOC reports that it has no record of what is from Gale and what is not. Therefore, the Bodleian list of books is highly useful and rare. For other works by James Scarth Gale outside the Rutt collection and available in the Bodleian, see Appendix 3. More materials and photos related to Gale are currently being processed.[54]

COLLECTIONS OF PHOTOGRAPHS RELATING TO THE HISTORY OF CHRISTIANITY IN THE BODLEIAN

Aside from documents, there is also a collection of interesting and rare photographs in the Bodleian Libraries, taken around the end of the 19th century and the beginning of the 20th century. Many of the pictures were taken by Anglican Church commissioners and show their activities, such as the building of churches and hospitals. There are also photographs taken by other people of the daily life of ordinary Korean people and officials. These include rare pictures of the exterior and interior of the Kanghwa Church designed by Bishop Trollope and completed in 1900; the first Korean priest, Kim Taegŏn; a royal funeral procession and a Korean wedding (with the couple in traditional costumes) at church. There is also a small collection of photographs of James Scarth Gale from Richard Rutt's donation, which the bishop obtained from Gale's family while preparing Gale's biography. As mentioned above, the entire USPG archive, including all the photos, are held in the Weston. The catalogues and the index cards to the photos (both albums and loose photographs) are in the David Reading Room.[55]

The fourth bishop in Korea was Alfred Cecil Cooper (1882–1964), and the fifth was John Charles Sydney Daly (1903–1993). Lee Cheon Hwan (Paul Lee, 1922–2010) was installed as the first Korean-born bishop in the diocese of Seoul in 1965.[56] From 1965, the Korean diocese was split into two: Seoul and Taejŏn), and from 1974, the diocese of Pusan was added. From 1993, the Anglican Church of Korea became a Province of the Anglican Communion. There are approximately 100 churches and 50,000 followers, and the Church is associated with Sungkonghoe University, the Anglican University. The current primate is the Most Reverend Moses Nagjun Yoo, Primate of Korea and Bishop of Daejeon.

Tenures of the first Anglican bishops to Korea

Tenure	Name (Korean name)	Lifetime
1889–1905	Charles John Corfe (고요한)	1843–1921
1905–10	Arthur Beresford Turner (단아덕)	1862–1910
1911–30	Mark Napier Trollope (조마가)	1862–1930
1931–54	Alfred Cecil Cooper (구세실)	1882–1964
1955–65	John Charles Sydney Daly (김요한)	1903–1993
1965–84	Lee Cheon Hwan (Bishop of Seoul) (이천환) (Right Reverend Paul Lee)	1922–2010
1968–73	Richard Rutt (Bishop of Taejön)	1925–2011

OTHER PHOTOGRAPHIC COLLECTIONS: THE HOWARTH COLLECTION

A large collection of some 2,425 A4-size high-quality photographs of Korea taken in the 1950s and 1960s at the time of Bishop Daly's tenure can be found in the Howarth Box 7 (six files of photographs: Korean I–XI, nos 1–2425).[57] Anthony Howarth was a photographer who undertook photography assignments for the USPG; there are also photographs of other countries by him. Many of these pictures are of village and street scenes, and people's daily life; most are of the Christian activities of building schools, hospitals churches and other projects. These also give us a glance of what Korea was like during this important period of the mid-20th century. Places of interest that appear in these photos are St Michael's Seminary, Inchön Church, Anjung Orphanage, St Bede's House Seoul, Seoul Cathedral of St Mary and St Nicholas, United Nations Day Ceremonial, St Andrew's Church Chonan, Ewha Women's University, the Church of St Gregory Ch'ongju, St John's College and Ch'ongju. A variety of missionaries are shown, as are prominent politicians, including General Park Chung-hee (who was later elected president of the Third Republic of South Korean in 1963) and Song Yochan (prime minister of South Korea from 3 July 1961 to 16 June 1962); there is also a photo of the bronze statue of the late General Douglas MacArthur erected in 1957 in Inchön. For more details, see Appendix 4: Howarth collection.

CONCLUSION

This chapter has surveyed the history of Christianity in Korea with a focus on the Anglican Church in Korea from the late 19th to the mid-20th century. Significant Korean engagement with Christianity did not appear until the late 18th to early 19th centuries and began from curious literati investigating an alternative path to understand the Dao. As a heterodox teaching that made believers vulnerable to accusations of social and political subversion, Christianity became entwined with politics. When Korean Christians appealed for foreign military intervention to protect converts, the heterodoxy became treasonous. When French priests enlisted the French navy to put pressure on the Korean government, Christianity and imperialism became almost synonymous. Despite these political problems and severe persecutions, the number of converts expanded, and the first ordained Korean priest (Father Kim Taegŏn) was martyred in 1846. The last persecution began in 1866 and lasted until 1871, resulting in the martyrdom of nine French priests. Such was the background to the arrival of Protestant missionaries in the 1880s.

Protestantism, though, had several fortuitous aspects that propelled it to become a major social force in 20th-century Korea and to retain that position in the Republic of Korea after the Korean War. The Protestant missionaries arrived with legal protection guaranteed by treaties, and they usually combined their ministry with medicine and education. The history of the Anglican Church in Korea has revolved around the establishment of clinics, hospitals and schools, and its priests became leading scholars of the Korean tradition, helping to establish the field of Korean studies in the West. The Bodleian Library has a rich store of rare materials on the history of the Anglican Church in Korea, replete with extensive internal correspondence, the personal papers of leading scholar-priests, and thousands of photographs that document the activities of the Church as well as Korean life over the 20th century up until the 1970s.

Bishop Trollope and staff or clergy at the ordination of three Koreans, St. Matthew's day. 1917

[WES] USPG Album 153a. p. 437. image 1159 (© United Society for the Propagation of the Gospel)

The late Bishop of Korea, Arthur Beresford Turner. February 1911

[WES] USPG Album 153a, p. 410, image 6618
(© United Society for the Propagation of the Gospel)

Bishop Charles John Corfe. May 1895

[WES] USPG Album 153a, p. 400, image 1806
(© United Society for the Propagation of the Gospel)

The Bishop in Korea, Right Rev. A.C. Cooper. November 1936

[WES] USPG Album 153a, p. 432, image 1354
(© United Society for the Propagation of the Gospel)

The Rev. Paul Lee. Warden of St. John's College for day church workers, talking to Mr. Francis the builder (centre) and Bishop John Daly. 1950s/1960s

[WES] USPG Howarth Photos – Korea 469
(© United Society for the Propagation of the Gospel)

The Rev. Richard Rutt, Warden of St. Bedes, having a discussion in the library with students. 1950s/1960s

[WES] USPG Howarth Photos – Korea 273
(© United Society for the Propagation of the Gospel)

Admiral of the Korean navy. 1901

[WES] USPG Album 153a, p. 330, image 1901
(© United Society for the Propagation of the Gospel)

The major of Seoul. c.1900

[WES] USPG Album 153a, p. 331, image 4708
(© United Society for the Propagation of the Gospel)

Archers shooting with bows and arrows. January 1904

[WES] USPG Album 153a, p. 403, image 4487 (© United Society for the Propagation of the Gospel)

**Officials in court dress.
May 1905**

[WES] USPG Album 153a, p. 405, image 4707
(© United Society for the Propagation of
the Gospel)

**Notice the wooden clogs
worn in wet weather.
In-patients, 'Chin-Chun'
hospital. 1911**

[WES] USPG Photo 875 (© United Society for
the Propagation of the Gospel)

Two Christian girls of Park-chun. Taken the day of their baptism. 1913

[WES] USPG Photo 732 (© United Society for the Propagation of the Gospel)

Kanghwa Church. The city can be seen to the right of the picture. 1915

[WES] USPG Photo 871 (© United Society for the Propagation of the Gospel)

Kanghwa Island – Priest walking about his village (The Rev. Isaiah Sou at Naeri). 1950s/1960s

[WES] USPG Howarth Photos – Korea 598
(© United Society for the Propagation of the Gospel)

The Rev. Stephen Yu (Kanghwa Island). 1950s/1960s

[WES] USPG Howarth Photos – Korea 500
(© United Society for the Propagation of the Gospel)

Bishop John Daly in a country village (among children). 1950s/1960s

[WES] USPG Howarth Photos – Korea 650
(© United Society for the Propagation of the Gospel)

Sister Maria and the Rev. Mother Phoebe. 1950s/1960s

[WES] USPG Howarth Photos – Korea 55
(© United Society for the Propagation of the Gospel)

Miners having a smoke, Hwangji-ri (?). 1950s/1960s

[WES] USPG Howarth Photos – Korea 1654
(© United Society for the Propagation of the Gospel)

Leper women preparing red peppers and man carrying pot in which pickles are made. 1950s/1960s

[WES] USPG Howarth Photos – Korea 1757
(© United Society for the Propagation of the Gospel)

General Park [Chung-hee]. The leader of the revolution of 1961. Early 1960s

[WES] USPG Howarth Photos – Korea 1653
(© United Society for the Propagation of the Gospel)

Seoul, United Nations Day Celebration. The Rt. Rev. John Daly having a chat with Prime Minister Song. Early 1960s

[WES] USPG Howarth Photos – Korea 1901
(© United Society for the Propagation of the Gospel)

CLOTHES AND ACCESSORIES

THE MUSEUMS OF the University of Oxford have a good selection of traditional Korean costumes, particularly those of officials and scholars, which reflect the class-structured society of the Chosŏn period which rewarded academic accomplishment. Upward social mobility was possible by passing the *kwagŏ* 科擧 (civil service examinations) and was the most desirable way for men to achieve a successful public career in Chosŏn society. While clothes for the upper classes were made of bright colours and indicated the wearer's social status, with various accessories completing the outfit – such as footwear, jewellery and headdresses or hairpins – commoners wore white, except during festivals and special occasions such as weddings. There was also little surface ornamentation.

changot 長衣 장옷 or *changŭi* 장의
(Woman's long garment of green gauze)
19th century. Length x width (centre back to sleeve end)
40 x 65 cm. Gauze and silk.
[PRM] 1896.62.206.3. S. Wakefield collection, purchased by PRM in 1907
(© Pitt Rivers Museum, University of Oxford)

A *changot* (literally a 'long garment') is a type of cloak worn by noble ladies in public during the Chosŏn period. It is similar to a *turumagi* 두루마기 (overcoat) which was worn by both men and women, but the *changot* has added *gŏdŭlji* 거들지 (white cuffs) and double-string red and purple ties. An interesting feature of the *changot* is that silk is used for both the inner and outer layers.[6] *Changot* were also used as veils to hide women's faces. When used as a veil, the arms are not inserted into the sleeves, and the upper part is drawn hood-wise over the head, making an effective veil. The face veil in this style began to disappear at the turn of the century due to the growing influence of Western culture.[7]

Previous page:

aengsam 鶯衫 앵삼

(Nightingale robe worn by successful applicants in the civil service examination)

19th century. Length x width (centre back to sleeve end) 130 x 90.5 cm. Silk

This yellow-green robe was worn by a man who passed the state examinations held to recruit officials. The highest scorer or *changwŏn* 壯元 (장원) in the government test received a red certificate, a *hongpae* 紅牌 (홍패) and a specially designed hat that was decorated with a double spray of paper flowers called an *ŏsahwa* 御賜花 (어사화), presented by the king. A three-day celebration followed the ceremony, during which the successful person paraded about with musicians, dressed in the same robe and hat, and visited their seniors, relatives and the administrators of the examination.[1]

The regular examinations were held every three years and consisted of five stages. At all stages the number of successful candidates was a fixed quota. The first two stages constituted the *sokwa* 小科 (소과) (lesser examination) and the *Ch'osi* 初試 (초시) (first test), which were taken locally in Seoul or in one of the eight provincial centres in the autumn. The successful candidates went on to take the *poksi* 覆試 (복시) (repeat test), in the following spring, at the Board of Rites in the capital. A successful candidate was considered a *saengwŏn* 生員 (생원) (classics licentiate) or *chinsa* 進士 (진사) (literary licentiate), depending on the type of examination (exegesis of classics or prose and poetry composition), and acquired the social status of *sŏnbi* 儒 or 士 (선비) (literatus or scholar without an official appointment). He could be appointed to a lower official post but was expected to matriculate into the Sŏnggyungwan 成均館 (성균관) (National Confucian Academy) in Seoul, and prepare for the next examination level. Many retired to their villages at this point, having acquired an elevated social status.

The more ambitious candidates presented themselves for the next three stages or the *taekwa* 大科 (대과) (the major examination), which was better known as the *munkwa* 文科 (문과) (civil service examination). Although these examinations were also held every three years, there were a number of irregular examinations. Again, candidates sat the *ch'osi* and the *poksi*. Among the passers of the *poksi*, thirty-three were selected to continue to the highest examination, the *chŏnsi* 殿試 (전시) (palace examination), where the king was present. The highest scorer or *changwŏn* was appointed to junior sixth rank in the civil service. Two others received *kapkwa* 甲科 (갑과) (first-class honours) and were appointed to the seventh rank, seven received *ŭlgwa* 乙科 (을과) (second-class honours) and were appointed to the eighth rank, while the remaining twenty-three received *pyŏnggwa* 丙科 (병과) (third-class honours) and were appointed to the ninth rank.[2]

Mugwa 武科 (무과) (military examinations) were held every year and military officials were recruited through the state examinations based on knowledge of military texts and skills in the military arts, such as archery and horsemanship. Chosŏn society placed academic learning and civil officials above military officials, thereby ensuring civilian control of the military. Civil officials were recruited through the civil service examinations that tested knowledge of Confucian classics and skill in writing poetry, prose and essays. They were not only given rights in the personnel administration of the civil side of the government but also the right to command in the military side. Therefore, the passing of the civil service examinations was considered the greatest of successes.[3]

noksa-bok 錄事服
(Blue gauze robe)
19th century. Length x width (centre back to sleeve
end) 134 x 90.5 cm. Silk or possibly cotton

[ASH] EAX.3834 (© Ashmolean Museum, University of Oxford)

This was a robe for a *noksa* 錄事 (recorder), a
low-ranked official, who was employed at a local
government office in the Chosŏn period.[4]

tallyŏng 團領 단령
(Official robe)

19th century. Length x width (centre back to sleeve end)
129 x 82 cm. Textile silk

[PRM] 1907.80.19.1. S. Wakefield Collection, purchased by PRM in 1907
(© Pitt Rivers Museum, University of Oxford)

The official garment of the court nobility in the Chosŏn period consisted of a gown with a rounded neckline, a chest band, emblematic squares or rank badges attached on the chest and back and a silken hat with wings. All of these reflected the rank of the wearer by material and design. An example of

an official dressed as this can be seen on p. 96 of Volume 1 of *Korean Treasures*. Towards the end of the Chosŏn period, these gowns were also worn by commoners as the wedding attire of the groom. The tradition continues today, and one can see the groom wearing a similar robe when the couple pay their respects to their parents as part of the wedding ceremony.

Shown in this picture is an official robe with two embroidered *hyungbae* 胸背 (흉배) (rank badges). One is afixed to the chest and the other to the centre of the back. The single crane on these embroidered badges indicates that the wearer is a lower civil official below the third rank. Two cranes

would indicate an official of upper-third rank and above. Cranes represented the loftiness of the spirit of a learned man of noble blood. The rank badge for a military official was a tiger, which suggested strength and valour. These rank indicators changed and there were no military officials above Upper 3rd rank. The high-quality embroidery is done on a purple-patterned satin damask. The crane with its wings open is holding the plant of eternal youth in its beak. There are clouds around the crane, and sea and waves below. Other objects include the Buddhist swastika. The edges of the insignia are embroidered with braided yellow thread.[5]

(above) *kapchu* 甲冑 갑주
(Military officer's silk coat with inner armour plates of lacquered leather that overlap like scales)
Max. length 102.5 cm. Silk, lacquer, hide, cotton and metal
[PRM] 1906.79.1. S. Wakefield collection, purchased by PRM in 1906
(© Pitt Rivers Museum, University of Oxford)

This is an unusual and rare armour with lacquered leather mail on the inside at the back as well as at the front. The exterior is made of dark blue silk with floral patterns and the inside is lined with plain light-blue cotton. There are two characters inside the armour, Kim Sam 金三 (김삼), which could be the name of the official. The neck is lined with beige leather. Each of the lacquered leather squares for the mail are constructed with three pieces of hide stuck together and held by studs on the inside of the armour. There is another known example in the Grassi Museum für Völkerkunde (Grassi Museum of Ethnology) in Leipzig, Germany. A note on the old Pitt Rivers Museum label states 'Officer's armour, coat & helmet. The coat is "armoured" inside with overlapping scales of lacquered hide ... The helmet has similar scales of lacquered copper.' Unfortunately the helmet is nowhere to be found.

(left) *tae-ch'ang-ŭi* 大氅衣 대창의
(Nobleman's robe with wide sleeves)
19th century. Length x width (centre back to sleeve end)
131 x 90 cm. Silk
[PRM] 1896.62.208.7. Robert T. Turley collection, purchased by PRM in 1896
(© Pitt Rivers Museum, University of Oxford)

The literati from the noble class in the Chosŏn period wore this robe for everyday wear, along with a three-tiered horsehair hat. The cord of the hat was braided and tied in front. The robe was also worn as an inner robe for official attire.

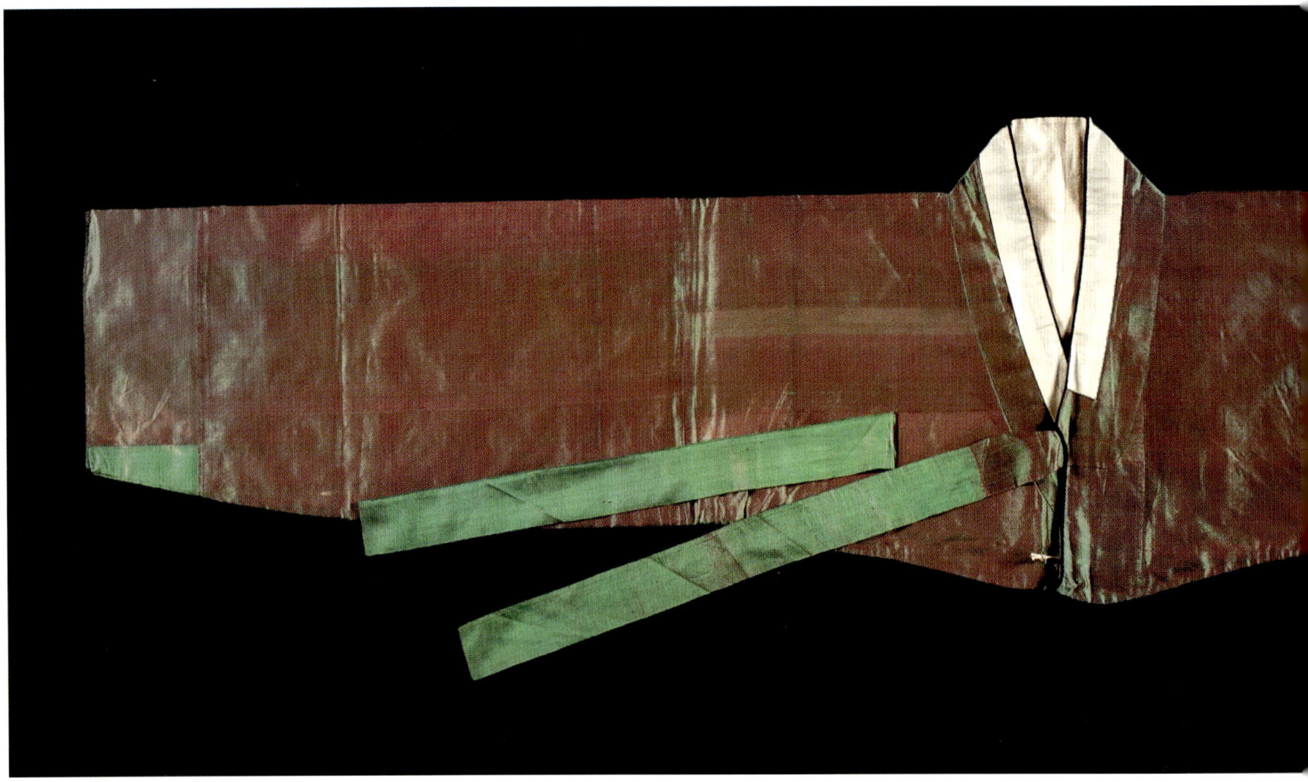

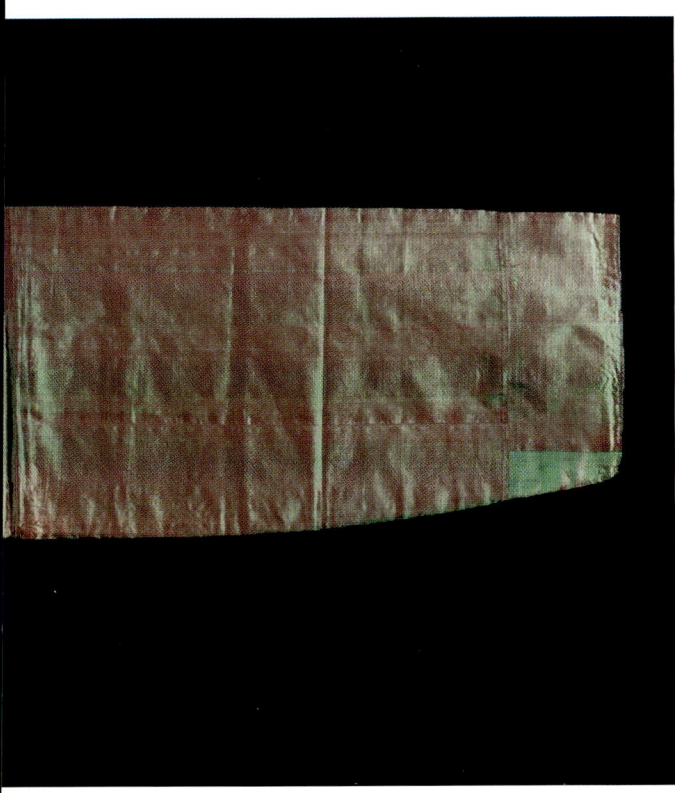

chŏgori 襦 저고리
(An upper jacket)

19th century. Length x width (centre back to sleeve end) 35 x 69 cm. Very short jacket of iridescent green with thin black trim. Silk

[PRM] 1896.62.206.2. Robert T. Turley collection, purchased by PRM in 1896
(© Pitt Rivers Museum, University of Oxford)

The *chŏgori* is a traditional Korean upper garment, worn by both men and women. It covers the arms and upper part of the body. The men's version is longer and stretches down to the waist. Women wear *chima* 치마 (skirts) while men wear *paji* 바지 (baggy pants). In the 15th century, Korean women began to wear longer *chŏgori* and skirts. The skirts were tied high up above the breast with a sash.[8] The *chŏgori* in the early period reached below the waist but became progressively shorter in later years and gradually shortened until it acquired its present length, just covering the breasts. This example is a very short jacket of iridescent green with thin black trim for a wealthy lady. The example below is even shorter.

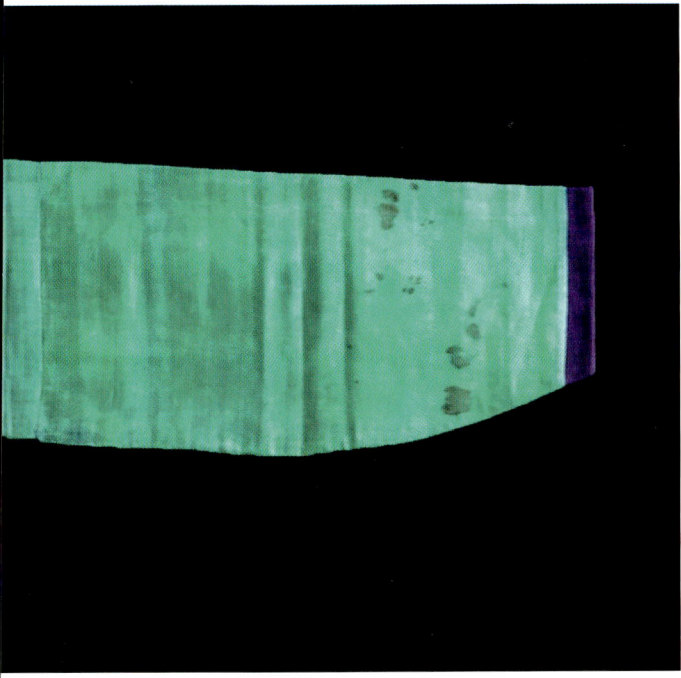

chŏgori 襦 저고리
(An upper jacket)

19th century. Length x width (centre back to sleeve end) 28 x 69 cm. Woman's very short emerald-green jacket with purple trim on cuffs. Silk

[PRM] 1896.62.206.1. Robert T. Turley collection, purchased by PRM in 1896
(© Pitt Rivers Museum, University of Oxford)

kŏdŭl-ch'ima 거들 치마
(Pleated skirt)
19th century. Max. height x width
138 x 148 cm. Gauze
[PRM] 1907.80.20.6 S. Wakefield collection, purchased by PRM
in 1907 (© Pitt Rivers Museum, University of Oxford)

The *kŏdŭl-ch'ima* skirt was worn by
unmarried girls of the privileged class in
the Chosŏn dynasty. It was about 30 cm
longer than normal skirts and had many
more pleats. The skirt had to be tucked
up in a sash at the waist for convenience
of movement.[9]

kokkal 曲葛 곡갈
(Triangular hood)
19th century. Max. length x height
27.5 x 22 cm. Woven rattan
[PRM] 1906.79.9. S. Wakefield collection, purchased in 1906
(© Pitt Rivers Museum, University of Oxford)

Buddhist monks and nuns wore this
triangular hood, usually made of folded
white paper or silk (of which examples
can be seen in the collection: [PRM] 1906.79.10
and [PRM] 1906.79.11). The way it was worn is
illustrated in the drawing attached to the
hood. The one shown here is unusual as it
is made of rattan. Today, this type of hood
is also worn by shamans and performers
of farmers' dances.

p'ungjam 風簪 풍잠
(Hat fastener)

19th century. Max. length x width
5.5 x 3 cm. Most likely animal horn

[PRM] 1896.62.117. Robert T. Turley collection, purchased by PRM in 1896 (© Pitt Rivers Museum, University of Oxford)

A catch for fixing a gentleman's hat to the headband to prevent the hat from falling forwards.

nambawi 남바위
(Winter cap)

19th century. Max. length x height
33 x 35 cm. Silk and fur

[PRM] 1896.62.217. S. Wakefield collection, purchased by PRM in 1907 (© Pitt Rivers Museum, University of Oxford)

This is a winter cap trimmed with fur, of a type worn by women of rank in the Chosŏn dynasty. They were usually made of silk, and the usual colours for this type of cap were purple and indigo blue; they are said to have been also worn by men of the noble class. It looks similar to another type of traditional Korean winter hat, *p'ungch'a* 風遮 (풍차), which has extra flaps to cover the temples.

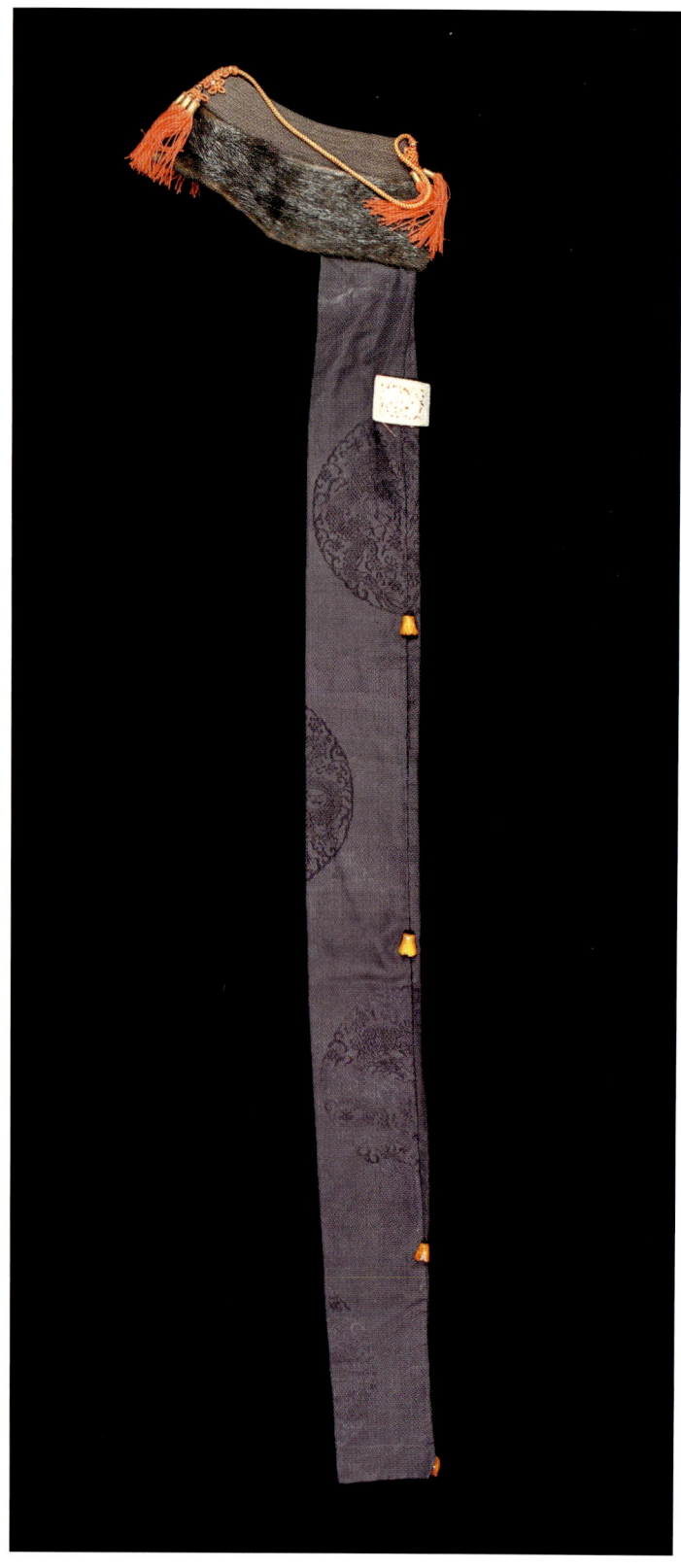

ayam 額掩 아얌[액엄]
(Women's open winter headdress)
19th century. Height x width 14 x 30 cm.
Silk, animal fur, cotton, metal wire, felt
and resin

[PRM] 1907.80.26. S. Wakefield collection, purchased by PRM in
1907. (© Pitt Rivers Museum, University of Oxford)

This is a winter headdress worn by Korean
ladies of higher-class nobility during the
Chŏson dynasty. It was mainly made of
black satin and was characterized by a
long streamer that hung down at the
back. This example is decorated with a
rectangular jade floral ornament and six
amber cicadas. Two other examples of
this type of headdress can be seen in the
collection: the [PRM] 1966.1.1336, collected
in November 1883 by Mr T. Miller and
donated by Miss Miller in 1929, and [PRM]
1886.5.1, collected by William Richard Carles
(Assistant Consul Shanghai) and donated
in 1886.

chŏngjagwan 程子冠 정자관
(Aristocrat's tiered hat)

Collected by 1896. Max. length x height
34 x 18 cm. Horsehair

[PRM] 1896.62.213. Robert T. Turley collection, purchased by
PRM in 1896. (© Pitt Rivers Museum, University of Oxford)

This is an example of a horsehair
headdress worn by scholars and
courtiers. These tiered hats could be
one tier, two tiers (such as this one) or
three tiers and were normally worn by
aristocrats and Confucian scholars in the
Chŏson period. They wore these hats
at home with a *changot* 長衣 (장옷)or
changŭi 장의 (long robe) or a *top'o* 道袍
(도포) (overcoat).

manggŏn 網巾 망건
(Headband for men)

19th century. Max. length (folded) x
height 29 x 8 cm. Horse hair, cotton
string, turtle shell (?)

[PRM] 1896.62.216. Robert T. Turley collection, purchased by
PRM in 1896 (© Pitt Rivers Museum, University of Oxford)

The *manggŏn* was a headband worn in
the Chŏson period by all classes of adult
men (of varying quality), indoors or out.
The hair was pulled up into a topknot and
the *manggŏn* wrapped tightly around
the head without covering the topknot,
and a hat was placed over this. They were
usually made of horsehair. The material
used for the cord loops indicated the
wearer's official rank or status.

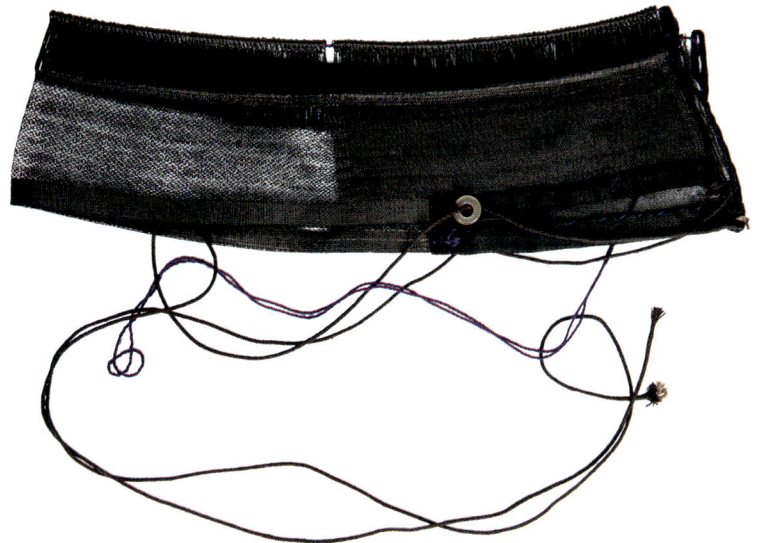

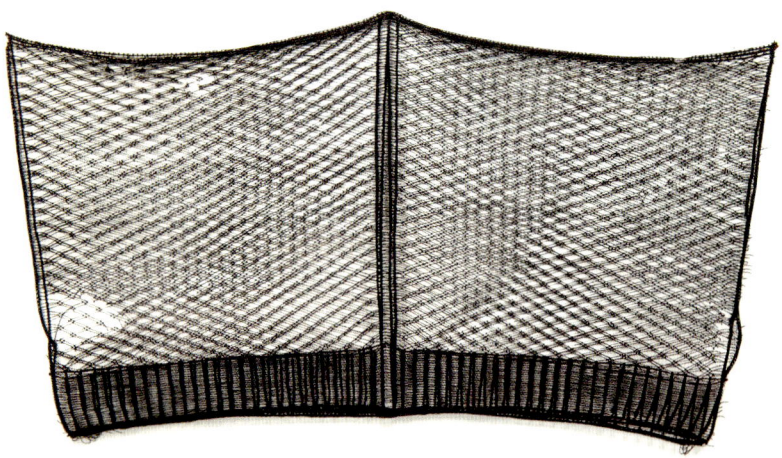

panggŏn 方巾 방건
(Confucian scholar's cubic cap)
19th century. Max. length x height
31 x 16 cm. Horse hair

[PRM] No: 1896.62.214. Robert T. Turley collection, purchased by PRM in 1896 (© Pitt Rivers Museum, University of Oxford)

This simple design of cap was worn by Confucian scholars of the Chŏson period when relaxing in their everyday life.

t'anggŏn 宕巾 탕건
(Indoor cap for noblemen)
19th century. Max. length x height
26.5 x 19 cm. Horse hair

[PRM] 1896.62.211. Collected by Robert T. Turley. Purchased in 1896 (© Pitt Rivers Museum, University of Oxford)

An Indoor cap made of horsehair, worn by men to cover their topknots. A *kat* 갓 (wide-brimmed horsehair hat) was worn over this when going out.

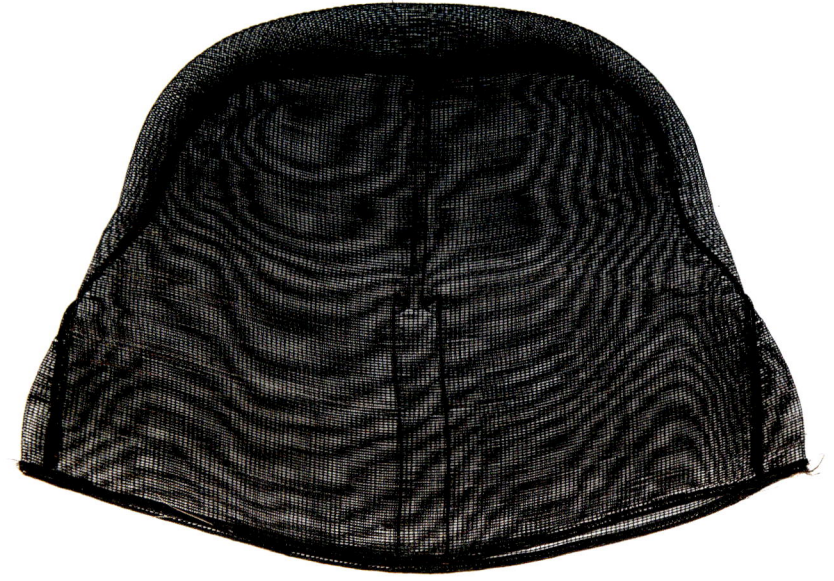

samo 沙帽 사모
(Courtier's silk hat)
Collected before 1907. Max. diameter x
height 17 x 17.2 cm. Horse hair, silk,
papier-mâché and cotton
[PRM] 1907.80.27 (© Pitt Rivers Museum, University of Oxford)

Silk hats with symbolic ear-flaps were
worn by courtiers for an audience with
the king. This is an example from the
late Chosŏn period, with a low crown
and short wings (missing). From the late
Koryŏ through the Chosŏn dynasties, the
nobility of the court wore hats in these
styles with their official robes. The hats
consisted of a two-stage crown with side
wings, which underwent slight changes in
style over time. Men of the common class
could wear these hats only once in their
life, together with the *tallyŏng* official robe
– when they married.

paengnip 白笠 백립
(Mourner's white hat)
Collected before 1907. Max. diameter x
height 30 x 10.5 cm. Cane, metal and
plant fibre
[PRM] 1907.36.3. Donated October 1907 by Mrs S. Wakefield
(© Pitt Rivers Museum, University of Oxford)

This kind of hat was worn by men during
state mourning periods.

t'ugu 투구
(Elaborately decorated gilt-mounted helmet)

19th century. Max. diameter (helmet only) 21.7 cm, approx.
max. height 24 cm, max. length (lapels) 32.5 cm. Leather, gilt
bronze, iron, silver, velvet and satin damask

[PRM] 1906.79.3. S. Wakefield collection, purchased by PRM in 1906
(© Pitt Rivers Museum, University of Oxford)

This helmet is similar to the one published in Volume I of
Korean Treasures, but this specimen is much more elaborately
decorated. Like the one in the first volume, it also has a symbol
of longevity inscribed on the front. This helmet was worn by
a military commander and likely to be ceremonial rather than
for actual battle, as indicated by the elaborate decorations. The
cone of the helmet is made of black lacquered leather and is
divided into four sections, with a pair of gilt dragons on the front
and a pair of phoenixes on the back. The gilt rim is engraved
with phoenixes at the front, cranes at the side and dragons at
the back. The brim at the front has an openwork decoration of
twin dragons. There are ear-flaps and a neck-flap made of red
velvet with a blue satin damask lining. The finial on the top of the
helmet is further decorated with dragons, phoenixes and cranes
among waves and clouds in an openwork design.

chŏllip 氈笠 전립
(Officer's felt hat)
19th century. Max. diameter x height
37 x 12 cm. Felt

[PRM] 1907.80.29. S. Wakefield collection purchased by PRM in 1907
(© Pitt Rivers Museum, University of Oxford)

Black felt hat with rough hairy surface worn by
military officers in the Chosŏn period. It is decorated
with red tassels on top.

hyŏpgŭmhye 夾金鞋 협금혜
(Bronze shoes)
End of 18th/19th century. Length 21.75 cm. Bronze

[PRM] No: 1906.79.8.1–2. S. Wakefield collection purchased by PRM in 1906
(© Pitt Rivers Museum, University of Oxford)

This is a pair of shoes made of bronze or brass, which were in fashion for a very short time at the end of the 18th century. They show the stitching of an ordinary shoe reproduced as a decorative feature. The soles are fitted with spikes on the heel and toe. The designs in black at the front and the back are similar to those on *t'aesahye* 太史鞋 (태사혜) (canvas shoes). The sides are lower than the heel and toe, which turn up, and cover very little. These are very rare.

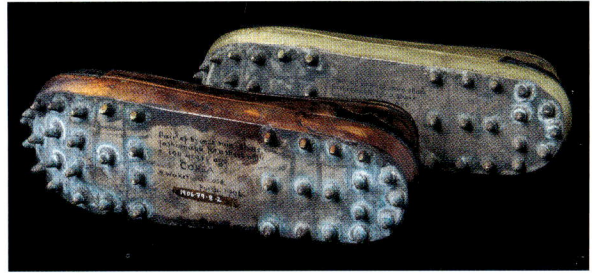

t'aesahye 太史鞋 태사혜
(Canvas shoes)

19th century. Length 22.5 cm. Canvas, textile
and leather

[PRM] 1896.62.43.1-2. R.T. Turley collection, purchased by PRM in 1896.
(© Pitt Rivers Museum, University of Oxford)

These canvas shoes are covered on the outside with
green material and lined with fine white leather. An
embroidered design in red decorates the toe and
heel and there is an edging around the top and
above the sole join. The sole curves up at the toe and
the uppers are very low at the sides inclining upwards
towards the heel. Another example in the collection is

[PRM] 1907.80.23.1–2. S. Wakefield collection, purchased by PRM in 1907.

namakshin 木履나막신
(Wooden clogs with design)
19th century. Length 19.3 cm. Wood

These wooden clogs, with soles elevated on double supports, were worn in wet weather in towns by men and women. They are cut from a solid large block with an upside-down V shape under the heel. The sides slope up to the toe and heel, the wood at the toe being comparatively thick and the recess shallow. There is a slight design on the toe, which is said to be for women. The pair below ([PRM] 1896.62.37.1–2) have no design and are said to be for men.

namakshin 木履나막신
(Wooden clogs without design)
19th century. Length 19.3 cm. Wood

mit'uri 麻鞋 미투리 [마혜]
(Ramie shoes)
19th century. Length 26 cm. Ramie, hemp and paper
[PRM] 1896.62.38.1 (© Pitt Rivers Museum, University of Oxford)

These are sandal-type shoes, woven from raw fibres of ramie,
worn by both noblemen and commoners. The sole is made of
hemp and paper string-work around the toes. Each string is
attached to the edge around the toe and to a string knotted to
two side-pieces with a cord encircling the heel. This is joined at
the back to a stiff strut that comes up at the back of the heel.

pŏsŏn 襪 버선 [말]
(Pair of women's socks)

19th century. Length from toe to heel 20.5 cm, from top to bottom of toe 26 cm. Cotton

[PRM] 1896.62.206.7.1–2 (© Pitt Rivers Museum, University of Oxford)

This is a pair of women's cotton socks with a seam down the front and back of the leg and along the bottom of the sole, being gathered under the instep and above the heel at the back. Socks have undergone few stylistic changes throughout their long history of use. It is recorded that people wore cloth socks similar to these during the Silla dynasty (*c.* 5th to 10th centuries CE). This is a type that was widely worn by women of various classes.

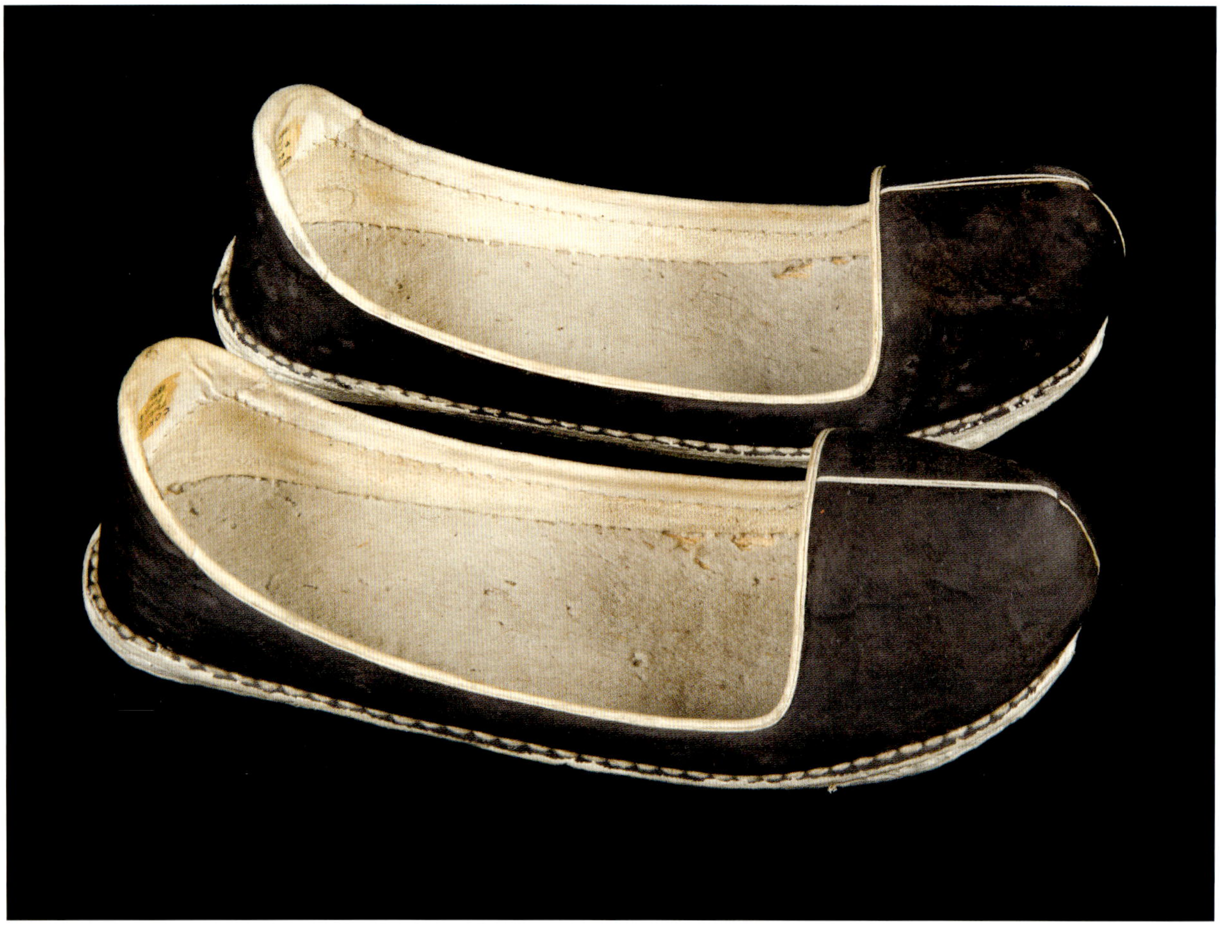

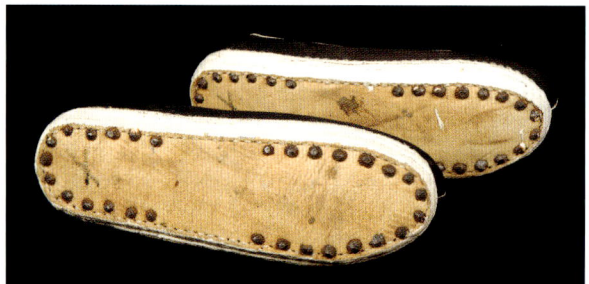

hŭkhye **黑鞋 흑혜**

(Black leather shoes)

19th century. Length 25.5 cm. Iron, leather, felt and pigment

[PRM] 1896.62.42.1–2 (© Pitt Rivers Museum, University of Oxford)

This pair of men's shoes has a thick sole studded with hob nails around the edge of the toe and heel. The uppers are completely plain black leather with white edging and a felt sole lining. The sides are low, sloping up to the back of the heel, at right angles to the edge going over the toes. These black leather shoes were used by upper-class men and women of the Chŏson period. Men's shoes have a broad toe, while women's shoes have a narrow, turned-up toe. Both have rounded heels.[10]

mokhwa 木靴 목화
(Flannel boots)

19th century. Length of sole x height 24 x 26.5 cm.
Textile, leather, felt, cotton, metal and wood

[PRM] 1907.80.22.1–2. S Wakefield collection, purchased in 1907
(© Pitt Rivers Museum, University of Oxford)

Court officials in the late Chŏson period wore these flannel boots
with their *tallyŏng* 團領 (단령) (official robe). They are decorated
with narrow strips of red or red and white, and the leather soles
are panelled with wood. The uppers are joined down the back
and front, leaving a small opening at the top of the back seam. A
strip of leather is doubled and let in along the joins and around
the foot in a curved line, with each side going down towards the
instep and up towards the toe and heel. The edge is bound with
purple felt and the inside is lined with cotton.

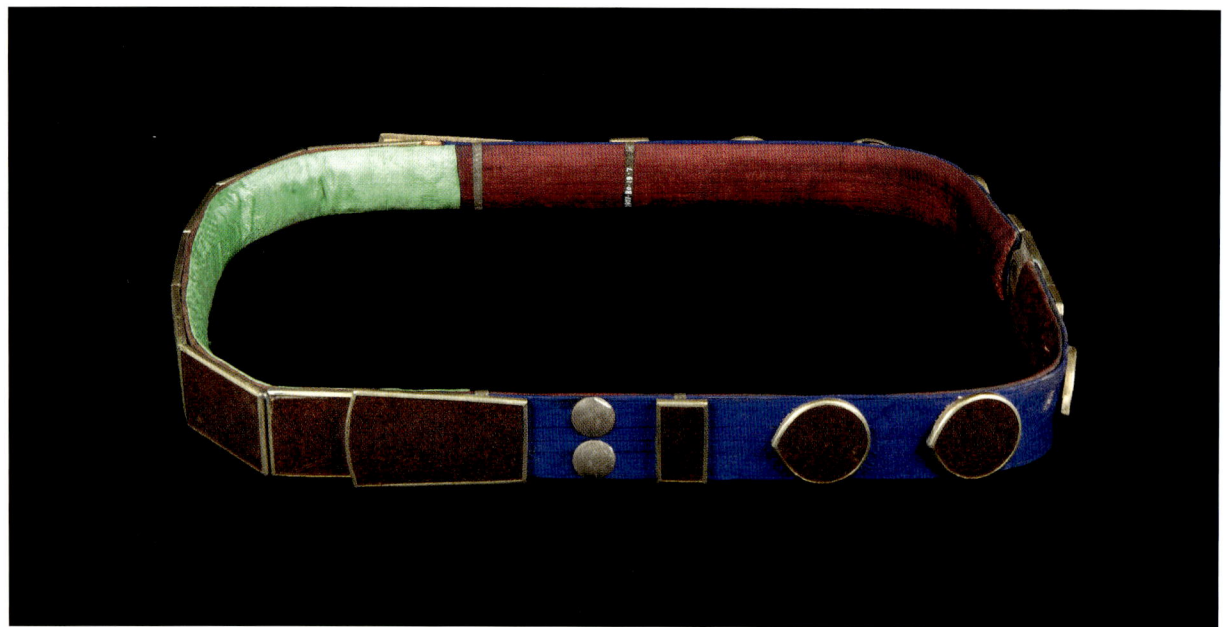

kaktae 角帶 각대
(Rank belt)

19th century. Max. diameter (diagonally across the oblong shape) 40 cm.
Textile, silk, metal and enamel

[PRM] 1907.80.19.7. S. Wakefield collection, purchased by PRM in 1907 (© Pitt Rivers Museum, University of Oxford)

This is a rank belt made of cloth with metal buttons and enamelled panels, also known as a man's girdle. This is quite an unusual example as rank belts were normally decorated with gilded attachments or carvings from buffalo horn, but this one is decorated only with metal buttons and an enamelled panel. The metal buttons are in various shapes such as circles, squares and rectangles. These belts were worn over various formal and ritual robes.

tŭngt'osi 藤吐手 등토[수]시
(Rattan wristlets)

Max. length x diameter 15 x 11 cm. Rattan

[PRM] 1896.62.209.1–2. Robert T. Turley collection, purchased by PRM in February 1896 (© Pitt Rivers Museum, University of Oxford)

These are Korean cuff frames to keep cuffs clean in hot weather. The frame has round openings at the top and bottom made by binding two strips of cane together with cane woven between them. These wristlets were worn by men in the summer to prevent clothes from clinging to the body. They were also helpful in protecting the skin from sweat. Wristlets were usually woven with wisteria rattan, while their frame was sometimes made with bamboo strips.

sopit 梳 [소] 빗
(Comb)
19th century. Max. length 9.5 cm.
Lacquer and horn

[PRM] 1896.62.112. Robert T. Turley collection, purchased by
PRM in 1896 (© Pitt Rivers Museum, University of Oxford)

Among the comb collection in the Pitt
Rivers Museum, this type of comb is the
most interesting and unusual. It has four
prongs and a semicircular top, coloured
bright red. This comb is for fixing in a
topknot to prevent the hat from falling
forwards. Another example of this type
of comb is [PRM] 1896.62.113, which is
coloured dark brown, also purchased in
1896 from the Turley collection.

pit-ch'igae 빗치개
(Comb cleaner)
19th century. Max. length 19.2 cm. Horn

[PRM] 1896.62.115. Robert T. Turley collection, purchased by
PRM in 1896 (© Pitt Rivers Museum, University of Oxford)

This horn hairpin with circular top was
used for cleaning combs and parting hair.

5

OTHER ITEMS

THE MUSEUMS OF Oxford contain a wide range of Korean objects stretching back to the 7th century CE. Many of these are miscellaneous items that caught the fancy of missionaries, diplomats and British businessmen, donated after their return to the United Kingdom or purchased because of their beauty by the Ashmolean Museum.

METALWORK

Metalworking culture spread from Manchuria into the peninsula, and the Korean bronze age began early in the first millennium BCE (*c.* 700 BCE). Extant artefacts include daggers, swords, spears, arrowheads, mirrors and small bells. Bronze items were probably possessed only by political and social elites. Iron deposits on the south-eastern coast attracted interest from the Chinese mainland and the Japanese islands, and trade was widespread. In the early centuries of the first millennium CE, metalworking technologies were transmitted from the continent to the peninsula, and highly skilled craftsmanship developed. Buddhist statuary and temple bells from the Silla period display these skills, which were refined in later centuries. Koryŏ-period bronze-working techniques produced more everyday objects, such as mirrors, household utensils, jewellery and other items. While iron and steel production was directed towards building materials and weaponry, bronzeware in the late Koryŏ and Chosŏn periods was used for rituals, printing, utensils and coinage.

ssangyong mun tonggyŏng
雙龍文銅鏡 쌍룡문동경
(Round bronze mirror with twin dragon design)
Koryŏ dynasty, diameter 23.5 cm.
Bronze
[ASH] EA1956.1571. Presented by Sir Herbert Ingram in 1956
(© Ashmolean Museum, University of Oxford)

This design of twin dragons chasing a jewel was popular during the Koryŏ period. Both dragons are illustrated swirling through clouds with their mouths wide open and eyes bulging, chasing the jewel that grants all wishes. The knob is at the centre of the inner ring, where there is a lotus design. There are twelve cloud designs decorating the outer rim.

ch'ŏngdong chong 青銅鐘 청동종
(Geometric-patterned bronze bell with loop)
6th century CE. Height 9.5 cm. Bronze

[ASH] EA 1970.213. Presented by E. H. Goddard in 1933 (© Ashmolean Museum, University of Oxford)

Small bronze bells such as this one were first made in Korea in the Bronze
Age and may have been horse trappings or used in shamanist rites or even
carried as a symbol of authority. The skill of bronze bell casting reached a
high level during the Unified Silla dynasty, especially in connection with large
bells produced for use in Buddhist temples. Bell casting was introduced
from Tang China, but like papermaking and ceramic manufacture, Korean
manufacture often excelled Chinese, and Korean craftsmen produced
exceptionally large and finely decorated examples.[1]

ch'ŏngdong sakto 青銅削刀 청동삭도
(Bronze razor)
Koryŏ dynasty. Length 13.5 cm. Bronze

[PRM] 1946.8.111. Collected by Charles Gabriel Seligman & Brenda Zara Seligman, donated in 1946 (© Pitt Rivers Museum, University of Oxford)

This is the bronze blade of a razor used during the Koryŏ period by Buddhist monks and nuns to shave their heads. It has a blackish and green patina that is the remains of some gilding and a hole at the end to which a handle was attached.

ch'ŏngdong-che yŏnmi-hyŏng sutkarak
青銅製燕尾形匙 청동제연미형 숟가락
(Bronze swallow-tailed-shaped spoons)
Koryŏ dynasty. Length 21.9 cm. Bronze

[PRM] 1923.38.1–3. Collected by Mrs Sprott, donated by Harry Geoffrey Beasley in 1923 (© Pitt Rivers Museum, University of Oxford)

This style of spoon was popular during the Koryŏ period with the end resembling the tail of a swallow. The end forms a 'Y' shape, and there is a small design carved just below the 'Y'. The overall shape forms a very elegant curve.

ch'ŏlje ŭn ipsa swaeyak 鐵製銀入絲鎖鑰 철제은입사쇄약
(Iron padlock with silver-inlaid designs)
19th century. Length 17 cm. Iron inlaid with silver

[PRM] 1907.80.1. S. Wakefield Collection, purchased in 1907
(© Pitt Rivers Museum, University of Oxford)

This massive iron padlock is rare: it is dated and possesses a more elaborate design and sturdy structure than examples in other museums. There are a couple of similar locks in museums in Korea, but none is as big and as elaborate as this one; neither are they dated. This is a padlock, cylindrical with a bar for locking mounted on one side. It is inlaid with silver. The silver forms very fine geometric patterns and is in excellent condition. The silver inlay presents squared characters for *su* 壽 (longevity) on the top right, and *bu* 富 (wealth) on the top left with the date of completion across the bar: 17th day of the fourth month of 1826 (丙戌四月十七日造). The padlock was signed by the artist using a stylized signature that is not his name (花押 화압). On the cylinder is the character *hŭi* 囍 (double happiness). This padlock was for securing chests containing valuables belonging to a bride.

ssangjo mun nŭnghyŏng tonggyŏng
雙鳥文稜形銅鏡 쌍조문릉형동경
(Flower-shaped bronze mirror with twin bird design)
Koryŏ dynasty. Diameter 12.2 cm. Bronze
[ASH] EA1956.1623. Presented by Sir Herbert Ingram in 1956
(© Ashmolean Museum, University of Oxford)

Another popular design on bronze mirrors during the Koryŏ
period was that of birds and flowers. Here, two birds are
depicted, one on each side of the mirror, and flowers fill up
all the space within the inner rim. The inner rim shape is the
same as that of the outer rim. There are eight floral patterns
between the inner and outer rims.

WATER DROPPERS

Porcelain writing implements, in particular water droppers, were popular in the 19th century. Water droppers were used to dilute the ink stick on the ink stone for use in painting and calligraphy. The Ashmolean Museum has a good selection of water droppers in various forms and designs, including round, square, hexagonal, octagonal and in the shape of fruit and fish. Most of these are from the collection donated in 1978 by Gerald Reitlinger, one of the great benefactors to the Museum during the 20th century.[2] None of these Korean droppers have ever been displayed.

yŏnjŏk 硯滴 연적
(Water dropper)
19th century. Height x width x depth 3.4 x 9.5 x
8.7 cm. Porcelain with cobalt blue underglaze
[ASH] EA1978.1200, Gift of Gerald Reitlinger, 1978
(© Ashmolean Museum, University of Oxford)

This porcelain blue and white water dropper is
decorated with a mountain landscape, with underglaze
painting in cobalt blue.

yŏnjŏk 硯滴 연적
(Water dropper)

19th century. Height x width x depth 2.9 x 8.1 x
7.4 cm. Porcelain with cobalt blue underglaze
and an unglazed base

[ASH] EA1978.1186. Gift of Gerald Reitlinger, 1978
(© Ashmolean Museum, University of Oxford)

A blue and white water dropper with landscape
decoration, in porcelain, with underglaze painting
in cobalt blue and an unglazed base.

yŏnjŏk 硯滴 연적
(Water dropper)

19th century. Max. height x width x depth 7.5 x 14 x
12.9 cm. Porcelain with cobalt blue underglaze

[ASH] 1978.1201. Gift of Gerald Reitlinger, 1978
(© Ashmolean Museum, University of Oxford)

A blue and white water dropper with foliage spray
decoration, in porcelain, with underglaze painting in
cobalt blue. There are four characters written on the side:
天一生水[3] (To be filled with water to form the world)[4]

yŏnjŏk 硯滴 연적
(Water dropper)

19th century. Max. height x width x depth 4.5 x
6.9 x 6.2 cm. Porcelain with cobalt blue glaze

[ASH] EA1978.1990. Gift of Gerald Reitlinger, 1978
(© Ashmolean Museum, University of Oxford)

Square water dropper with blue glaze decoration,
in porcelain, slab-built, and with cobalt blue glaze.

yŏnjŏk 硯滴 연적
(Ceramic peach shaped water dropper)
19th century. Height x width x depth
11 x 9.3 x 9 cm. Ceramic with cobalt blue
and copper red underglaze

[ASH] EA1978.1860. Gift of Gerald Reitlinger, 1978
(© Ashmolean Museum, University of Oxford)

Decorated with an underglaze of cobalt
blue and copper red. Branches and leaves
were made separately and attached. The
leaves were coloured with cobalt blue,
while the branches were highlighted with
copper red. A hole near the top of the
peach was made to put water in, and a hole
at the top end of the branch at the back
was for pouring water.

yŏnjŏk 硯滴 연적
(Water dropper)
19th century. Height x width x depth
3 x 7.7 x 7.2 cm. Porcelain with blue
glaze

[ASH] EA1961.3. Presented by Cyril A. de Costa Andrade, 1961
(© Ashmolean Museum, University of Oxford)

A water dropper in the form of a carp, in
porcelain, with blue glaze.

ROOF TILES AND BRICKS

The most common traditional roofing form in Korea was thatch, but ceramic roof tiling was introduced from China during the later Three Kingdoms period (approx. 4th to 7th centuries CE) and became popular and widespread among the elite classes and for government and religious buildings. Important houses, palaces and Buddhist temples started to have tiled roofs. Although styles developed differently in each of the three kingdoms of Silla, Paekche and Koguryŏ, by the time of the Unified Silla dynasty (668–936 CE), tiles reached new heights in sophistication and artistry. The examples here preserved in the Ashmolean Museum are from the Unified Silla period.[5]

yŏnhwamun wŏnwadang
蓮花文圓瓦當 연화문원와당
(Circular roof end-tile with lotus design)
Second half of the 7th century CE. Max. height x width x depth 13.7 x 12.7 x 3.2 cm. Ceramic

[ASH] EA1983.234. Purchased with the assistance of the Victoria and Albert Museum Fund and the Friends of the Ashmolean Museum, 1983 (© Ashmolean Museum, University of Oxford)

yŏnhwamun wŏnwadang
蓮花文圓瓦當 연화문원와당
(Circular roof end-tile with lotus design)
Second half of the 7th century CE. Height x
width x depth 14.8 x 14.3 x 6 cm. Ceramic

[ASH] EA1983.233. Purchased with the assistance of the Victoria and
Albert Museum Fund and the Friends of the Ashmolean Museum.
1983 (© Ashmolean Museum, University of Oxford)

yongmun p'yŏngwadang
龍文平瓦當 용문평와당
(Roof end-tile with running dragon design)
Second half of the 7th century CE. Height x
width x depth 7 x 19 x 4.5 cm. Ceramic

[ASH] EA1983.232. Purchased with the assistance of the Victoria and
Albert Museum Fund and the Friends of the Ashmolean Museum, 1983
(© Ashmolean Museum, University of Oxford)

nokmunjŏn 鹿文塼 록문전
(Brick with opposing deer)
Second half of the 17th century.
Ceramic

[ASH] EA1983.235. Purchased with the assistance of
the Victoria and Albert Museum Fund and the Friends
of the Ashmolean Museum, 1983 (© Ashmolean
Museum, University of Oxford)

DOLLS

The Pitt Rivers Museum possesses a collection of dolls collected between 1900 and 1925 by Lady Jordan, whose husband, Sir John Jordan, was the first British Minister to Korea (1901–5). Sir John Jordan also served in Beijing between the years 1906 and 1920. The collection was donated by Lady Dorothea Hosie to the Pitt Rivers Museum in 1953. These dolls are made of wood with painted faces and hair, movable legs and arms, and are dressed in colourful textile clothes.

Left:
inhyŏng 人形 인형
(Doll)
19th/20th century. Height 28 cm.
Wood and textiles
[PRM] 1953.3.8.1. Donated by Lady Dorothea Hosie to PRM in 1953 (© Pitt Rivers Museum, University of Oxford)

Wooden male doll with painted face and hair, with yellow and blue textile clothes and a red sash.

Opposite:
inhyŏng 人形 인형
(Doll)
19th/20th century. Height 28 cm.
Wood and textiles
[PRM] 1953.3.9. Donated by Lady Dorothea Hosie to PRM in 1953 (© Pitt Rivers Museum, University of Oxford)

Wooden male doll with painted face and hair, wearing black and green textile clothes and with wooden, movable legs and arms.

inhyŏng 人形 인형
(Doll)

19th or early 20th century. Height 28 cm. Wood and textiles

[PRM] 1953.3.10.1. Donated by Lady Dorothea Hosie to PRM in 1953
(© Pitt Rivers Museum, University of Oxford)

Wooden female doll with painted face and hair, wearing a
yellow bodice, red skirt and white girdle.

inhyŏng 人形 인형
(Doll)

19th/20th century. Height 28 cm. Wood and textiles

[PRM] 1953.3.11. Donated by Lady Dorothea Hosie to PRM in 1953

(© Pitt Rivers Museum, University of Oxford)

Wooden female doll with painted face and hair, wearing a
yellow bodice, green skirt and white girdle.

FANS

Hand-held fans are common in East Asia, and Korea developed its own styles of *puch'ae* 부채 (fan), used by both men and women.

***chŏpsŏn* 摺扇 접선**
(Folding fan)
19th century. Length 25.9 cm. Cane and paper
[PRM] 1892.18.3. Donated in 1892 by William Richard Carles
(© Pitt Rivers Museum, University of Oxford)

This folding fan has thirteen leaves and two guard sticks of cane painted with a fine geometric pattern. The leaves are wider than the guard sticks and are of a red-ochre colour. The paper of the leaves is plain. There is a brass metal pin and eye at the base.

misŏn 尾扇 미선
(Fishtail-shaped fan)

19th century. Max. length 37.5 cm. Split bamboo and mulberry paper

[PRM] 1888.41.4. Donated in 1888 by Thomas Watters, Director of the Royal Botanic Gardens, Kew (© Pitt Rivers Museum, University of Oxford)

This fan has the shape of a fish's tail, with its top edges finished with two curved lines. Green mulberry paper has been pasted onto split bamboo, with chrysanthemum and other flower designs symmetrically drawn for decoration.

t'aegŭksŏn 太極扇 태극선
(_T'aeguk_ fan)

19th century. Max. length 35.2 cm. Split bamboo, mulberry paper and lacquer

[PRM] 1888.41.3. Donated in 1888 by Thomas Watters, Director of Royal Botanic Gardens, Kew (© Pitt Rivers Museum, University of Oxford)

The round face is decorated with a three-lobed _t'aegŭk_ 太極 in three colours, green, red and yellow, on mulberry paper. The _t'aegŭk_ refers to the Supreme Ultimate of Confucian cosmology and is most commonly thought of as the yin–yang symbol. A similar symbol is the central element of the flag of the Republic of Korea. The handle of this fan is thickly lacquered in black.

WEAPONS

The Oxford museums possess numerous Korean weapons, suits of
armour and other military paraphernalia such as flint, steel and tinder
used with muskets.

t'onggae chŏntong 筒箇箭筒 통개전동
(Quiver set)

19th century. Max. length 89 cm. Stout
paper, wood, antler, feather and iron

[PRM] 1911.57.2.1–16. Purchased from Glendining's Auction
Rooms in 1911 (© Pitt Rivers Museum, University of Oxford)

This is a quiver with a cap made of stout
paper and wooden ends. Attached by a
thong is an 'arrow straightener' made of
antler. There are fourteen arrows in the
quiver.

pusittol, kangch'ŏl, pul
부싯돌, 강철 [鋼鐵], 불
(Flint, steel and tinder)

19th century. Flint max. length 2.5 cm; Steel max. length 7.6 cm. Flint, steel and tinder

[PRM] 1900.1.12.1–3. Collected by Rev. James Scarth Gale and presented to PRM by Sir Cuthbert Edgar Peek in 1900 (© Pitt Rivers Museum, University of Oxford)

Used with muskets or for making fire. The flint is a small rough flake of irregular shape and yellowish colour. The steel is a flat and plain piece of iron. The tinder is made from scrapings of the scurf of Artemisia (?)

kakkung 角弓 각궁
(Horn bow)

19th century. Linear length of unstrung and recurved bow 124.5cm. Horn, velvet, silk and bark

[PRM] 1894.54.1.1. Donated by William George Aston in 1894 (© Pitt Rivers Museum, University of Oxford)

A short composite traditional bow made of a combination of materials. It is unstrung and recurved almost into a circle. Since it is unstrung, the limbs are curved with the inner side of the limbs when strung now showing on the outer side. It is a light, very strongly reflexed bow with very broad ears. The water buffalo horn of the belly is exposed; the back is covered in bark. Velvet-covered bridges for the string are fixed at the elbows. Although not shown here, there is a peacock-blue silk bow-string made of many strands, wound between sinew loops. The strands are left loose except at the nocking point, which is bound.

MISCELLANEOUS ITEMS

The museums of Oxford hold a number of miscellaneous, singular items that were donated over the period from the 19th century to the present.

karo 座燈 가로
(Floor lanterns)

19th century. Max. height x depth x width 100.5 x 30.7 x 31 cm. Wood, canvas, brass and metal

[PRM] 1908.51.1.1. Presented by Mr and Mrs Wakefield in 1908
(© Pitt Rivers Museum, University of Oxford)

This is a pair of rare large floor lanterns, made of wood, carved and painted red and black. They are rectangular with canvas screens and open fretwork decoration for the windows. There is one hinged panel for each door, with a single candle pricket within. The lanterns are on bases with four legs with horizontal struts between each. There is a single drawer with brass ring-pull below the hinged panel. The bevelled roof has a swastika on the flat top and a jointed metal stirrup handle over the top.

chumŏni 주머니
(Pouch)

19th century. Max. length x width 12.8 x 14cm. Cotton

[PRM] 1966.1.1173. Collected by the late Mr T. Miller in 1883 and presented by Miss Miller in 1929 (© Pitt Rivers Museum, University of Oxford)

A small mushroom-shaped cotton bag, red on one side, green on the other. A small piece of notepaper was found inside the bag: 'Sundry bag, carried round the waist with the baggy pouch by all Koreans – [signature?] 1883'.

churumak 주루막
(String-work bag)
19th century. Max. width x height 55 x 29.5 cm.
String and bark

[PRM] 1906.79.12. S. Wakefield collection, purchased by PRM in 1906
(© Pitt Rivers Museum, University of Oxford)

This string-work bag, made of eight knottings, would
have been used for carrying game and other things.
The bag has drawstring handles or carrying straps
made from string. They pass through loops on the top
of the bag and attach to two loops bound with bark
that are attached to the bottom corners of the bag.

chŏnggwe 頂 櫃 정궤
(House chest and safe)
19th century. Height x width x depth
42 x 59 x 30 cm. Wood and brass
[ASH] EA1958.111. Presented by Miss M. G. Hobson in 1958
(© Ashmolean Museum, University of Oxford)

This house chest with brass fittings has four tiers:
there is one drawer on the first tier, two drawers on
the second, three drawers on the third, and four
drawers on the top tier. Most of the brass fittings are
decorated with a wave pattern. The handles on both
doors are in the pattern of a bat. The chest to the left
was a kind of safe to store valuables or documents
and could also be used as a medicine cabinet.

sutkarak 匙
(Spoon)

19th century. Max. length 12 cm.
Horn and beads

[PRM] 1896.62.18. R.T. Turley collection, purchased by PRM in 1896 (© Pitt Rivers Museum, University of Oxford)

This spoon is made from a small brown horn with incised lines and two inlaid red beads. It is a chemist's spoon and was used to measure quantities of pharmaceuticals.

t'ujŏn 鬪牋 투전
(Traditional Korean playing cards)

19th century. Max. length 8.3 cm.
Oiled paper and ink

[PRM] 1900.1.9.1--6. Presented to PRM by Sir Cuthbert Edgar Peek in 1900 (© Pitt Rivers Museum, University of Oxford)

This along with five other packs of cards was collected by Rev. James Scarth Gale and John Harington Gubbins. T'ujŏn 鬪牋 (contest slips) are traditional Korean playing cards, made of thick oiled paper. They are now rare. A deck might contain sixty or eighty cards, but forty is usual. There are nine numeral cards and one *chang* 將 장 (general) to each suit; these are shown by peculiar narrow, black ink-figures. The suits and their generals are as follows: *saram* 사람 (man), *mulkogi* 물고기 (fish), *kamagwi* 까마귀 (crow), *kkwŏng* 꿩 (pheasant), *noru* 노루 (roe deer), *pyŏl* 별 (star), *t'okki* 토끼 (hare) and *mal* 말 (horse). The backs are usually decorated with a stylized feather design.[6]

angyŏng 眼鏡 안경 **and** *an-gyŏnggap* 眼鏡匣 안경갑 **or** *an-gyŏngjip* 안경집 (Dark eyeglasses and case)

19th century. Glasses (folded) max. length 11 cm, case max. length 15 cm. Horn, crystal, silk and cloth

[PRM] 1907.80.8.1–2. S. Wakefield collection, purchased PRM in 1907 (© Pitt Rivers Museum, University of Oxford)

The case is covered by silk and the outline is fitted with a black cloth. The pair of spectacles are made of dark crystal lenses and the frames are made of horn. It is a simple design, much prized on account of the crystal, worn by men against the glare of the sun, to give them dignity.

changsingu – p'odo songi 裝身具 장신구 – 포도송이 (Trinket – bunch of grapes in silver)

19th century. Max. length x width 6.8 x 3.4 cm. Silver and enamel

[PRM] 1907.80.14. S. Wakefield collection, purchased by PRM in 1907 (© Pitt Rivers Museum, University of Oxford)

This silver trinket's design of a bunch of grapes was made from silver and enamel. It would have been worn by a woman, attached to her girdle. The grapes are silver balls covered with two multicoloured enamelled leaves, two small blue enamelled leaves and two yellow enamelled animals.

pegae 枕 베개
(Pillow)
19th century. Max. length x diameter 68 x 27.5 cm.
Textiles and wood

[PRM] 1907.36.2. (© Pitt Rivers Museum, University of Oxford)

This pillow belonged to Mrs Yang, the wife of a
customs interpreter and was presented to the
Pitt Rivers Museum by Mrs Wakefield in 1907. The
pillowcase is embroidered at both circular ends with
pok 福 (good fortune) and *su* 壽 (long life) characters
in the middle. Rounded fret designs circle around on
the outer ring with designs of bats between the inner
and outer rings. The pillowcase is made from cream-
coloured textiles with a hole in the centre to insert
the pillow. The ends have a circle of wood stitched to
the inside of the pillowcase to add stability for shape.

NOTES

Chapter 1

1   Gari Ledyard, 'Cartography in Korea', in J.B. Harley and David Woodward (eds), *The History of Cartography, Volume 2, Book 2: Cartography in the Traditional East and Southeast Asian Societies,* Chicago and London, University of Chicago Press, 1994, pp. 177–576, p. 238.

2   Ledyard, 'Cartography in Korea', p. 245. For a detailed description of the *Kangnido* and a discussion of its date of production, see Kenneth R. Robinson, 'Chosŏn Korea in the Ryūkoku "Kangnido": dating the oldest extant Korean map of the world (15th century)', *Imago Mundi* 59:2 (2007): 177–92.

3   Ledyard, 'Cartography in Korea', p. 247.

4   Ledyard, 'Cartography in Korea', p. 269. For a detailed discussion of the maps contained in the *Haedong chegukki*, see Takahashi Kimiaki, 'Birth of new perspectives through integration of origin maps: the case of "Haedong cheguk ch'ongdo"', *Kokusai kaihatsu kenkyū Fōramu* 国際開発研究フォーラム *(Forum of International Development Studies)* 44 (2014): 17–35.

5   See: www.ssu.ac.kr/web/museum/exhibit_d;jsessionid=LaaWgz24q1AmQvmOIJyveThq MsxYJTt3T1NMdXIO7fu69W1os49SJr06FAQ cSbic?p_p_id=EXT_MUSEUM&p_p_lifecycle= 0&p_p_state=normal&p_p_mode=view&p_p_col_id=column-1&p_p_col_count=1&_EXT_MUSEUM_struts_action=%2Fext%2Fmuseum%2Fview&_EXT_MUSEUM_vPage=relic&_EXT_MUSEUM_orderSelection=TITLE_KR&_EXT_MUSEUM_subjectId1=32&_EXT_MUSEUM_subjectId2=322&_EXT_MUSEUM_relicId=394 (accessed 6 September 2018).

6   Ki-baek Yi, *A New History of Korea,* Cambridge, MA, Harvard University Press, 1984, p. 241.

7   Jongtae Lim, 'Representing an ideal world order of the past: the cultural function of the Jesuit world maps in the 18th-century Korean government', lecture at Institute of History and Philology, Academia Sinica, 2016, www2.ihp.sinica.edu.tw/bulletinDetail. php?TM=1&M=2&sM=1&C=&bid=920 (accessed 6 September 2018).

8   Shannon McCune, *Art of the Korean Map,* Gainesville, FL, Grinter Gallery, University of Florida, 1977.

9   After nine years of detention in Shenyang as a hostage, the Korean crown prince Sohyŏn 昭顯 世子 was released by the Manchus in 1645. He stayed in Beijing for two months before returning to Korea. There he became a close acquaintance of the Jesuit Johann Adam Schall von Bell (1592–1666). Adam Schall gave the prince books on astronomy and mathematics and a globe, as well as religious writings and articles.

10 Three maps in the Korean map collection at the British Library have the maps in a different order: Korean maps are placed right at the front before the map of the world and maps of China.

11 Ledyard, 'Cartography in Korea', p. 267.

12 'Terra Australis (Latin for *South Land*) is a hypothetical continent that first appeared on maps between the 15th and 18th centuries. The existence of Terra Australis was not based on any survey but rather on the idea that land in the Northern Hemisphere should be balanced by land in the Southern Hemisphere. This theory has been documented as early as the 5th century CE on maps by Macrobius, who uses the term Australis on his maps', https://en.wikipedia.org/wiki/Terra Australis (accessed 27 July 2018).

13 The earliest known human settlement in Tierra del Fuego dates from around 8,000 BCE. Europeans first explored the islands during Ferdinand Magellan's expedition of 1520; Tierra del Fuego and similar names stem from sightings of the many bonfires that the natives built (https://en.wikipedia.org/wiki/Tierra_del_Fuego, accessed 27 July 2018).

14 For a high resolution image of Ricci's map, see: https://upload.wikimedia.org/wikipedia/commons/7/71/Kunyu_Wanguo_Quantu_%28 E5%9D%A4E8%BC%BFE8%90%AC%E5%9C%8B%E5%85%A8%E5%9C%96%29.jpg (accessed 13 August 2018).

15 Takejirō Akioka 秋岡武次郎, 'An Kanae-fuku (An Chŏng-bok) [1712–1791] hitsu Chikyū giyō sekai chizu: Tōyō seisaku no ko Chikyū giyō funegata-zu no hiitotsu 安鼎福筆地球儀用世界地圖: 東洋製作の古地球儀用丹形図の一', *Rekishi chiri* 歴史地理 61:2 (1933): 107–15, p. 111. This attestation and map is again reproduced in No Chŏng-sik 盧禎埴, 'Han'guk ŭi ko segye chido yŏn'gu (韓國의 古世界地圖 研究)', unpublished PhD dissertation, Hyosŏng Yŏja Taehakkyo, 1992, p. 82.

16 Chai Shin Yu, *The Founding of Catholic Tradition in Korea,* Mississauga, OT, Korean and Related Studies Press, 1996, p. 56.

17 Yasui Santetsu, also known as Shibukawa Harumi 渋川春海 and Motoi Santetsu 保井算哲, was a Japanese scholar, *go* player, and the first official astronomer appointed in the Edo period.

18 Although Nakamura Hiroshi published a collection of maps in English (Hiroshi Nakamura 中村拓, *East Asia in Old Maps,* Tokyo, Centre for East Asian Cultural Studies, 1962), he does not include this map. The preface states, 'This is an abridged version in English of Dr. Hiroshi Nakamura's treatise entitled "Tōa no kochizu 東亜 の古地図" (History of East Asian Maps) published in the *Journal of Yokohama Municipal University,* Series A-19, No. 88, March 1958.' I have been unable to confirm if it is included in the original journal article.

19 *Rekishi chiri* 歴史地理, 17:4 (1899).

20 Email correspondence 25 January 2018.

21 Shannon McCune, 'Some Korean maps', *Transactions of the Royal Asiatic Society Korea Branch* 50 (1975): 79–80.

22 McCune, *Art of the Korean Map,* p. 23.

23 https://en.wikipedia.org/wiki/Nanjing (accessed 26 July 2018).

24 https://en.wikipedia.org/wiki/Ning%27an (accessed 26 July 2018).

25 https://en.wikipedia.org/wiki/Shenyang (accessed 26 July 2018).

Chapter 2

1   The Korean coin collection has been documented by Lyce Jankowski. The Japanese coin collection has been documented by Nobuhisa Furuta, Shin'ichi Sakuraki and Lyce Jankowski.

2   See www.britishmuseum.org/research/collection_online/search.aspx?search Text=Korean+coins (accessed 6 September 2018).

3   See http://webapps.fitzmuseum.cam.ac.uk/explorer/index.php?do=Search&qu=Korean%20 coins&fi=%7B%22term%22%3A%7B%22Production PlaceName.asterm%22%3A%22Korea%22%7D%7D (accessed 6 September 2018).

4   See http://harbour.man.ac.uk/mmcustom/NSContactSheet.php?QueryName=BasicQuery&QueryPage=%2Fmmcustom%2FZooQuery.php&any=SummaryData%7CAdmWebMetadata&taxonomy=TaxTaxonomyLocal%7CIdeTypeStatus_tab&notes=NotNotes&place=SitSiteLocal_tab&QueryTerms=Korean+coin&QueryOption=any&Submit=Search&StartAt=61 (accessed 6 September 2018).

5   Dr Shinichi Sakuraki, Professor of Japanese History, Faculty of Economics, Shimonseki City University, has been providing consultation for years.

6   See http://hcr.ashmus.ox.ac.uk/collection/8 (accessed 6 September 2018).

7   Shin'ichi Sakuraki et al., *Catalogue of the Japanese Coin Collection (Pre-Meiji) at the British Museum: With Special Reference to Kutsuki Masatsuna,* London, British Museum, 2010.

8 Kim In-sik 金仁植 (ed.), *Han'guk hwapye kagyŏk torok* 韓國貨幣價格圖錄, Seoul, Osŏng K&C (오성K&C), 2017, p. 41.

9 Wybrand Op den Velde and David Hartill, *Cast Korean Coins and Charms*, Sandy, Bright Pen, 2013, p. 16.

10 J.B. Harley and David Woodward (eds), 'Cartography in the traditional East and Southeast Asian societies', *History of Cartography, Volume 2, Book 2*, Chicago and London, University of Chicago Press, 1987, p. 240.

11 Kim, *Han'guk hwapye kagyŏk torok*, p. 41.

12 Kim, *Han'guk hwapye kagyŏk torok*, p. 41.

13 Op den Velde and Hartill, *Cast Korean Coins and Charms*, p. 16.

14 Op den Velde and Hartill, *Cast Korean Coins and Charms*, p. 18.

15 See Su-hwan Chŏng 정수환, *Chosŏn hugi hwapye yut'ong kwa kyŏngje saenghwal* 조선후기 화폐유통과 경제생활, Seoul, Kyŏngin munhwasa, 2013, for an extensive study of the production and distribution of coins in the late Chosŏn period.

16 Keith Pratt and Richard Rutt (eds), *Korea: A Historical and Cultural Dictionary*, Richmond, Curzon Press, 1999, p. 76.

17 Pratt and Rutt, *Korea: A Historical and Cultural Dictionary*, pp. 123–4.

18 Pratt and Rutt, *Korea: A Historical and Cultural Dictionary*, pp. 483–4.

19 Won Yu Han, *Money: Traditional Korean Society*, Seoul, Ewha Women's University Press, 2006, p. 88.

20 Han, *Money*, p. 91.

21 Han, *Money*, pp. 99–101.

22 Op den Velde and Hartill, *Cast Korean Coins and Charms*, p. 247.

23 H.A. Ramsden, *Corean Coin Charms and Amulets*, Yokohama, Jun Kobayagawa Co., 1910, p. ii.

24 Shiyuan Chen, *Wandering Spirits: Chen Shiyuan's Encyclopedia of Dreams*, trans. Richard E. Strassberg, Berkeley, University of California Press, 2008, p. 211.

Chapter 3

1 The Center for the Study of Global Christianity, 'Christianity in its Global Context, 1970-2020', June 2013, p. 36, 40. https://www.gordonconwell.edu/ockenga/research/documents/ChristianityinitsGlobalContext.pdf. Last accessed 24/01/2019. According to this report, all areas of East and Southeast Asia show an increase in Christian populations, except Japan, and China has shown the highest average annual growth rate from 1970 to 2013 at nearly 11 per cent. 'Christian' in these statistics includes Anglicans, Independents, Marginals (Jehovah's Witnesses and the Church of Jesus Christ of Latter-day Saints), Orthodox, Protestants and Roman Catholics.

2 For a discussion of early contacts, see Franklin D. Rausch, 'The Jesuits in Korea: influence without presence', *World History Connected* 10:3, http://worldhistoryconnected.press.uillinois.edu/10.3/forum_rausch.html (accessed 6 September 2018).

3 For broad descriptions of Christianity in Korea, see Kwang Cho, 'The meaning of Catholicism in Korean history', *Korea Journal* 24:8 (August 1984): 14–27; Kwang Cho, 'Human relations as expressed in vernacular Catholic writings of the late Chosŏn dynasty', trans. Timothy S. Lee, in Robert E. Buswell and Timothy S. Lee (eds), *Christianity in Korea*, Honolulu, University of Hawai'i Press, 2006, pp. 29–37; Kwang Cho 조광, *Chosŏn hugi sahoe wa Ch'ŏnjukyo* 조선후기 사회와 천주교, Seoul, Kyŏng'in munhwasa, 2010; Kwang Cho, 'The Chosŏn government's measures against Catholicism', in Chai-shin Yu (ed.), *The Founding of Catholic Tradition in Korea*, Mississauga, ON, Korean and Related Studies Press, 1996, pp. 103–14; Kwang Cho, 'The meaning of Catholicism in Korean history', in Chai-shin Yu (ed.), *The Founding of Catholic Tradition in Korea*, Mississauga, ON, Korean and Related Studies Press, 1996, pp. 115–40; Suk-woo Choi, 'Korean Catholicism yesterday and today', in Chai-shin Yu (ed.), *The Founding of Catholic Tradition in Korea*, Mississauga, ON, Korean and Related Studies Press, 1996, pp. 141–60; James Huntley Grayson, 'A quarter-millennium of Christianity in Korea', in Robert E. Buswell and Timothy S. Lee (eds), *Christianity in Korea*, Honolulu, University of Hawai'i Press, 2006, pp. 7–25; Han-sik Kim, 'The influence of Christianity on modern Korean political thought', *Korea Journal* 23:12 (1983): 4–17; Andrew E. Kim, 'Protestantism in Korea and Japan from the 1880s to the 1940s', *Korea Journal* 45:4 (winter 2005): 261–90; Andrew E. Kim, 'Korean religious culture and its affinity to Christianity: the rise of Protestant Christianity in South Korea', *Sociology of Religion* 61:2 (summer 2000): 117–33; Ok-hy Kim, 'Women in the history of Catholicism in Korea', *Korea Journal* 24:8 (August 1984): 28–40; Sebastian C.H. Kim and Kirsteen Kim, *A History of Korean Christianity*, Cambridge, Cambridge University Press, 2015; Chang-t'ae Kŭm, 'The doctrinal disputes between Confucianism and Western thought in the late Chosŏn period', in Chai-shin Yu (ed.), *The Founding of Catholic Tradition in Korea*, Mississauga, ON, Korean and Related Studies Press, 1996, pp. 7–44; Sung-Deuk Oak, *The Making of Korean Christianity: Protestant Encounters with Korean Religions, 1876–1915*, Waco, TX, Baylor University Press, 2013; and George Nak-chun Paik 백낙준, *The History of Protestant Missions in Korea, 1832–1910*, Pyeng Yang, Union Christian College Press, 1929.

4 Juan Ruiz de Medina, *The Catholic Church in Korea: Its Origins, 1566–1784*, trans. John Bridges, Seoul, Royal Asiatic Society, 1991, pp. 34–5.

5 de Medina, *The Catholic Church in Korea*, pp. 47–50.

6 de Medina, *The Catholic Church in Korea*, pp. 56–7.

7 Kim, 'The influence of Christianity', p. 5.

8 Wŏn-sun Yi, 'The Sirhak scholars' perspectives on *sŏhak* in the later Chosŏn society', in Chai-shin Yu (ed.), *The Founding of Catholic Tradition in Korea*, Mississauga, ON, Korean and Related Studies Press, 1996, pp. 45–101.

9 Kyoung Bae Min 민경배, *Han'guk Kidokkyohoesa* 한국기독교회사, Seoul, Yonsei Taehakkyo Ch'ulp'anbu, 2007, pp. 61–5. Hongyŏl Yu, 유홍렬, *Han'guk Ch'ŏnju Kyohoesa* 한국천주교회사, Seoul Kat'ŏllik ch'ulp'ansa, 1962, pp. 81–91 for details and documents quoted liberally from Charles Dallet, *Histoire de l'église de Corée*, 2 volumes, Paris, Librarie Victor Palmé, 1874.

10 Jai-Keun Choi, *The Origin of the Roman Catholic Church in Korea: An Examination of Popular and Governmental Responses to Catholic Mission in the Later Chosŏn Dynasty*, Cheltenham, Hermit Kingdom Press, 2006, p. 51.

11 For a discussion of the legalities of suppression, see Pierre-Emmanuel Roux, 'The great Ming code and the repression of Catholics in Chosŏn Korea', *Acta Koreana* 15:1 (2012): 73–106

12 Ki-bok Ch'oe, 'The abolition of ancestral rites and tablets by Catholicism in the Chosŏn dynasty and the basic meaning of Confucian ancestral rites', *Korea Journal* 24:8 (August 1984): 41–52, p. 45. See also Don Baker, 'A different thread: orthodoxy, heterodoxy, and Catholicism in a Confucian world', in JaHyun Kim Haboush and Martina Deuchler (eds), *Culture and the State in Late Chosŏn Korea*, Cambridge, MA, Harvard University Asia Center, 1999, pp. 217–20.

13 See Baker, 'A different thread', and Kevin Cawley, 'Deconstructing hegemony: Catholic texts in Chosŏn's neo-Confucian context', *Acta Koreana* 15:1 (2012): 15–42, for discussions of philosophical differences between Catholicism and Korean Confucianism.

14 See Don Baker and Franklin Rausch, *Catholics and Anti-Catholicism in Chosŏn Korea*, Honolulu, University of Hawai'i Press, 2017, for an annotated translation of the entire 'Silk Letter' with discussion of historical circumstances. For an excerpted translation, see Don Baker, 'Hwang sayŏng: an appeal for aid', in Peter H. Lee et al. (eds), *Sourcebook of Korean Civilization, Volume 2: From the 17th Century to the Modern Period*, New York, Columbia University Press, 1996, pp. 147–50.

15 Baker, 'Hwang sayŏng', p. 149.

16 For a close examination of one of the people named in the 'Silk Letter', see Gari Ledyard, 'Kollumba Kang Wansuk, an early Catholic activist and martyr', in Robert E. Buswell and Timothy S. Lee (eds), *Christianity in Korea*, Honolulu, University of Hawai'i Press, 2006, pp. 38–71.

17 Hongyŏl Yu, 유홍렬, *Han'guk Ch'ŏnju Kyohoesa* 한국천주교회사, Seoul, Kat'ollik ch'ulp'ansa, 1962, p. 316.

18 Choi, *The Origin*, p. 182; Yu, *Han'guk Ch'ŏnju Kyohoesa*, p. 399.

19 Yu, *Han'guk Ch'ŏnju Kyohoesa*, pp. 431–6.

20 Yu, *Han'guk Ch'ŏnju Kyohoesa*, pp. 468–72.

21 Yu, *Han'guk Ch'ŏnju Kyohoesa*, pp. 476–86.

22 Yu, *Han'guk Ch'ŏnju Kyohoesa*, pp. 624–5.

23 Yi Hangno's arguments present the ideological threat. See Chai-sik Chung, *A Korean Confucian Encounter with the Modern World: Yi Hang-no and the West*, Berkeley, Institute of East Asian Studies, University of California, Center for Korean Studies, 1995, and Baker, 'A different thread'. See also Franklin D. Rausch, 'Like birds and beasts: justifying violence against Catholics in late Chosŏn Korea', *Acta Koreana* 15:1 (2012): 43–71.

24 The canonization was delivered with a papal visit (Pope John Paul II, 1984 and 1989). Another papal visit (Pope Francis, 2014) was celebrated with beatifications and museum exhibitions. See Seoul Yŏksa Pangmulgwan 서울역사박물관, *Sŏsomun pyŏlgok* 서소문별곡, *Ode to the West Small Gate*, exhibition catalogue, Seoul, Seoul Yŏksa Pangmulgwan, 2014.

25 Yu, *Han'guk Ch'ŏnju Kyohoesa*, pp. 677, 697.

26 Yu, *Han'guk Ch'ŏnju Kyohoesa*, pp. 705–24. Many of these books (儀軌 의궤) are illustrated records of court protocol and were being kept at a royal library (外奎章閣 외규장각). They were taken to the Bibliothèque Nationale de France. In 2011, an agreement was reached between the Republic of Korea and the French Republic to repatriate the stolen books.

27 The crew of the *General Sherman* had sailed their ship up the Taedong River in an attempt to establish trade relations; they engaged in provocative behaviour and finally ran aground near P'yŏngyang. The ship was set alight and destroyed by local Korean militia and the peasantry with the loss of all on board.

28 Jae-eun Kang, *The Land of Scholars: Two Thousand Years of Korean Confucianism*, trans. Suzanne Lee, Paramus, NJ, Homa & Sekey Books, 2006, p. 388.

29 Yonsei University Health System, 'History', www.yuhs.or.kr/en/about_yuhs/yuhs/YUMC_history (accessed 6 September 2018).

30 Donald N. Clark, 'Christianity in modern Korea', *Education about Asia* 11:2 (autumn 2006): 35–9, p. 12. For an extensive bibliography on the subject, see UCLA Online Archive Korean Christianity. http://koreanchristianity.cdh.ucla.edu (accessed 6 September 2018).

31 Writings by other Christian missionary women can be seen in Missionary Sisters of the Community of St Peter, Kilburn, 'Extracts from the sisters' letters, August 11th to December 29th, 1895', Project Canterbury, http://anglicanhistory.org/asia/kr/sisters_letters1895.html (accessed 6 September 2018).

32 Spencer J. Palmer, *Korea and Christianity: The Problem of Identification with Tradition*, Seoul, Royal Asiatic Society Korea Branch, 1986, pp. 51–2.

33 By 2016, there were 27,000 Korean missionaries outside the country: *Christianity Daily*, 'Over 27,000 Korean missionaries worldwide, according to study', 8 June 2016, www.christianitydaily.com/articles/8179/20160608/over-27-000-korean-missionaries-ministering-worldwide-according-study.htm (accessed 6 September 2018). See also Center for the Study of Global Christianity, 'Christianity in its global context', p. 76, which counted 20,000 missionaries in 2010, making South Korea the sixth largest exporter, after the US, Brazil, France, Spain and Italy, but the fifth largest exporter per million church members, after Palestine, Ireland, Malta and Samoa.

34 Brother Anthony of Taizé, 'The early years of the RASKB: 1900–1920', http://hompi.sogang.ac.kr/anthony/RASKBHistory1940.html (accessed 7 September 2018).

35 There is a complete run of the *Transactions of the Royal Asiatic Society Korea Branch*, shelfmark AS559.R7 TRA 1900 in the Korean Studies Library, Oriental Institute. For indices to the complete series please see 'Indices to the complete series of the Transactions of the Royal Asiatic Society Korea Branch', http://anthony.sogang.ac.kr/Transactions.htm (accessed 6 September 2018).

36 There is a growing number of outstanding online resources for Christianity in Korea and for Anglicanism. See the UCLA Online Archive Korean Christianity.

37 For more details on authorship, see Korean Bible Society, 'Korean Bible translations', http://en.bskorea.or.kr/?page_id=106 (accessed 9 September 2018).

38 Minh Chung, *Korean Treasures: Rare Books, Manuscripts and Artefacts in the Bodleian Libraries and Museums of Oxford University*, Oxford, Bodleian Library, 2011, pp. 11–17.

39 Ross did not work alone. His team consisted of John Macintyre, Yi Ŭngch'an 이응찬 (李應贊), Paek Hungjun 백홍준 (白鸿俊), Sŏ Sangnyun 서상륜 (徐相崙) and Yi Sŏngha 이성하 (李成夏), Korean Bible Society, 'Korean Bible translations'.

40 *Yesu syŏnggyo syŏngsyŏ, Yoannui po' kŭm* (Gospel of John) (N.T. Corean e. 4)
Yesu syŏnggyo syŏngsyŏ, Nuga po' kŭm, Teja haengjyŏk (Gospel of Luke and Acts) (N.T. Corean e.5)
Yesu syŏnggyo chyŏnsyŏ (New Testament) (N.T. Corean e.1)
Yesu syŏnggyo syŏngsyŏ, Malko po' kŭm (Gospel of Mark) (N.T. Corean e.3)
Yesu syŏnggyo syŏngsyŏ Mattae po' kŭm (Gospel of Matthew) (N.T. Corean e.2)

41 *Corean primer: being lessons in Corean on all ordinary subjects*, transliterated on the principles of the 'Mandarin primer', by the same author, 1877 (Cor. e.8).
History of Corea, ancient and modern, 1879 (OC) 246 e.579).
Korean speech: with grammar and vocabulary, 1882 (Cor. e.2).
The Corean language,1890 (Cor. d.7).
Yesu syŏnggyŏ chyŏnsyŏ (New Testament), 1956 (Korean Research Collection, BSF).
See also John Ross and Kyŏng-suk Hong 홍경숙, *Jon Rosŭ ŭi Han'guksa: Sŏyang ŏnŏ ro kirok toen ch'oech'o ŭi Han'guk yŏksa* 존로스의 한국사: 서양 언어 로 기록 된 최초의 한국역사, Kyŏnggi-do P'aju-si, Sallim Ch'ulp'ansa, 2010.

42 John C. Corfe, *The Anglican Church in Corea*, London, Livingstones; Seoul, Seoul Press, 1905, http://anglicanhistory.org/asia/kr/corfe.html (accessed 6 September 2018), p. 8. See also Hamish C. Ion, *The Cross and the Rising Sun, Volume 2: The British Protestant Missionary Movement in Japan, Korea and Taiwan, 1865–1945*, Waterloo, ON, Wilfrid Laurier University Press, 1993, pp. 86ff.

43 London, Church of England Mission to Korea, *The Morning Calm*, 1890–1936 (Bod Per. 1335 e.124, 172).

44 Many of Bishop Corfe's other works are available in the Bodleian: 'Magnificat and Nunc Dimittis for men's voices'; 'The Anglican Church in Corea, documents, original and translated, issued during the episcopate of the first bishop between 1889 and 1905, with an intr. by C.J. Corfe'; and 'Yŏngguk Sŏnggonghoe sŏn'gyosa ŭi nun e pich'in Han'gugin ŭi sinang kwa p'ungsok'.

45 Bodleian shelfmark: Corean 20. A digitized version is online at https://databank.ora.ox.ac.uk/misccoll/datasets/Corean20/Corean20.pdf (accessed 9 September 2018). The digitization was kindly paid for by Professor Ross King of the University of British Columbia and the Friends of the Bodleian.

46 Korean Mission (Church of England), *The Anglican Church in Korea*, London, Korean Mission, 1963, pp. 10–11.

47 Chung, *Korean Treasures*, p. 102.

48 Fifteen years before his death, he wrote a general work on the Church. See Mark N. Trollope, *The Church of Corea*, London, A.R. Mowbray, 1915, https://archive.org/stream/

churchincorea00troluoft#page/22/mode/2up (accessed 6 September 2018).

49 Chung, *Korean Treasures*, p.22.

50 Works by Bishop Trollope available at the Bodleian include: 'Translation: notes on the imperial Chinese mission to Corea, 1890', compiled by a private secretary of the imperial commissioners [M.N. Trollope], 1892 (BOD 38494 d.4); 'A memoir of the family of Trollope', 1897 (BOD 2182 T. d.6, Box B000000485388); 'The Church in Corea', 1915 (BOD 1335 f.23); 'A charge delivered by Mark … bishop in Corea to the clergy of the English Church mission in that country …', 1915 (BOD 1005 d.12/8); 'A charge delivered by Mark … bishop in Corea to the clergy of the diocese …', 1917 (BOD 1005 d.12/9); 'Charles John Corfe: naval chaplain, bishop', by Bishop Montgomery; with an introduction by Mark Napier Trollope, 1927 (BOD 1335 e.215); '"The peace of Jerusalem": reflections on … reunion', 1930 (BOD (RHO) USPG 182); 'A biography by his sister: Constance Trollope: Mark Napier Trollope', London, SPCK, 1936 (BOD 1335 e.291); papers published in RASKB *Transactions*: 'Kang-wha [Kanghwa]' Part I, II (1902): 1–36; 'Introduction to the study of Buddhism in Korea', VIII (1917): 1–41; 'Arboretum Coreense, being a preliminary catalogue of the vernacular names of fifty of the commonest trees and shrubs found in Chōsen', Part I, IX (1918): 69–90 and Part II, XI (1920): 39–100; 'Corean books and their authors, being an introduction of Corean literature', XXI (1932): 1–58; 'Book production and printing in Corea', XXV (1936): 101–7.

51 The United Society for the Propagation of the Gospel was first given a royal charter in 1701 and named the Society for the Propagation of the Gospel in Foreign Parts (SPG), acting as a missionary wing of the Church of England. It was renamed in 1965 as the United Society for the Propagation of the Gospel (USPG). From November 2012 until 2016, it was called the United Society or US. From 2016, the United Society was renamed the United Society Partners in the Gospel (USPG).

52 Brother Anthony of Taizé's obituary on Monsignor Cecil Richard Rutt can be seen at: www.koreatimes.co.kr/www/news/special/2011/08/178_92085.html (accessed 9 September 2018).

53 Richard Rutt's works available in the Bodleian include: *Korean Works and Days: Notes from the Diary of a Country priest*, 1964 (BOD 247191 e.219); *Korean Works and Days: Notes from the Diary of a Country Priest*, 2nd edn, 1978 ([KSL] DS904 RUT 1978); 風流韓國 리처드 • 러드著. *P'ungnyu Han'guk Rich'ŏdŭ Rŏt'ŭ chŏ*. 1965 (BOD Cor. e.2484); 孤獨의愛像: 이것이코리어더 / 리처드 • 러트 盧大榮著. *Kodok ŭi aesang: Igŏsi K'oriŏ ta / Rich'ŏdŭ, Rŏt'ŭ No Tae-yŏng chŏ*, 1965 (Korean Research Collection, BSF); *The Bamboo Grove: An Introduction to Sijo*, edited and translated by Richard Rutt, 1971 ([KSL] PL984.E3.R8 RUT 1971); *James Scarth Gale and his History of the Korean People: A New Edition of the History Together with a Biography and Annotated Bibliographies*, by Richard Rutt, 1972 ([KSL DS907 GAL 1972]; *James Scarth Gale and his History of the Korean People: A New Edition of the History Together with a Biography and Annotated Bibliographies*, by Richard Rutt, 2nd edn, 1983 ([KSL] DS907 GAL 1987); *The Green People: Thirty Sijo Poems, by Yi Unsang*, translated by Richard Rutt, 1973 ([KSL] PL991.9.U5 A6 YI 1973); *Virtuous Women: Three Classic Korean Novels*, translated by Richard Rutt and Kim Chong-un, 1974 ([KSL] PL980.A2 VIR 1979); *Godparents: A Report*, by Richard Rutt, 1984 (BOD M08.F03702); *Virtuous Women: Three Masterpieces of Traditional Korean Fiction*, translated by Richard Rutt and Kim Chong-un, 1974 (Cor. d.163).

54 Queries regarding materials and photos related to James Scarth Gale should be sent to the librarian at minh.chung@bodleian.ox.ac.uk.

55 They carry the following shelfmarks: SPG photographs 732, 868, 869, 870, 871, 873, 874, 875, 4001 and 5519; albums 123, 153 and 158. For a specialized work on missionary photography, see Donald Clark, *Missionary Photography in Korea: Encountering the West through Christianity*, Seoul, Korea Society, 2009.

56 The Right Reverend Paul Lee's obituary in *Morning Calm* is available at www.koreanmission.org/mc/2010_no45_september.pdf (accessed 9 September 2018).

57 Howarth Box 7 used to be in one large box (which was how it was received from the USPG) but it has been housed into six smaller archive boxes before being moved to the Weston Library from Rhodes House.

Chapter 4

1 Kim Yong-suk 金英淑 and Son Kyong-ja 孫敬子, *Chosŏn wangjo Han'guk poksik togam* 朝鮮王朝韓國服飾圖鑑 (*An Illustrated History of Korean Costume*), Seoul, Yŏgyŏng sanŏpsa, 1984, Vol. 1, p. 88.

2 Keith Pratt and Richard Rutt (eds), *Korea: A Historical and Cultural Dictionary*, Richmond, Curzon Press, 1999, p. 106.

3 National Folk Museum of Korea, *National Folk Museum of Korea*, Seoul, National Folk Museum of Korea, 2009, pp. 264–6.

4 Kim and Son, *Chosŏn wangjo Han'guk poksik togam*, Vol. 1, p. 106.

5 Kim and Son, *Chosŏn wangjo Han'guk poksik togam*, Vol. 1, pp. 152–4.

6 Kim In-gyu 김인규, Pak Tae-nam 박대남, Sŏ Hŏn-gang 서현강 and Son Chun-ho 손준호, *Korean Collections at the British Museum*, London, British Museum, 2016, p. 225.

7 Kim and Son, *Chosŏn wangjo Han'guk poksik togam*, Vol. 2, p. 80.

8 Kim and Son, *Chosŏn wangjo Han'guk poksik togam*, Vol. 2, p. 60.

9 Kim and Son, *Chosŏn wangjo Han'guk poksik togam*, Vol. 2, p. 68.

10 Kim and Son, *Chosŏn wangjo Han'guk poksik togam*, Vol. 1, pp. 160–1.

Chapter 5

1 Keith Pratt and Richard Rutt (eds), *Korea: A Historical and Cultural Dictionary*, Richmond, Curzon Press, 1999, pp. 23–4.

2 For details of Gerald Reitlinger, see Ashmolean Museum, 'Gerald Reitlinger (1900–1978), biography', www.jameelcentre.ashmolean.org/collection/6/671 (accessed 9 September 2018).

3 These characters refer to the Yellow River Diagram 河图 and the Nine Halls Diagram 九宮圖, which are mathematical and divinatory schemes derived from the *Yijing* 易經 (*Book of Changes*). The phrase is the first phrase of a longer reference that describes the symbolic meaning of hexagrams and the basic elements (water, wood, metal, fire and earth). Hexagrams are formed by the throwing of yarrow stalks to produce trigrams for divination: 天一生水，地六成之；地二生火，天七成之；天三生木，地八成之；地四生金，天九成之；天五生土，地十成之. In its original context it is part of a cosmological, astrological, geomantic and numerological system and is deliberately arcane and obscure and designed to enhance a sense of mystery.

4 Translated by Kang Kyung Nam, assistant curator, National Museum of Korea.

5 Pratt and Rutt, *Korea: A Historical and Cultural Dictionary*, pp. 388–9.

6 Pratt and Rutt, *Korea: A Historical and Cultural Dictionary*, p. 351.

APPENDICES

Appendix 1:
Works related to Christianity in the Rutt collection

1 *Sŏnggyo richŭng* 聖教理證. Keijō, Seikōkai shuppansha (Sŏnggonhoe ch'ulp'ansa 聖公會出版社), Taishō 2, 1913

2 *Mokcha sŏng* 牧者鏡: *Mirror of pastors.* Keijō, Seikōkai shuppansha (Sŏnggonhoe ch'ulp'ansa 聖公會出版社), Taishō 13, 1924

3 *Kŭidomun* 긔도문 (祈祷文). Keijō, Keijō Rokoku Seikyōdō (Kyŏngsŏng Noguk Chŏnggyodang 京城露國正教堂, Seoul Russian Orthodox Church), Taishō 2, 1913

4 *Chŏndogyo ŭijŏl, Paek Se-myŏng* 天道教儀節, 白世明. Seoul, Chŏndogyo ch'ongbu kyŏngniwŏn 天道教總部經理院, Potŏk 布德 87, 1946

5 *Sŏng Benedikto ŭi sudo kyuch'ik* 성베네딕도의수도규칙. Waegwan, Sŏng Benedikto Sudowŏn 성베네딕도수도원, 1962

6 *Oju sŏngch'e pohyŏl yeŭi* 吾主聖體寶血禮儀. Keijō-fu, Chōsen Seikōkai (Chosŏn Sŏnggonghoe 朝鮮聖公會), Showa 14, 1939

Appendix 2:
Materials by James Scarth Gale (1863–1937) obtained by Richard Rutt from Gale's family while preparing Gale's biography

A)
Manuscript, 'Translation of the bible into Korean (Proverbs, preacher, song of songs)' [in Hangul], Dr Gale, given to Richard Rutt by Mrs J. Lloyd-Kirk, 22 August 1971

B)
Typewritten copy, *Along the Trans-Siberian*, J.S. Gale, written on the way 1903, copy 1916

C)
1 Various book lists by J.S. Gale

1.1 Catalogue of books in Korean

1.2 Another list

1.3 Korean language study

2 A photocopied article, 'Pioneer missionary to Korea – Death of Dr. James Scarth Gale', *Bath Weekly Chronicle and Herald*, Saturday 6 February 1937, one page

3 A photocopy of typewritten notes entitled 'Death of Rev. James S. Gale', one page

4 Biographical note about Rev. Dr James Scarth Gale, by Mrs J.S. Gale

D)
1 *Poems and essays by Yi Kyoo-bo* (1168–1241 AD), translated by James S. Gale

2 *A Korean contemporary of King Richard, Coeur de Lion* (1157–1199 AD), translated by James S. Gale

3 *Francis of Assisi* (1182–1226 AD), translated by James S. Gale

4 *Genghis Khan* (1162–1227 AD), translated by James S. Gale

E)
1 A letter from James Gale to Horace, 27 April 1933

2 Wedding invitation card of Ada Louisa & Gale

3 Commission as Christian Missionary, University College, YMCA, Toronto, J.S. Gale, 1888

4 Doctor of Divinity Degree, Howard University, Washington, D.C., Dr James S. Gale, June 1904

5 Bachelor of Arts Degree, University of Toronto, J.S. Gale, 12 June 1888

6 Letter from Gale to Sunday School Scholars and Teachers, Seoul Chŏson, 28 November, 1924

7 Letter from Howard University to certify J.S. Gale was awarded an honorary degree in Divinity in 1904

8 Copy of Dr James S. Gale's Doctorate of Divinity certificate

9 Copy of Dr James S. Gale's appointment and credentials from University College, YMCA, Toronto

F)
1 Typewritten pages written while in Bath entitled 'Life of James Scarth Gale', JSG, 1932–3, seven pages

2 Typewritten pages entitled 'Bishop Trollope visits downside Abbey', James S. Gale, four pages

3 'Early manufacture of movable types in Korea', JSG

4 A photocopy of a handwritten page entitled 'Books done by J.S. Gale', listing books in English and Korean written by him, J.S. Gale, one page

5 Typewritten pages entitled 'Marriage in Korea', James S. Gale, three pages

G)
1 A letter from Y. Sakai to Monsignor Rutt, 2 March 1971

2 A letter from Key P. Yang to Monsignor Rutt, 1 February 1971

3 A letter from Marion Heel to Monsignor Rutt, 11 December 1970

4 A letter from Marion Hell to Monsignor Rutt, 4 January 1971

5 A letter from George J.M. Gale to Monsignor Rutt, 5 October 1970

6 Four letters from Mrs Annie H. Gale to Monsignor Rutt, 3 September 1970– 20 January 1971

7 A letter from George J.M. Gale to Monsignor Rutt, 14 July 1970

8 A letter from George J.M. Gale to Monsignor Rutt, 25 August 1970

9 A letter from Annie H. Gale to Monsignor Rutt, 18 June 1971

10 A letter from George J.M. Gale to Monsignor Rutt, 3 August 1988

11 A letter from S.B. Murphy to Monsignor Rutt, 14 August 1972

12 A letter from Mrs J. Lloyd-Kirk to Richard Rutt, 7 November 1972

13 A letter from Robert A. Kinney to Monsignor Rutt, 5 December 1971

14 An extract from *Knox College Monthly*; letter from James S. Gale, 12 January 1890

H)
1 A letter from Mrs Esson Gale to Bishop and Mrs Rutt, 29 December 1971

2 A letter from Mrs J. Lloyd-Kirk to Monsignor Rutt, 15 May 1970

3 A letter from Mrs J. Lloyd-Kirk to Monsignor Rutt, 9 January 1972

4 'Mrs James S. Gale memorial minutes', adopted by the Presbyterian Board of Foreign Missions, 21 April 1953, two copies along with a short biography

5 A letter from William Scott to Monsignor Rutt, 4 November 1970

6 A letter from Gerald W. Gillette to Monsignor Rutt, 10 November 1971

7 A letter from Charles H. Moffett to Rev. Malcolm Shields, 5 October 1971

8 A letter from Miss K.J. Cann to Monsignor Rutt, 10 November 1970

9 A letter from Dr William Scott to Monsignor Rutt, 17 November 1970

10 A letter from Dr William Scott to Monsignor Rutt, 27 November 1970

11 A letter from Dr William Scott to Monsignor Rutt, 3 December 1970

12 A letter from Dr William Scott to Monsignor Rutt, 22 December 1970

13 A letter from Dr William Scott to Monsignor Rutt, 15 January 1971

I)

1 A letter to Mr Kinney from Monsignor Rutt (?), 10 December 1971

2 A letter to Mr Kinney from Monsignor Rutt (?), 17 February 1972

3 A letter to Allen [Clark] from Monsignor Rutt (?), 13 October 1972

4 A letter from Annie Gale to Monsignor Rutt, 16 April 1973

5 A letter from Annie Gale to Joan and Richard Rutt, 21 February 1971

6 A letter from Samuel H. Moffett to Richard Rutt, 22 June 1970

7 A letter from Samuel H. Moffett to Richard Rutt, 23 November 1971

8 A letter from 요한 Yohan (or John) to Richard Rutt, 16 January 1972

9 A letter from Harold F. Cook to Monsignor Rutt, 22 April 1970

10 Two letters from Chewon Kim to Monsignor Rutt, 2 May 1970 and 28 April 1970

11 A letter from Harold F. Cook to Monsignor Rutt, 8 May 1970

12 A letter from 김양선대리 이흥근 Kim Yang-sŏn Taeri (or Deputy Kim Yang-sŏn) to 노대영주교 Noh Tae-yŏng Chugyo (or Bishop Noh Tae-yŏng), 9 September 1970

13 A letter from Malcolm Shields to Charles H. Moffett, 2 October 1970

14 A letter from Pierre Song to Monsignor Rutt, 2 October 1970

J)

1 A letter from Pierre Song to Monsignor Rutt, 26 September 1970

2 A letter from Pierre K. Choi to Monsignor Rutt, 18 August 1967

3 A letter from Kathleen Cann to Monsignor Rutt, 8 December 1970

4 A letter from Allen [Clark] to Monsignor Rutt, 27 October 1970

5 A collection of letters: a letter from (?) to Rev. William Scott, 16 December 1970; a letter from Harold Stough to Bishop Rutt, 27 January 1972; a letter from William Scott to Richard and Joan [Rutt], 12 September 1972; a letter from Bishop Rutt to Mr Gale (son of James S. Gale), 8 February 1973; a letter from Bishop Rutt to Earnest Fisher, 8 February 1973; a letter from Earnest Fisher to Bishop Rutt, 23 February 1973; a letter from Bishop Rutt to Earnest Fisher, 5 March 1973; a letter from Earnest Fisher to Bishop Rutt, 12 May 1973 and a letter from Albert and Coby Keble to Bishop Rutt, 4 September 1973

6 A letter from R.N. Hachaens to Rev. William Scott, 16 December 1970

7 A letter from 김양선 Kim Yang-sŏn to 노대영주교 Noh Taeyŏng chugyo (Bishop), 21 February 1972

8 A letter to Monsignor Rutt, 10 January 1972

9 A letter to Monsignor Rutt, 20 January 1972

10 A letter from Mrs Janice E. Pearson to Monsignor Rutt, 13 September 1972

11 A copy of a letter from Monsignor Rutt to Mr Sauer, 6 September 1972

12 A letter from Ethel Kueck to Mrs Janice E. Pearson, 4 October 1972

13 A letter from Mrs Sutton to Mrs Janice E. Pearson, 25 September 1972

14 A letter from Mrs Janice E. Pearson to Monsignor Rutt, 6 October 1972

K)

1 A letter from Monsignor Rutt to an archivist, 5 September 1972

2 A letter from Monsignor Rutt to Mrs Janice E. Pearson, 31 October 1972

3 A letter from Monsignor Rutt to Mrs Sutton, 31 October 1972

4 A letter from Monsignor Rutt to Mrs Sutton, 17 November 1972

5 A letter from Anne Davidson to Monsignor Rutt, 1 February 1971

6 A letter from Harry A. Rodes, 'In memoriam' of James S. Gale, 26 July 1937

7 A letter from George J. Gale to Rev. John T. Watson; a typewritten page entitled 'Books done by J.S. Gale' listing books in English and Korean written by him, J.S. Gale, 4 July 1960, one page

8 A letter from J.M. Dent & Sons Limited, 5 December 1912

9 A letter from Richard Rutt to Dr Cook, 4 December 1971

10 A letter from Dr H.F. Cook to Mr Robert A. Kinney, 6 December 1971

11 A letter from L. George Paik to Monsignor Rutt, 25 February 1972

12 A letter from Mrs Lloyd-Kirk to Monsignor Rutt, 29 March 1972

13 P.S., 14 September 1970

14 A letter from Director Won-Yong Kim to Monsignor Rutt, 25 September 1970

15 Invoice to Monsignor Rutt, 11 August 1972

L)

1 A letter from Michael Cooks to Monsignor Rutt, 26 June 1972

2 A letter from Rev. James Pong to Monsignor Rutt, 14 July 1970

3 A letter from Myrtle M. Clemmer to Monsignor Rutt, 27 April 1970

4 A letter from Myrtle M. Clemmer to Monsignor Rutt, 22 June 1970

5 A letter from Catherine Booth to Monsignor Rutt, 23 November 1971

6 A letter from Robert K. Anderson to Monsignor Rutt, 31 May 1971

7 A letter from James Grayson to Monsignor Rutt, 3 February 1973

8 A letter from Giuliano Bertuccioli to Monsignor Rutt, 8 November 1972

9 A letter from Mrs J. Lloyd-Kirk to Monsignor Rutt, 11 October 1970

10 A letter from Mrs J. Lloyd-Kirk to Monsignor Rutt, 5 December 1971

11 A letter from Mrs J. Lloyd-Kirk to Monsignor Rutt, 10 September 1970

12 A letter from George Gale to Monsignor Rutt, 24 September 1972

13 A letter from Mrs J. Lloyd-Kirk, 31 October 1971

14 A letter from William B. Miller to Monsignor Rutt, 10 August 1970

15 A letter from L.G. Paik to Monsignor Rutt, 12 February 1973

M)

1 A memo from Kim Chi-hŏn 金知憲 to Rev. Richard Rutt (?)

2 A letter from Samuel H. Moffett to Rev. Richard Rutt, 19 June 1970

3 A letter from James Gale to the International Committee Young Men's Christian Associations, 9 July 1906

4 A letter from (?) to Mr Levering, 6 April 1908

5 A letter from (?) to Richard Rutt, 27 December 1971

6 A letter from Edward B. Adams to Rev. Richard Rutt, 27 July 1970

7 A letter from the British Museum to Rev. the Lord Bishop of Taejon, 6 May 1970

8 A letter from Burton Watson to Monsignor Rutt, 7 December 1971

9 A letter from [Bishop Rutt] to Dr Scott, 23 January 1971

10 A letter from William C. Carrol to Monsignor Rutt, 12 March 1971

11 A letter from the Presbyterian Theological Seminary to Rev. Richard Rutt, 24 May 1972

12 A letter from Bill Wentham (?) of University of Hawaii to Monsignor Rutt, 15 May 1972

13 A letter from (?) to Andersen, 24 November 1907

14 A letter from (?) to F.S. Brock, 18 March 1908

15 A photocopy of a handwritten certificate, University College, YMCA, Toronto, for Mr James Scarth Gale, [no date]

N)

1 A typewritten page entitled 'Biographical data – Rev. James Scarth Gale'

2 A photocopied typewritten page entitled 'Extracts from report of Rev. James S. Gale, D.D. 1917 Korea'

3 An article, 'Korea: the Hermit Nation',

4 An article, 'Good cheer from Korea', *Knox College Monthly*, James S. Gale, June 1889, pp. 111–13

5 Typewritten pages entitled 'In memoriam – the Reverend James Scarth Gale, D.D.', John McNab with words sent by the widow on Gale's death, [no date], two pages

6 Photocopied pages entitled 'Touching farewell party for Dr and Mrs Gale', International Friendly Association Entertains, [no date]

7 A handwritten note

8 A handwritten note on a small piece of paper

9 A handwritten list and summary

10 A handwritten note

11 Two typed accounts about Dr Gale

12 Biographical notes on Dr James S. Gale, three pages

13 Materials used for biography and bibliography, four pages

O)

1 A photocopied page from *Who was who, 1916–1928*

2 A photocopied page from *The Missionary Review of the World*, July 1900

3 A photocopied page from *Korea Report*, 1905

4 Photocopy of a typewritten page entitled 'Rev. James S. Gale D.D. June 1925', issued by the Foreign Missions Library, New York, 19 October 1965

5 Book review, *Korean Repository*, 1895, Vol. 2, p. 230

6 Two photocopies of a leaflet entitled 'Commemorative service in memory of the Rev. Dr. James Scarth Gale (1863–1937), St. Andres's Presbyterian Church, ALMA, 5 June 1988', each four pages

7 An article, 'Gale: learned missionary', *Korea Times*, 5 November 1972

8 A photocopy of pages from the *Encyclopedia of World Methodism*, Nashville, United Methodist Pub. House, c.1974, with information on William Arthur Noble (1866–1945) and Willard Gliden Cram (1875–1969), three pages

9 A photocopied article, 'Mr. and Mrs. D.L. Gifford, James S. Gale' *The Evangelist*, 18 October 1900

10 Danish translations

11 Book review from *Korean Repository*, 1895, Vol. 2, pp. 230–1

12 Two photocopied pages from *The Missionary*, May 1910

13 Two photocopied pages from *The Church at Home and Abroad*, Vol. 16, July 1894

14 An article, 'Korean history paper IV', *Korean Repository*, James S. Gale, May 1986, pp. 183–8

15 A photocopied chapter taken from the book *The Christian Movement in Japan, Korea and Formosa*, 1923, pp. 456–71

16 A photocopied chapter, 'Survey of Christian literature' by J. S. Gale taken from the annual periodical, *The Christian Movement in the Japanese Empire*, Tokyo, Published for the Conference of Federated Missions, 1918

P)

1 A photocopied chapter taken from a book, 'What Korea has lost', *The Christian Movement in Japan, Korea and Formosa*, James S. Gale, 1926, pp. 375–82

2 Biography

3 A photocopied photo of G.S. Gale, Yi Won-Mo, Yi Kyo-Seung and Yi Chang-Jik, July 1927

4 Two photocopied biographies about James S. Gale, 10 October 1985

5 A typewritten biography, 'Harold Wilson Harkness is the son of Robert Harkness'

6 Typewritten notes on 'Articles in Korean'

7 Photocopied booklet taken from the book *The Christian Movement in the Japanese Empire*, 1918

8 Two photocopied pages from *Children's Work for Children*, August 1893, Vol. 18, No. 8, pp. 132–3

9 Photocopied pages from *Japan and Korea*

10 A typewritten page entitled 'Bibliography addenda'

11 A photocopied article, 'About new books', *Canadian Magazine*, James S. Gale, June 1904, XXIII, pp. 184–5

12 Photocopies from *Annual Report of the Librarian of Congress 1919*, pp. 28–31; *Annual Report of the Librarian of Congress 1920*, pp. 192–3; *Annual Report of the Librarian of Congress 1927*, pp. 276–7; *Annual Report of the Librarian of Congress 1928*, pp. 298–309

13 Photocopied pages from *Woman's Work*, August 1908, Vol. XXIII, No. 8, pp. 173–4

14 Photocopied articles about Japan in Korea

15 A photocopied page from 'World Service', *Latourette*, Kenneth Scott, New York, Association Press, 1957, p. 41

16 Four photocopied pages from the University of Toronto Annual Report, 1888–93

Q)

1 Three typed pages entitled 'Book chat' introducing books written by James Gale, with no name of the author

2 Photocopied entry for Robert Pilkington in *Dictionary of National Biography*, Vol. 15, p. 1186

3 A photocopied page from *The Canadian Men and Women of the Time: A Handbook of Canadian Biography of Living Characters*, Henry James Morgan (ed.), Toronto, W. Briggs, 1912, p. 428

4 Portrait of James Gale by J. Bruce in Toronto

5 An article, 'Koreans have revised copy of bible', *The Continent*, 1 April 1926

6 An article, 'Korea, the Hermit Nation, two missionaries sent from Toronto'

7 An article, 'Noted missionary visiting Toronto'

8 An article, 'Dr Gale, here from Korea is honoured at a luncheon'

9 An article, 'A Canadian translator: an ambassador to the Hermit Kingdom', Rev. John McNab

10 A typewritten article, 'Korea's first English instructor a Britton', Harold F. Cook

11 An article, 'Pioneers of modernization (13), Gale: learned missionary', *The Korea Times*, 5 November 1972

12 An article, 'My Korean friend Yee', J.S. Gale

13 A photocopied article, 'A Korean story of a nose', translated by Rev. James S. Gale, *Over Sea and Land*, November 1900, Vol. 25, p. 212

R)

1 *Ambassador to the Hermit Kingdom*, The Thorn Press, Toronto, 1939

2 Typewritten pages, 'Footprints of the wildgoose' (pages numbered 1 to 25)

3 A typewritten article, 'His Majesty the King, Esson Third', seven pages

4 A typewritten article, 'Trip to Japan', Shin Yoo-han, two pages

5 Photocopied pages from *Korean Literature*, J.S. Gale

6 An article, 'Korean history paper II', *Korean Repository*, James S. Gale, March 1986 (?), pp. 14–19

7 Photocopied pages from *The Korean Magazine*, September 1917, pp. 404–14

8   An article, 'Korean history paper III', *Korean Repository*, James S. Gale, March 1986, pp. 95–100

9   A photocopy of a handwritten letter from James [no surname] in Seoul to James [no surname], 1 January 1926, two pages

10 A photocopied article, 'A Korean story, *The Outlook*, James S. Gale, February 1902, pp. 916–19

11 A typewritten article, 'Korean playing cards'

12 Typewritten pages, 'Pre-Gutenberg art printing,' Paul Hennig, Notebook 1, 1914, seven pages

13 A photocopied article, 'Vorgutenbergiche Buchdruckerkunft'

14 A photocopied article, 'Early manufacture of movable types in Chōsen', J.S. Gale, Seoul Press, 11 October 1913

15 A photocopied article, 'Early use of movable types in Chōsen', *Japan Daily Mail*, 15 October 1913

S)

1   A photocopied article, 'Korea – after forty years', James S. Gale, *Presbyterian Witness*, 11 September 1924

2   A photocopied article, 'Ambassador to the Hermit Kingdom', *In Other Tongues*, Gale

3   Photocopied pages from the magazine *The Korean Field*, November 1904, pp. 214–21

4   A photocopied chapter from a book, 'What Korea has lost', *Korea*, J.S. Gale, pp. 375–81

5   A photocopied chapter from a book, 'The Christian movement in Korea', *Korea*, J.S. Gale, pp. 331–5

6   An article, 'Korean literature', *The Korea Magazine*, July 1918, pp. 297–9

7   A photocopied page, 'Two poems, from the Korean of Yi Kyoobo', *The Quarterly Review*, translated by James S. Gale, 2 February 1946, p. 156

T)

1   Booklet, 'The centenary of the granting of the charter of Knox College,' Knox College, Toronto, 1858–1958

2   Photocopied pages in Korean, *Chŏngsin Yŏja Kodŭng Hakkyo* 정신여자 고등학교 학교연혁 (History of Chungshin Girls' High School), two pages

3   Booklet, 'ALMA through the years 1948–1967'

U)

1   Collection of handwritten notes

V)

1   Two handwritten pages in Chinese about inscription on a bronze mirror

2   Chŏkpyŏk-ka (적벽가)

3   Poem by Chʻoe-ssi about An Kwison's husband

4   A letter written in Chinese from Zhong Yingmei 鍾應梅 (Xianggang zhong wen da xue song ji xue yuan 香港中文大學宋基學院) to De Ming 德明, 21 September [no year]

5   Two handwritten pages in Chinese about opium banning

6   A typewritten page entitled 'The McAll Board of Direction in Paris'

7   A photocopied article, 'Disput des Nichijō mit dem Pater'

8   Photocopied pages in Chinese

W)

List of books sent by Gale to Library of Congress on his retirement

X)

Photos of James S. Gale

Appendix 3:
Other works by James Scarth Gale available in the Bodleian Library

1   *A Concise Dictionary of the Korean Language: in Two Parts, Korean-English & English-Korean*, Horace Grant Underwood; assisted by Homer B. Hulbert, James S. Gale, 1890 (BOD Cor. e.3)

2   *Sagwa Chinam* (*Korean Grammatical Forms*), James S. Gale. 1894 (CCL PL911 G35 GAL 1894 Stacks)

3   韓英字典 (*A Korean-English Dictionary*), James S. Gale, 1894 (BOD Cor. d.6)

4   *Korean sketches*, James S. Gale, 1898 (BOD M09.G00371)

5   James Gale's draft manuscripts: 'Translations from Yi Kyubo', Draft A, (probably made in Seoul 1913–27); 'Poems and essays by Yi Kyubo', Draft B, (apparently made in Bath 1928–36); 'Selections from the writings of Yi Kyubo', Draft C, (apparently made in Bath 1928–36); List of contents for 'Tonguk Yi Sangguk Chip, I – XXXIII kwŏn' (probably made in Seoul about 1921), (apply to the Librarian)

6   *Korean reader* (*Yumong chʻŏnja*), James S. Gale, 4 Vols, 1909 (Korean Research Collection, BSF)

7   *Chŏllo yŏkchŏng* 텬로력뎡 (*Pilgrim's progress*), translated from the English by Rev. James S. Gale (?)

8   *Han-Yŏng sajŏn* (*A Korean-English Dictionary*), James Scarth Gale, 1911 ([KSL] PL937.E5 G3 GAL 1911 Ref.)

9   *Korean Folk Tales: Imps, Ghosts and Fairies*, translated from the Korean of Im Bang and Yi Ryuk, James S. Gale, 1913 (?), (BOD 932 e.34)

Appendix 4:
Howarth Collection

Korean I   nos 1–329
Korean II   nos 330–781
(The first two files include: Chonan, Anjung, Onsuri, Chʻŏngju, Inchʻŏn, Buddhist temple, Umsong, Yonsei University, Ewha University, Seoul, St John's College, Chʻŏngju, Kanghwa Island, Naeri village, Anjung, Chin Chou farming resettlement project and others [Spelling is as appears on photographs.])
Korean III   nos 782–1318
Korean IV   nos 1319–1727
(The second two files include: Farmers' resettlement project, Chinchon, Chungchu, Masok, Seoul National University, Hangui Project, Kanghwa, Sansu resettlement village – pottery, Hanghi, Inchʻŏn, school in Seoul, Holy Canaan, Hangni, Suwŏn, Seoul, new mining area and others [Spelling is as appears on photographs.])
Korean V   nos 1728–2139
Korean VI   nos 2140–2425
(The last two files include: Coalmining area, Hwangdu, school, railway construction, Masok, Seoul, Yonsei University, United Nations Day ceremonies, Seoul National University, Chonan, Hangni, Kanghwa and others)

Missionaries and Church figures included in these photographs:
Rev. John Daly
Rev. Charles Goodwin
Rev. Archer Torrey
Rev. Roger Tennant
Rev. Clifford Smart
Rev. Richard Rutt
Rev. Lionel Beere
Rev. William Austin
Rev. Stephen Yu (Parish Priest of Kangwha)
Rev. Stephen Chou (Vicar of Inchʻŏn)
Rev. Fred Phipps (Vicar of Onsuri)
Rev. Aiden Kang
Rev. Paul Lee (Warden of St. John College)
Rev. Paul Ko (Parish Priest of Chʻŏngju)
Rev. Mother Phoebe (first Korean superior)
Sister Maria (of the Society of the Holy Cross)
Miss Jo Roberts (Mothers' Union)
Rev. Mark Pae (Vicar of Chonan)

ADDRESSES

LIBRARIES

The University of Oxford's Bodleian Library is renowned worldwide and provides an important resource for scholars across all the arts and sciences. Listed below are libraries that have Korean-related materials. For access to any of the libraries please visit: www.bodleian.ox.ac.uk/bodley/services/admissions.

Bodleian China Centre Library

Dickson Poon Building
Canterbury Road, Oxford, OX2 6LU
Phone: +44 (0)1865 280430
Email: china.centre.library@bodleian.ox.ac.uk
Website: www.bodleian.ox.ac.uk/ccl
Essentially, a library for Chinese Studies but has a fair amount of Korean books.

Bodleian Oriental Institute Library

Pusey Lane, Oxford, OX1 2LE
Phone: +44 (0)1865 278202
Email: oriental.institute@bodleian.ox.ac.uk
Website: www.bodleian.ox.ac.uk/oil
The Korean-language collection started in the late 19th century and the Korean Studies Library was established with the support of the project 'Window On Korea' in 2013.

Sackler Library

1 St John Street, Oxford, OX1 2LG
Phone: +44 (0)1865 278092
Email: enquiries@saclib.ox.ac.uk
Website: www.bodleian.ox.ac.uk/sackler
Books related to art and archaeology are located here.

Bodleian Library – Weston Library

Broad Street, Oxford, OX1 3BG
Phone: +44 (0)1865 277150
Email: specialcollections.enquiries@bodleian.ox.ac.uk
Website: www.bodleian.ox.ac.uk/weston
Houses the library's Special Collections (including the Korean manuscripts and antiquarian printed books previously housed in the Radcliffe Science Library and also Korean sources related to the history of Christianity previously housed in Rhodes House).

MUSEUMS

The University of Oxford's museums are world-famous and offer scholars an important resource. They welcome visits from members of the public and are visited by more than a million people every year. Listed below are museums that have Korean-related materials. Admission is free to any of the museums. For more details please visit: www.ox.ac.uk/about_the_university/museums_and_collections/index.html.

Ashmolean Museum of Art and Archaeology

Beaumont Street, Oxford, OX1 2PH
Phone: +44 (0)1865 278002
Email: eastern-art@ashmus.ox.ac.uk
Website: www.ashmolean.org
Established in 1683. It is the oldest museum in the UK and one of the oldest in the world. It houses the University's extensive collections of art and antiquities, ranging back over four millennia.

Museum of the History of Science

Broad Street, Oxford, OX1 3AZ
Phone: +44 (0)1865 277280
Email: museum@mhs.ox.ac.uk
Website: www.mhs.ox.ac.uk
The world's oldest surviving purpose-built museum building, housing an unrivalled collection of early scientific instruments.

Oxford University Museum of Natural History (OUMNH)

Parks Road, Oxford, OX1 3PW
Phone: +44 (0)1865 272 950
Email: info@oum.ox.ac.uk
Website: www.oum.ox.ac.uk/index.htm
Houses the university's scientific collections of zoological, entomological, palaeontological and mineral specimens. With 4.5 million specimens, it is the largest collection of its type outside of the national collections.

Pitt Rivers Museum

The entrance to the Pitt Rivers Museum is through the OUMNH on Parks Road, Oxford, OX1 3PW. The entrance is at the far wall of the OUMNH. Visitors need to walk across the ground floor to reach it.
Phone: +44 (0)1865 270927
Email: prm@prm.ox.ac.uk
Website: www.prm.ox.ac.uk/index.html
Holds one of the world's finest collections of anthropological and archaeological objects, with objects from every continent and from throughout human history.

SELECT BIBLIOGRAPHY

Maps

Akioka, Takejirō 秋岡武次郎, 'An Kanae-fuku (An Chŏng-bok) [1712–1791] hitsu Chikyū giyō sekai chizu: Tōyō seisaku no ko Chikyū giyō funegata-zu no hitotsu 安鼎福筆地球儀用世界地圖: 東洋製作の古地球儀用丹形図の一', *Rekishi chiri* 歴史地理 61:2 (1933): 107–15.

Ledyard, Gari, 'Cartography in Korea', in J.B. Harley and David Woodward (eds), *The History of Cartography, Volume 2, Book 2: Cartography in the Traditional East and Southeast Asian Societies,* Chicago and London, University of Chicago Press, 1994, pp. 177–576.

Lim, Jongtae, 'Representing an ideal world order of the past: the cultural function of the Jesuit world maps in the 18th-century Korean government', lecture at Institute of History and Philology, Academia Sinica, 2016, www2.ihp.sinica.edu.tw/bulletinDetail.php?TM=1&M=2&sM=1&C=&bid=920 (accessed 6 September 2018).

McCune, Shannon. 'Some Korean maps', *Transactions of the Royal Asiatic Society Korea Branch* 50 (1975): 79–80.

McCune, Shannon, *Art of the Korean Map*, Gainesville, FL, Grinter Gallery, University of Florida, 1977.

Nakamura, Hiroshi 中村拓, *East Asia in Old Maps*, Tokyo, Centre for East Asian Cultural Studies, 1962.

No, Chŏng-sik 盧禎埴, 'Han'guk ŭi ko segye chido yŏn'gu (韓國의 古世界地圖 研究)', unpublished PhD dissertation, Hyosŏng Yŏja Taehakkyo, 1992.

Rekishi chiri 歴史地理, 17:4 (1899): frontispiece.

Robinson, Kenneth R., 'Chosŏn Korea in the Ryūkoku "Kangnido": dating the oldest extant Korean map of the world (15th century)', *Imago Mundi* 59:2 (2007): 177–92.

Takahashi, Kimiaki, 'Birth of new perspectives through integration of origin maps: the case of "Haedong cheguk ch'ongdo"', *Forum of International Development Studies* 44 (2014): 17–35.

Yang, Zhiyi, 'Zhu Xi as poet', *Journal of the American Oriental Society* 132:4 (2012): 605–7.

Yi, Ki-baek, *A New History of Korea,* Cambridge, MA, Harvard University Press, 1984.

Yu, Chai-Shin. *The Founding of Catholic Tradition in Korea*, Mississauga, ON, Korean and Related Studies Press, 1996.

Coins, amulets and chatelains

Chen, Shiyuan, *Wandering Spirits: Chen Shiyuan's Encyclopedia of Dreams*, trans. Richard E. Strassberg, Berkeley, University of California Press, 2008.

Chŏng, Su-hwan 정수환, *Chosŏn hugi hwapye yut'ong kwa kyŏngje saenghwal* 조선후기 화폐유통과 경제생활, Seoul, Kyŏngin munhwasa, 2013.

Han, Won Yu, *Money: Traditional Korean Society*, Seoul, Ewha Women's University Press, 2006.

Harley, J.B. and David Woodward (eds), 'Cartography in the traditional East and Southeast Asian societies', *History of Cartography, Volume 2, Book 2*, Chicago and London, University of Chicago Press, 1987.

Kim In-sik 金仁植 (ed.), *Han'guk hwapye kagyŏk torok* 韓國貨幣價格圖錄, Seoul, Osŏng K&C (오성K&C), 2017.

Pratt, Keith and Richard Rutt (eds), *Korea: A Historical and Cultural Dictionary*, Richmond, Curzon Press, 1999.

Ramsden, H.A., *Corean Coin Charms and Amulets*, Yokohama, Jun Kobayagawa Co., 1910.

Sakuraki, Shin'ichi, Helen Wang and Peter Kornicki, with Nobuhisa Furuta, Timon Screech and Joe Cribb (eds), *Catalogue of the Japanese Coin Collection (Pre-Meiji) at the British Museum: With Special Reference to Kutsuki Masatsuna*, London, British Museum, 2010.

Shijing, trans. Gladys Yang, Beijing, Waiwen chubanshe, 2001.

Op den Velde, Wybrand and David Hartill, *Cast Korean Coins and Charms*, Sandy, Bright Pen, 2013.

Sources related to the history of Christianity in Korea

Baker, Don, 'Hwang Sayŏng: an appeal for aid', in Peter H. Lee et al. (eds), *Sourcebook of Korean Civilization, Volume 2: From the 17th Century to the Modern Period*, New York, Columbia University Press, 1996, pp. 147–50.

Baker, Don, 'A different thread: orthodoxy, heterodoxy, and Catholicism in a Confucian world', in JaHyun Kim Haboush and Martina Deuchler (eds), *Culture and the State in Late Chosŏn Korea*, Cambridge, MA, Harvard University Asia Center, 1999, pp. 217–20.

Baker, Don, 'The Korean Catholic Church's first hundred years: guest editor's introduction', *Acta Koreana* 15:1 (2012): 1–14.

Baker, Don and Franklin Rausch, *Catholics and Anti-Catholicism in Chosŏn Korea*, Honolulu, University of Hawai'i Press, 2017.

Brother Anthony of Taizé, 'The early years of the RASKB: 1900–1920', http://hompi.sogang.ac.kr/anthony/RASKBHistory1940.html (accessed 7 September 2018).

Cawley, Kevin, 'Deconstructing hegemony: Catholic texts in Chosŏn's neo-Confucian context', *Acta Koreana* 15:1 (2012): 15–42.

Center for the Study of Global Christianity, Gordon Conwell Theological Seminary, 'Christianity in its global context, 1970–2020: society, religion, and mission', www.gordonconwell.edu/ockenga/research/ documents/2Christianity initsGlobalContext.pdf (accessed 18 September 2018).

Cho, Kwang, 'The meaning of Catholicism in Korean history', *Korea Journal* 24:8 (August 1984): 14–27.

Cho, Kwang, 'Human relations as expressed in vernacular Catholic writings of the late Chosŏn dynasty', trans. Timothy S. Lee, in Robert E. Buswell and Timothy S. Lee (eds), *Christianity in Korea*, Honolulu, University of Hawai'i Press, 2006, pp. 29–37.

Cho, Kwang 조광, *Chosŏn hugi sahoe wa Ch'ŏnjukyo* 조선후기 사회와 천주교, Seoul, Kyŏng'in munhwasa, 2010.

Cho, Kwang, 'The Chosŏn government's measures against Catholicism', in Chai-shin Yu (ed.), *The Founding of Catholic Tradition in Korea*, Mississauga, ON, Korean and Related Studies Press, 1996, pp. 103–14.

Cho, Kwang, 'The meaning of Catholicism in Korean history', in Chai-shin Yu (ed.), *The Founding of Catholic Tradition in Korea*, Mississauga, ON, Korean and Related Studies Press, 1996, pp. 115–40.

Ch'oe, Ki-bok, 'The abolition of ancestral rites and tablets by Catholicism in the Chosŏn dynasty and the basic meaning of Confucian ancestral rites', *Korea Journal* 24:8 (August 1984): 41–52.

Choi, Jai-Keun, *The Origin of the Roman Catholic Church in Korea: An Examination of Popular and Governmental Responses to Catholic Mission in the Later Chosŏn Dynasty*, Cheltenham, Hermit Kingdom Press, 2006.

Choi, Suk-woo (Ch'oe Sŏk-u), 'Korean Catholicism yesterday and today',

in Chai-shin Yu (ed.), *The Founding of Catholic Tradition in Korea*, Mississauga, ON, Korean and Related Studies Press, 1996, pp. 141–60.

Chung, Chai-sik, *A Korean Confucian Encounter with the Modern World: Yi Hang-no and the West*, Berkeley, Institute of East Asian Studies, University of California, Center for Korean Studies, 1995.

Chung, Minh, *Korean Treasures: Rare Books, Manuscripts and Artefacts in the Bodleian Libraries and Museums of Oxford University*, Oxford, Bodleian Library, 2011.

Clark, Donald, *Missionary Photography in Korea: Encountering the West through Christianity*, Seoul, Korea Society, 2009.

Clark, Donald N., 'Christianity in modern Korea', *Education about Asia* 11:2 (autumn 2006): 35–9.

Corfe, C. John, 'The Anglican Church in Corea', London, Livingstones; Seoul, Seoul Press, 1905, http://anglicanhistory.org/asia/kr/corfe.html (accessed 6 September 2018).

de Medina, Juan Ruiz, *The Catholic Church in Korea: Its Origins, 1566–1784*, trans. John Bridges, Seoul, Royal Asiatic Society, 1991.

Grayson, James Huntley, 'A quarter-millennium of Christianity in Korea', in Robert E. Buswell and Timothy S. Lee (eds), *Christianity in Korea*, Honolulu, University of Hawai'i Press, 2006, pp. 7–25.

Ion, A. Hamish, *The Cross and the Rising Sun, Volume 2: The British Protestant Missionary Movement in Japan, Korea and Taiwan, 1865–1945*, Waterloo, ON, Wilfrid Laurier University Press, 1993.

Japan Guide, 'Christianity', 7 May 2018, www.japan-guide.com/e/e2298.html (accessed 6 September 2018).

Kang, Jae-eun, *The Land of Scholars: Two Thousand Years of Korean Confucianism*, trans. Suzanne Lee, Paramus, NJ, Homa & Sekey Books, 2006.

Kim, Han-sik, 'The influence of Christianity on modern Korean political thought', *Korea Journal* 23:12 (1983): 4–17.

Kim, Andrew E., 'Protestantism in Korea and Japan from the 1880s to the 1940s', *Korea Journal* 45:4 (winter 2005): 261–90.

Kim, Andrew E., 'Korean religious culture and its affinity to Christianity: the rise of Protestant Christianity in South Korea', *Sociology of Religion* 61:2 (summer 2000): 117–33.

Kim, Ok-hy, 'Women in the history of Catholicism in Korea', *Korea Journal* 24:8 (August 1984): 28–40.

Kim, Sebastian C.H. and Kirsteen Kim, *A History of Korean Christianity*, Cambridge, Cambridge University Press, 2015.

Korean Bible Society, 'Korean Bible translations', http://en.bskorea.or.kr/?page_id=106 (accessed 9 September 2018).

Kŭm, Chang-t'ae, 'The doctrinal disputes between Confucianism and Western thought in the late Chosŏn period', in Chai-shin Yu (ed.), *The Founding of Catholic Tradition in Korea*, Mississauga, ON, Korean and Related Studies Press, 1996, pp. 7–44.

Ledyard, Gari, 'Kollumba Kang Wansuk, an early Catholic activist and martyr', in Robert E. Buswell and Timothy S. Lee (eds), *Christianity in Korea*, Honolulu, University of Hawai'i Press, 2006, pp. 38–71.

Lee, Peter H. et al. (eds), *Sourcebook of Korean Civilization, Volume 2: From the 17th Century to the Modern Period*, New York, Columbia University Press, 1993–96.

Min, Kyoung Bae 민경배, *Han'guk Kidokkyohoesa* 한국기독교회사, Seoul, Yonsei Taehakkyo Ch'ulp'anbu, 2007.

Missionary Sisters of the Community of St Peter, Kilburn, 'Extracts from the sisters' letters, August 11th to December 29th, 1895', Project Canterbury, http://anglicanhistory. org/asia/kr/sisters_letters1895.html (accessed 6 September 2018).

Oak, Sung-Deuk, *The Making of Korean Christianity: Protestant Encounters with Korean Religions, 1876–1915*, Waco, TX, Baylor University Press, 2013.

Paik, George Nak-chun 백낙준, *The History of Protestant Missions in Korea, 1832–1910*, Pyeng Yang, Union Christian College Press, 1929.

Palmer, Spencer J., *Korea and Christianity: The Problem of Identification with Tradition*, Seoul, Royal Asiatic Society Korea Branch, 1986.

Project Canterbury, 'Anglicanism in Korea', http://anglicanhistory.org/asia/ kr/index.html (accessed 7 September 2018).

Rausch, Franklin D., 'Like birds and beasts: justifying violence against Catholics in late Chosŏn Korea', *Acta Koreana* 15:1 (2012): 43–71.

Rausch, Franklin D., 'The Jesuits in Korea: influence without presence', *World History Connected* 10:3, http:// worldhistoryconnected.press.uillinois. edu/10.3/forum_rausch.html (accessed 6 September 2018).

Ross, John and Kyŏng-suk Hong 홍경숙, *Jon Rosŭ ŭi Han'guksa: Sŏyang ŏnŏ ro kirok toen ch'oech'o ŭi Han'guk yŏksa* 존로스의 한국사: 서양 언어 로 기록 된 최초의 한국역사, Kyŏnggi-do P'aju-si, Sallim Ch'ulp'ansa, 2010.

Roux, Pierre-Emmanuel, 'The great Ming code and the repression of Catholics in Chosŏn Korea', *Acta Koreana* 15:1 (2012): 73–106.

Seoul Yŏksa Pangmulgwan 서울역사박문관, *Sŏsomun pyŏlgok* 서소문별곡, *Ode to the West Small Gate*, exhibition catalogue, Seoul, Seoul Yŏksa Pangmulgwan, 2014.

Trollope, Mark N., *The Church of Corea*, London, A. R. Mowbray,
1915, https://archive.org/stream/ churchincoreaootroluoft#page/22/ mode/2up (accessed 6 September 2018).

UCLA Online Archive Korean Christianity, http://koreanchristianity. cdh.ucla.edu (accessed 6 September 2018).

Yi, Wŏn-sun, 'The Sirhak scholars' perspectives on Sŏhak in the later Chosŏn society', in Chai-shin Yu (ed.), *The Founding of Catholic Tradition in Korea*, Mississauga, ON, Korean and Related Studies Press, 1996, pp. 45–101.

Yonsei University Health System, 'History', www.yuhs.or.kr/en/about_ yuhs/yuhs/YUMC_history (accessed 6 September 2018).

Yu, Hongyŏl 유홍렬, *Han'guk Ch'ŏnju Kyohoesa* 한국천주교회사, Seoul, Kat'ŏllik ch'ulp'ansa, 1962.

Clothes and accessories

Kim, In-gyu 김인규, Pak Tae-nam 박대남, Sŏ Hŏn-gang Sŏ 서헌강 and Son Chun-ho 손준호, *Korean Collections at the British Museum*, London, British Museum, 2016.

Kim, Yong-suk 金英淑 and Kyong-ja Son 孫敬子, *Chosŏn wangjo Han'guk poksik togam* 朝鮮王朝韓國服飾圖鑑 (*An Illustrated History of Korean Costume*), Seoul, Yŏgyŏng sanŏpsa, 1984, Vols 1 and 2.

National Folk Museum of Korea, *National Folk Museum of Korea*, Seoul, National Folk Museum of Korea, 2009.

Pratt, Keith and Richard Rutt, *Korea: A Historical and Cultural Dictionary*. Richmond, Curzon Press, 1999.

Metalwork, water droppers, roof tiles and bricks, dolls, fans, weapons and other items

Ashmolean Museum, 'Gerald Reitlinger (1900–1978), biography', www.jameel centre.ashmolean.org/collection/6/671 (accessed 9 September 2018).

Pratt, Keith and Richard Rutt, *Korea: A Historical and Cultural Dictionary*, Richmond, Curzon Press, 1999.

INDEX

aengsam 鶯衫 앵삼 106
Aleni, Giulio (1582–1649) 9–11, 17
Allen, Newton Horace (1858–1932) 82, 84
American diplomatic legation 82
Amnokgang River 鴨綠江 40
An, Chŏng-bok 安鼎福 (1712–1791) 11–13, 156, 165
ancestral rites 77, 157, 166
Anglican cathedral 85
Anglican Church 74, 84–5, 88–90, 158, 166
Anglican diocese 85
Anglican University 85, 88
angyŏng 眼鏡 안경 154
Anjung Orphanage 89, 100
anti-foreign steles 斥和碑 척화비 81
Appenzeller, H.G. (1858–1902) 84
Ashmolean Museum of Art and Archaeology 5–6, 44–5, 64, 132, 137, 140, 164, 167, 176
Australia 17
Avison, Oliver R. (1860–1956) 84
ayam 額掩 아얌 116

Bank of Korea Money Museum 한국은행 화폐박물관 47, 49
Battle of Sekigahara 75
Beijing 北京 9–10, 14–15, 17, 23–4, 26, 28, 43, 76–8, 142, 156, 165
Benson, Edward White, Archbishop (1829–1896) 85
Berneux, Siméon-François, Bishop (1814–1866) 79
Board of Rites 106
British Museum 44–5, 156, 159

Calais, Father (1833–1884) 80
Catholic 74–80, 82, 87, 156–8, 165–7
changot 長衣 장옷 102, 117
changsin'gu – p'odo songi 裝身具 장신구 – 포도송이 154
changŭi 장의 *see changot* 長衣 장옷
changwŏn 壯元 장원 106
Chiguŭiyong chuhyŏngdo 地球儀用舟形圖 10, 12
Chikyū giyō funegata sekai chizu 地球儀用舟形 世界地圖 12
ch'ima 치마 113
chinsa 進士 진사 106
Ch'oe, Pangje 崔方濟 (1820?–1837) 78
Ch'oe, Yangŏp 崔良業 (1821–1861) 78
chŏgori 襦 저고리 113
chŏhwa 楮貨 저화 46
chŏlje ŭn ipsa swaeyak 鐵製銀入絲鎖鑰 철제은입사쇄약 135
Ch'ŏljong, King 哲宗 (1831–1864) 79
chŏllip 氈笠 전립 122
Chŏng, Yakyong 丁若鏞 (1762–1836) 75–7
chŏngdong 青銅 청동 47
chŏngdong-che yŏnmi-hyŏng sutkarak 青銅製燕 尾形匙 청동제연미형 숟가락 135
chŏngdong chong 青銅鐘 청동종 134
chŏngdong sakto 青銅削刀 청동삭도 135
chŏnggwe 正櫃 정궤 152
chŏngjagwan 程子冠 정자관 117
Chŏngjo, King (1752–1800) 正祖 75–7, 81
Chŏnha-do 天下圖 13

Chŏnjamun 千字文 49
chŏnp'ye 箭幣 전폐 48
chŏnsi 殿試 전시 106
chŏpsŏn 摺扇 접선 146
ch'osi 初試 초시 106
Chosŏn t'ongbo 朝鮮通寶 45, 48, 53
Chosŏn wangjo sillok 朝鮮王朝實錄 15
Chou, Stephen, Rev. 163
Christianity 3–4, 74–7, 79, 81, 83, 87–90, 157–60, 164–7
chumŏni 주머니 150
Church of St Gregory Ch'ŏngju 89
Church of St Mary the Virgin and St Nicholas 85
Church of St Peter and St Paul *see* Kanghwa Church
churumak 주루막 151
civil service examination 64, 102, 106,
Confucian 11, 24, 39, 50, 64–5, 67, 75–7, 81, 106, 117–18, 147, 157–8, 165–6
Cooper, Alfred Cecil, Bishop (1882–1964) 88–9, 91
Corfe, Charles John, Bishop (1843–1921) 85, 87, 89, 91, 158–9, 166

Da Ming yi tong 大明一統 10
Daly, John Charles Sydney, Bishop (1903–1993) 92, 98, 100–1
Daoism 67
Daveluy, Bishop (1838–1866) 79
Diqiu shi'erchang yuanxing-tu 地球十二長圓形 圖 10
dolls *see inhyŏng* 人形 인형
Dutch 9

East Asian War 9, 75
Enlightenment Party 82
Evidential Learning 75–6
Ewha Women's University 82, 89, 157, 163, 165

Feron, Father (1827–1903) 80
filial piety 65, 77
Fitzwilliam Museum 45

Gale, James S. (1863–1937) 84, 87–8, 149, 153, 159–63
Gardner, C.T. 45
globe gore 9, 10, 11, 12, 17
Gospel of John 84, 158
Gospel of Luke and Acts 84, 158
Gospel of Mark 84, 158
Gospel of Matthew 84, 158
Grassi Museum 13, 111
Great Wall 21, 22
Gregorio de Céspedes (1551–?) 75, 81

Haedong 海東 45, 52
Haedong chegukki 海東諸國紀 9, 156
Haedong chungbo 海東重寶 46, 52
Haedong t'ongbo 海東通寶 46, 52
han'gŭl 한글 83–4
Hankan, Leon 75
Hansŏng 漢城 48
Hanyang 漢陽 14, 28–9, 48

Heberden Coin Room 45
ho 戶 호 46, 61
Hogu ch'ongsu 戶口叢數 15
hongpae 紅牌 홍패 106
Honil kangni yŏktae kukto chido 混一疆理歷代 國都地圖 8
Hŏnjong, King 憲宗 (1827–1849) 79
Howarth, Anthony 89, 92, 96–101
hŭkhye 黑鞋 흑혜 128
Hulbert, Homer B. (1863–1949) 84, 163
Hun tian yi shuo 渾天儀說 12, 13
Hŭngsŏn Taewŏn'gun Yi Haŭng 興宣大院君李 昰應 79
Hwang, Sayŏng (1775–1801) 黃嗣永 77–8, 81, 157, 163
Hwanghae 黃海 14, 28, 34, 47–9
hyŏpgŭmhye 夾金鞋 협금혜 123
hyungbae 胸背 흉배 108

Imanishi, Ryū 今西龍 11–12
Inch'ŏn Church 89
inhyŏng 人形 인형 142–5
Injo, King 仁祖 (1595–1649) 48, 79
Israel 17

Jesuits 74–6, 157, 167
Jones, George Heber (1867–1919) 84

Kaesŏng 開城 39, 45–7
Kaewŏn t'ongbo 開元通寶 45
kakkung 角弓 각궁 149
kaktae 角帶 각대 130
Kang, Jae-eun 82, 166
Kanghwa Anglican Cathedral 85
Kanghwa Church 85, 88, 95
Kanghwa Island 80, 85, 97, 163
Kanghwa Treaty 82
Kangnido 疆理圖 8–9, 156, 165
kapchu 甲胄 갑주 111
kapkwa 甲科 갑과 106
Kapsin Coup 82
karo 座燈 가로 150
kat 갓 118
Keijō 京城 160
Keijō Daigaku 京城大学 12–13
Kim, Andong 79
Kim, Okkyun 金玉均 (1851–1894) 82
Kim, Taegŏn 金大建 (1821–1846) 78
kŏdŭl-ch'ima 거들 치마 114
Koguryŏ 高句麗 7–8, 140
Kojong, King 高宗 (1852–1919) 79
kokkal 曲葛 곡갈 114
Konishi, Yukinaga 小西行長 (1555?–1600) 75, 81
Kŏnwŏn chungbo 乾元重寶 45
Koryŏ 高麗 7, 12, 46, 119, 132, 135–6
Kunyu wanguo quantu 坤輿萬國全圖 9–10, 156
Kuroda, Nagamasa 黑田長政 (1568–1623) 75
Kuroda, Yoshitaka 黑田孝高 (1546–1604) 75
Kutsuki, Masatsuna 朽木昌綱 (1750–1802) 45, 156, 165
Kyŏnggi Province 京畿道 14, 30, 46–8, 64, 80
kwagŏ 科擧 과거 102

Kwŏn, Sang'yŏn 權尙然 (1751–1791) 77
Kwŏn, Ton'in (1783–1859) 權敦仁 79

Landis, Eli (1865–1898) 85–6
Landis Library 86
Lee, Paul, Rev. （1922–2010) 88
leper women 99
Liangyi xuanlan tu 兩儀玄覽圖 9

MacArthur, Douglas, General (1880–1964) 89
Magellan, Ferdinand (1480–1521) 11, 17, 156
Malan, Solomon Caesar, Rev. (1812–1894) 84
Manchu 10, 14–15, 40, 43, 48, 132, 156
manggŏn 網巾 망건 117
Maria, Sister 98, 163
Maubant, Philippe, Father 78
Min, Yŏngik (1860–1914) 閔泳翊 82
Ming 明 7, 10, 27, 43, 48, 157, 167
misŏn 尾扇 미선 147
Missionaries 9, 74, 76, 78–80, 82–4, 89–90, 132,
    158, 162–3
mit'uri 麻鞋 미투리 126
mokhwa 木靴 목화 129
Morning Calm, The 85
mugwa 武科 무과 106
munkwa 文科 문과 106

namakshin 木履 나막신 125
nambawi 남바위 115
Nam'in 南人 76
Nanjing 南京 10, 14–15, 17, 24, 27, 156
National Library of Korea 4, 12, 176
New Testament 84, 158
Ning'an 寧安 14–15, 40, 168
Ningguta 寧古塔 14, 15, 40
nokmunjŏn 鹿文博 록문전 141
noksa 錄事 록사 107
noksa-bok 錄事服 록사복 107

Oppert, Ernst J. (1832–1903) 80
ŏsahwa 御賜花 어사화 106
ouyat blossoms 51

Paektusan Mountain 白頭山 40
paengnip 白笠 백립 119
paji 바지 113
p'algwae 八卦 팔괘 50
panggŏn 方巾 방건 118
Park, Chung-hee (1917–1979) 89
Park, Esther (1876?–1910) 金點童 82
pegae 枕 베개 155
persecution of 1866–71 79
Phoebe, Rev. 98, 163
pit-ch'igae 빗지개 131
poksi 覆試 복시 106
Portuguese 9
pŏsŏn 襪 버선 [말] 127
Protestantism 74, 82, 90, 157, 166
P'ung Island 豊島 80
p'ungch'a 風遮 풍차 115
p'ungjam 風簪 풍잠 115
pusittol, kangch'ŏl, pul 부싯돌, 강철 [鋼鐵],불 149
P'yŏng'an 平安 9, 14–15, 17, 28, 35, 47–9
pyŏnggwa 丙科 병과 106
P'yŏngyang 平壤 8, 13, 35, 83, 158

Qing 清 7, 10, 40, 43, 75, 76, 82

Ricci, Matteo 9–12, 156
Ridel, Father (1830–1884) 80
Rodgers, J., Admiral (1812–1882) 80
Rome 11, 17
Ross, John (1842–1915) 84–5, 158, 167
Royal Asiatic Society Korea Branch 84, 87, 156,
    158, 165, 167
Roze, Pierre-Gustave, Admiral (1812–1883) 80
Rutt, Cecil Richard, Monsignor (1925–2011) 87–9,
    92, 157, 159–61, 163, 165, 167
Rutt, Richard, Bishop *see* Rutt, Cecil Richard Rutt,
    Monsignor
Ryūkyū 琉球 13–14, 21, 28, 42

Saenamtŏ 새남터 (or 沙南基 사남기) 78–9
saengwŏn 生員 생원 106
Sahae chibang sŭnggae chi do chŏn 四海地方勝
    槩之圖全 14
Sahae chido 四海地圖 14, 21
St Andrew's Church Chonan 89
St Bede's House Seoul 89
St Francis Xavier *see* Xavier, St Francis
St John's College Ch'ŏngju 89
St Michael's Seminary 성미가엘신학원 85, 89
Sam Han 三韓 45, 53
Sam Han chungbo 三韓重寶 45, 53
Sam Han t'ongbo 三韓通寶 45, 53
Samguk sagi 三國史記 8
samo 沙帽 사모 119
sangp'yŏngch'ŏng 常平廳 48
Sangp'yong t'ongbo 常平通寶 45, 48–50, 53–60,
    66, 71
Schall, Adam (Johann Adam Schall von Bell)
    10–13, 17, 156
Scranton, Mary F. (1832–1909) 82
Sejo, King 世祖 (1417–1468) 48
Severance Hospital 82
Shanhaijing 山海經 10
Shanhaiguan 山海關 22
Shengjing 盛京 14, 15, 43, 168
Sherman, General 80, 158
Smart, Clifford, Rev. 100, 163
Sŏ, Chaep'il 徐載弼 (1864–1951) 82
Sŏ, Yoshitoshi 宗義智 (1568–1615) 75
Society for the Propagation of the Gospel 85–6,
    90–101, 159, 176
sŏhak 西學 서학 12, 157, 167
sokwa 小科 소과 106
sŏnbi 儒士 선비 106
Song, Yochan (1918–1980) 89
Sŏnggonghoe University 성공회 대학교 (聖公會
    大學校) 85, 88
Sŏnggyungwan 成均館 성균관 106
sopit 梳 [소] 빗 131
Sou, Isaiah, Rev. 97
so-ŭnbyŏng 小銀図 소은병 47
ssangjo mun nŭnghyŏng tonggyŏng 雙鳥文稜形銅
    鏡 쌍조문릉형동경 136
ssangyong mun tonggyŏng 雙龍文銅鏡
    쌍룡문동경 132
Sukjong, King (r. 1095–1105) 肅宗 45
Sungkonghoe University *see* Sŏnggonghoe
    University
sutkarak 匙 숫가락 135, 153

swaeŭn 碎銀 쇄은 47

tae-ch'ang-ŭi 大氅衣 대창의 111
Taedongbŏp 同法 46, 48
T'aegŭksŏn 太極扇 태극선 147
taekwa 大科 대과 106
t'aesahye 太史鞋 태사혜 123–4
Taewŏn'gun *see* Hŭngsŏn Taewŏn'gun Yi Haŭng
    興宣大院君李昰應
tallyŏng 團領 단령 108, 119
t'anggŏn 宕巾 탕건 118
Tan'gun 檀君 12, 28
Tennant, Roger, Rev. 100, 163
Tenri University 天理大学 12, 13
Terminations of the Verb (하다) 85
Tokugawa, Ieyasu (1543–1616) 75
t'onggae chŏntong 筒箇箭筒 통개전동 148
Tongguk 東國 45, 52
Tongguk chungbo 東國重寶 45, 52
Tongguk t'ongbo 東國通寶 45, 52
Tongnae 東萊 28
Tongsa kangmok 東史綱目 12
Trollope, Mark Napier, Bishop (1862–1930) 16,
    84–90, 158–60, 167
Tsushima 對馬 28, 41, 75
t'ugu 투구 121
t'ujŏn 鬪牋 투전 153
Tuman River 豆滿 40
tŭngt'osi 藤吐手 등토[수]시 130
Turner, Arthur, Bishop (1862–1910) 85, 89, 91
turumagi 두루마기 102

ŭlgwa 乙科 을과 106
Underwood, Horace G. (1859–1916) 82, 84, 163

Wanguo quantu 萬國全圖 9–10, 156
water droppers *see* yŏnjŏk 硯滴 연적
weapons 4, 6, 148, 167
Western learning *see* sŏhak 西學

Xavier, St Francis (1506–1552) 75

Yalu River *see* Amnokgang
yangban 兩班 양반 77
Yasui, Santetsu 安井算哲 12, 13, 156
Yi, Ik 李瀷 (1681–1763) 11, 12
Yi, Sŭnghun 李承薰 (1756–1801) 76
Yijing 易經 49–50, 159
Yŏjido 輿地圖 14
yŏlsoep'ye 열쇠폐 69
Yŏnggo yanggye Yodong chŏndo 寧古兩界遼東全
    圖 9, 10, 12, 17
Yŏngjo, King 英祖 (1694–1776) 24, 75
Yongmun p'yŏngwadang 龍文平瓦當 141
Yŏnhwamun wŏndawang 蓮花文圓瓦當 140–1
yŏnjŏk 硯滴 연적 137–9
Yonsei University 82, 86, 158, 163, 167
Yoo, Moses Nagjun, Rev. 88
YMCA 83, 160, 162
Yu, Stephen, Rev. 97, 163
Yun, Chich'ung (1759–1791) 尹持忠 77

Zhifang waiji 職方外紀 9
Zhou, Xingsi (470–521) 周興嗣 49
Zhu, Xi 朱熹 14, 24, 165
Zuo Zhuan 左傳 50

ACKNOWLEDGEMENTS

I am deeply indebted to many colleagues, specialists, scholars and friends for their help. I would like to express my especial appreciation to Dr James Lewis again for his invaluable advice, criticisms and many improvements during the preparation of this publication. I would also like to thank Dr Robert Chard, Dr James McMullen, Dr Gui Mengqiu and Yuki Kissick for their linguistic opinions and help.

I am grateful to many colleagues and curators for their help and permission to reproduce images of the objects in their museums and collections: Nicholas Crowe, Suzy Prior and colleagues (Pitt Rivers Museum); Dr Shailendra Bhandare, Alessandra Cereda, Unity Coombes and colleagues (Ashmolean Museum); James Allan and Nick Cistone (Imaging Services, Bodleian Library); Stephen Hebron, Sam Lindley and Lucy McCann (Bodleian Special Collections); and Catherine Wakeling (United Society for the Propagation of the Gospel).

My acknowledgement also goes to Dr Samuel Fanous, Deborah Susman, Dot Little, Su Wheeler and colleagues (Bodleian Library Publishing) for their support and for accepting this manuscript for publication. I would also like to mention Liu Po (Project Accountant Bodleian Libraries), as well as Jessica Cuthbert-Smith and Steve Williamson for their editorial help and Ocky Murray for his design.

I would also like to express my gratitude to the Bodley's Librarian Richard Ovenden, Dr Gillian Evison, Keeper of the Oriental Collections and a Subject Librarian for Classical Indian Studies, and James Legg, Head of Bodleian Humanities Libraries, for their support of this publication and Korean studies in general; without their support, the rapid development of the Korean collection and other Korea-related projects in Oxford would not have been possible.

My sincere thanks go to scholars and specialists in Korea and other institutes for their help and support: Professor Yang Young-kyun and Dr Shin Jeongso of the Academy of Korean Studies; Director Cha Gyeong-Lye, Director Kim Heesoon and Nanyoung Kye of the National Library of Korea; Dr Koo Ja-Hun, Dr Han Minsub and Ms Jung Jeehye of Korea University; Professor Yang Bo-Kyung of Sungshin Women's University; Dr Kang Moon-shik of the Kyujanggak, Seoul National University; Lyeon Gyeonghwa, Rho Sunhee and Lee Jihye of the National Museum of Korean Contemporary History; Lee Kiwon and Dr Choi Eun Soo of the National Folk Museum of Korea; Cindy Kim and Kang KyungNam of the National Museum of Korea; Professor Hideo Ishii of Teikyo University, Japan; Soojin Kwon of the Korean Cultural Centre, UK; Hyun Soo-ah of the British Museum; and Hamish Todd of the British Library.

This publication was supported by the Academy of Korean Studies Grant (AKS-2018-P08).